WILLIE WALLACE
HEART OF A LION

The Life and Times of Lisbon Lion William Wallace

Best Wishes

William Wallace

25th May

WILLIE WALLACE
HEART OF A LION

The Life and Times of Lisbon Lion William Wallace

Edited by Michael Knowling

Foreword by Rod Stewart

Feature by Brogan Rogan Trevino and Hogan from CQN

Tribute by Archie Macpherson

Statistics by Pat Woods

Introduction by Paul Brennan

Published by Quick News Publishing, 2013
www.celticquicknews.co.uk

CQN Books is a trading name of Quick News Publishing Limited
Cover design by Julie Robertson. CQ inSight, Australia
www.cqinsight.com.au
Special thanks to Nikki Warrington @ CQN Books

ISBN 978 0 9576171 0 0

Printed and bound by CPI Group (UK) Ltd, Croydon, CR0 4YY

ACKNOWLEDGEMENTS

Writing this book has given me a fantastic trip down memory lane, starting from my schooldays and travelling all the way forward to my last professional game of football with Ross County Football Club in 1977. This is the story of that trip, although my career did continue in coaching football and management and maybe, some day, I will write about those experiences.

My competitive playing career began as a twelve-year-old. School and Boys' Brigade football took up my first four years and secondary juvenile (under 21 years) the next twelve months. From there, I moved into senior professional football until my final game at 37 years of age. During my twenty-one years as a professional, I believe I was lucky in my choice of football clubs. In Scotland, they included Kilsyth Rangers, Stenhousemuir, Raith Rovers, Heart of Midlothian, Celtic, Dumbarton and Ross County, in England there was Crystal Palace in London and in Australia APIA Leichhardt in Sydney. I experienced fair treatment from all these clubs, except perhaps for my last few months at Heart of Midlothian. I was fortunate enough to play with and against fantastic players during my twenty-one years and I know I could write many books from my experiences.

Here I have tried to offer an insight into what was a long and happy career. Thanks go to my wife Olive and our daughters Lynn and Fiona, as they made many moves and sacrifices over this time. Special thanks to Olive for putting these words on to paper – thank goodness she learned to type in school!

I would like to thank Jim Craig, ex-Celtic player, my friend and colleague, for his patience, help and guidance in starting this book and Michael Knowling and Julie Robertson for their encouragement, support and expertise in editing and presenting all my ideas. Special thanks to Michael for his endless patience researching and checking the games, places and people I have mentioned. I appreciate also the assistance of Pat Woods for compiling the facts and figures of my time at each club; and thanks to our publisher CQN Books, especially David Faulds, for making my ideas a reality.

Special thanks, too, to the American Celtic Supporters' Federation for their hospitality in Las Vegas over the years and to the Celtic supporters clubs throughout Australia and the UK for many memorable occasions. I am the patron of Brisbane Celtic Supporters' Club and have spent many a pleasant hour in their company.

Importantly, my appreciation and thanks go to everyone who reads my story. I really do hope you enjoy the trip.

Willie Wallace,
Gold Coast, Australia.

CONTENTS

WILLIE WALLACE – HEART OF A LION

www.celticquicknews.co.uk

WILLIE WALLACE – AN AUTOBIOGRAPHY

WILLIE WALLACE – THE CQN FEATURE
(Brogan Rogan Trevino and Hogan)

WILLIE WALLACE - THE TRIBUTE
(Archie Macpherson)

"*The roots, the people, and of course the fact that they had become the first British Team to have won the European Cup—an amazing achievement for a Scottish Team of locals.*

I make no apology for the fact that the team, the club and the fans have come to mean so much to me over the years, and when we (Celtic) recently defeated the mighty Barcelona— said to be the best team in the world—at Celtic park I was caught shedding buckets of tears—of joy I hasten to add."

FOREWORD
by Rod Stewart

As a young man in the early years of my own career, I became a great fan of Scottish football, both at league and international levels. My father was a devoted Hibernian FC supporter, so I had the "green side" of Scottish football already in my blood.

I remember when Willie Wallace was transferred from Hearts to Celtic in November, 1966, This move was to make the already very strong group of players at Celtic FC even stronger and, as things turned out, it didn't take Willie long to fit into Celtic's style of play. Willie was part of what I think was one of the best teams Celtic has produced throughout the club's history. And, very important, he continued to score goals, as had been his habit during his years at Hearts.

Willie's successful career at Heart of Midlothian carried on to be an outstanding one during his time with Celtic. As a Celtic supporter, I can recall enjoying watching Willie play in many memorable games. He was also capped for Scotland and I particularly remember his contribution to the game at Wembley in April, 1967, when Scotland beat the world champions England 3–2; I think it should have been more! It's worth a mention that Jim Baxter and Willie both played in this match, carrying their pairing on to the highest international level after they had spent time together at Raith Rovers much earlier in their football careers.

On a recent tour of Australia, I had the great pleasure of meeting Willie and his lovely wife Olive. We talked about the current Celtic side and the future of the game we both love.

I am pleased to announce to the worldwide Celtic family that Willie bleeds green and, to my star-struck eyes, might as well have had a four-leaf clover as a heart. He's also a proud Scot through and through and a nicer, more humble man I've yet to meet.

Bless you, Mr Wallace.

By Rod Stewart, April 2013

"I have explained that tearful outburst since—but you see at the final whistle I thought of my dad, my affection for this club and the players and the fans and the people that go to make up Celtic, the history and all of the emotions which go with supporting this club—and yes that entire experience takes me back to those childhood dreams of being a footballer—the guy who pulls on the shirt, who scores the goal, who makes the tackle or whatever it takes to help the local team beat the best team in the world. That is what footballing dreams are made of."

Officially launched on the 25th May 2013

INTRODUCTION

Celtic were 79 years old when the Lisbon Lions took to the field in 1967. Fans already had their legends and memories, but in the days following that magnificent triumph, all realised, this was the greatest moment of them all. The club have now played more games after that date than before it but the achievements of Simpson, Craig, Gemmell, Murdoch McNeill, Clark, Johnstone, Wallace, Chalmers Auld and Lennox remain irrefutably the most spectacular and audacious any Scottish athlete has ever got near.

As such, it is an incredible honour for Celtic Quick News first book to be Willie Wallace's autobiography. This story is a huge part of why we are all so invigorated by the team we love. In coming to Celtic Quick News with his book, Willie demonstrates the connection with Celtic fans you feel every time you meet a Lion. CQN is published by and for Celtic fans, and despite having their name on a stand, no other Celtic team has made the effort to connect with fans more than the Lisbon Lions.

Willie's story is unique in a number of ways. He left Scotland a few years after Lisbon and established a new life in Australia. The Aussie

Celtic fans gain was a loss to those of us in Scotland. Willie became a well-known face to Celtic fans in Australia but most of us seldom got to hear his stories. He was also unique in that he was the only Lion Jock Stein signed for Celtic. All the others were already at the club when Stein arrived in 1965 but Stein needed phenomenal a striker with pace and Wallace was his man.

As well as Willie's recollections of his life, Jock Stein's close friend, Archie Macpherson, has written a chapter, giving the historical perspective on Willie and the forces which made him the only player the manager could add to an immensely talented squad. We also have a fantastic contribution from Brogan Rogan, which I know you will enjoy, and a foreword from Rod Stewart, a lad from London who remains as inspired by the Lisbon Lions today as he was in May 1967.

By Paul Brennan, Celtic Quick News, May 2013

"I was hoping I would play well and that we would win, so putting two good goals in the net for Celtic was a bonus, as I felt I was repaying some of the outlay made by the club in bringing me to Parkhead."

Celtic vs Aberdeen, Hampden Park, Glasgow, 29 April 1967.

Chapter 1

SEVENTEEN DAYS, FIVE GAMES; ONE GOLDEN SPELL

12 April 1967:
Celtic 3–1 Dukla Prague, European Cup semi-final 1st leg, Parkhead

15 April 1967:
England 2–3 Scotland, Wembley Stadium

19 April 1967:
Celtic 0–0 Aberdeen, Scottish First Division championship, Parkhead

25 April 1967:
Dukla Prague 0–0 Celtic, European Cup semi-final 2nd leg, Juliska Stadium

29 April 1967:
Celtic 2–0 Aberdeen, Scottish Cup final, Hampden Park

In the careers of many professional footballers, there are spells when the fates seem to smile down and success just comes your way, whether you expect it or not. In my five-year stint at Celtic Park, one 17-day, five-match period in April, 1967 turned out that way.

I had joined Celtic in the early days of December, 1966. As this was after the recognised deadline day for player registration with a new club, I was not eligible to play against the Yugoslavian (now Serbian) team Vojvodina Novi Sad in the quarter-final of the European Cup. I travelled with the team to Yugoslavia as a spectator for the first leg of the tie and trained with the boys as I normally would.

From what we were able to see, areas of that part of the country appeared remarkably backward. The main roads of the city of Novi Sad, for instance, were of tarmac but the streets leading into them were just packed earth. Our hotel, thankfully, was very modern and, on our first visit to Vojvodina's ground, we were surprised by the quality of the floodlighting, very definitely among the best we had ever seen. Unfortunately, though, the pitch wasn't in such great shape; on the day of the game it was rock hard and very difficult to play on.

I sat on the bench during the game and felt terrible, my nerves getting the better of me. When we lost a goal in 69 minutes, the condition of the pitch played a big part as a short back pass by Tommy Gemmell was cut off by the Vojvodina striker, who rounded Ronnie Simpson in goal and rolled the ball into an empty net. My heart sank as I watched it and I prayed we would equalise but there were no more goals. However, d espite losing 1–0 the boys were still in good form on the way home and quite confident about the return game.

Remarkable enough, recently I met a gentleman from the former Yugoslavia who was actually at that game in Novi Sad in 1967. Bogdean Antic now lives at Burleigh Waters, part of Queensland's Gold Coast in Australia, no further than half a mile from my own home. I first met Bogdean in 2009 when I was coaching an under-19 side in the local league, a team which included his then 16-year-old son. Since we met, we have had a few chats about that game in Novi Sad. He said the reason he could remember me was an announcement made at the ground before the game, that Celtic's new signing, Willie Wallace from Hearts, was on the bench but would not play due to not meeting the signing deadline. Bogdean recalled being pleased that Vojvodina had won on the day but said he had remained worried after the game that the 1–0 result would not be enough for them to defend in the second leg in Glasgow. He was right.

Still ineligible to play, I sat in the stand for the second leg at Parkhead, just behind the directors' box. In those days, only one substitute was allowed in these matches and that was the goalkeeper, so around me sat the rest of the first-team squad, all equally disappointed to be missing out on such a marvellous occasion with over 70,000 fans in the ground. I was so wrapped up in the game that I can't remember who was sitting next to me on the night but I do remember that some what might be called selfish thoughts briefly passed through my mind. After all, I was used to matches in the UEFA Cup with Heart of Midlothian but this was the big one – the European Cup – and if the team out there on the pitch couldn't overcome that 1–0 defeat in Novi Sad, I was in danger of missing out on the chance to play in it! I went through some anxious moments until Steve Chalmers scored – then I was up on my feet along with the thousands of others at the game. It was all square and when Charlie Gallagher took a corner kick very late in the game and Billy McNeill met the cross perfectly with his head and scored, I was up again, now sure that the chance to play in the semi-final of the European Cup had moved a big step closer.

Two days later, we were drawn against Dukla Prague, of Czechoslovakia, in one semi; Inter Milan, of Italy, would meet CSKA Sofia, of Bulgaria, in the other. My worry now was whether I would be selected in the team that would meet the Czechs. As things turned out, I was chosen to play against Dukla in the first leg at Parkhead on Wednesday, 12 April, 1967 – a day that held extra significance as it was our daughter Lynn's first birthday. I was particularly nervous before the game and couldn't wait to get out of the changing rooms and on to the field. I knew I would settle down once I was out there in front of a full house of Celtic supporters.

It was quite an even first half, in which Jimmy Johnstone gave us the lead before their outside-right equalised just before the break. Instead of being level, we should have been leading 2–1 at half-time as we had a perfectly good goal disallowed by the referee. The goal was disallowed for a high foot – in this case, the referee chose to apply a European rule that was not used in Scotland as long as both players had their feet up, as had been the case here. Anyway, I thought the goal should have stood.

In the second half, it felt like the forward runners such as myself were being given more space by the Dukla defenders. I thought maybe they were content with a 1–1 result to take back to Prague for the return match – but that little bit of extra space was just what I wanted. My first goal came when I chased a long ball from the back and managed to go past my marking defender. As I raced towards the ball, I noticed I was outside the Dukla keeper's right-hand post and realised I would have to take the chance quickly, before the angle narrowed even further. So I chose to strike the ball with the outside of my right foot – it wasn't an easy chance but I managed to make sweet contact with the ball and, much to my delight, it fairly flew into the roof of the net. My second goal came from a direct free kick outside the penalty box, to the right of centre. Bertie Auld or Bobby Murdoch usually took those free kicks around the box and – for some unknown reason – I was standing next to Bertie, who was placing the ball, when he said: "Can you see the hole they've left at the far post?" "Aye," I said. Bertie went on: "OK, I'll square it to you and you just find the hole". Bertie then shimmied over the ball and slipped it to me. Again, I struck it sweetly but not with a great deal of pace – just enough to send it smoothly into the corner of the net.

Those two second-half goals – made all the more special by it being my European debut for Celtic and my daughter's birthday – gave us a 3–1 win. It was just a fantastic feeling. My first goals in the European Cup had also helped to make it a great night for the Parkhead fans. Later, when we left the stadium making for the car park, thousands of them were still milling around and cheering.

On the drive home, my wife Olive asked if we were in the final. "Not yet," I said. We still had to play Dukla in Prague but we had a good lead to take there and, as long as something didn't go badly wrong, we would be in the final. I was surprised she should have asked a question like that and even more so when her next comment was simply "good". She was normally more inquisitive than that. Maybe I should have encouraged Olive to come to more Celtic games – but that would have interfered with her own Saturday sport as a hockey player with Lenzie Academy FP (Former Pupils).

Next morning at training, we were all buzzing after the previous night's win and the atmosphere in the training ground at Barrowfield could only be described as brilliant. Not only were we reliving the Dukla game, we were also talking about the forthcoming clash between England and Scotland at Wembley Stadium. In just three days' time, the two countries would meet for the first time since England had become world champions by defeating Germany at Wembley in 1966.

When I returned to Celtic Park for a shower after training, I noticed Jimmy Johnstone on the treatment table, so I popped into the room and asked him when he was flying down to London. He told me he wasn't fit and I would be going down in his place. "Aye, right," I said, certain he was winding me up and left for my shower. Just as I'd managed to cover myself almost completely in soap, "The Boss" – manager Jock Stein – came in and said: "Get yourself home and get yourself organised to be on the five o'clock flight to London. You'll be taking Jimmy's spot in the squad." Driving home, I remember wearing a big, wide smile at having been included, even if I would be among the reserves. At the very least, I would have the chance to watch the game live and enjoy a weekend in London.

I returned to Parkhead about 3 o'clock, received my instructions and proceeded to the airport for the flight to London. Arriving at Heathrow airport, I caught a cab to the Hendon Bridge Hotel in Golders Green, where the Scottish party was staying. When I got there, the boys had all gone to the movies but one of the staff had stayed behind, waiting for me to arrive. I booked in and discovered I was to share a room with my Celtic team-mate "TG" – Tommy Gemmell. I dropped off my gear and went back downstairs for dinner, then watched TV for about an hour. Around 10.30pm, the squad, most of whom I already knew, arrived back from the movies. I think the only player I hadn't met before was Jim McCalliog. After a light supper, we all retired for the night. Before dropping off to sleep, TG told me about what had happened before I arrived. Surprisingly, it didn't seem to amount to very much.

On the Friday morning, we were up around 7.30am, washed, shaved, fed and went training at 10.00am at the ground of Hendon FC, just five minutes from the hotel. We trained for a couple of hours – nothing too strenuous – then we were called to the centre of the field by the team manager, Bobby Brown. He proceeded to read out the team that would start the match and, to my absolute surprise, I was included at outside-right. To complete a Celtic quartet, Ronnie Simpson was in goal, Tommy Gemmell at left-back and Bobby Lennox at outside-left. I hadn't played in a wide position for quite a while – four years, to be precise – so I was stunned for two reasons but, once it all began to sink in, I was just over the moon. To be playing at Wembley for Scotland was every wee boy's dream and here I was, about to do it.

Not surprisingly, I didn't have a great night's sleep but next morning I was ready to go. We left the hotel around 1pm to drive to Wembley, which was also not so far from the hotel. It was quiet until we reached Wembley Way and then – what a sight – Scottish supporters and flags flying everywhere. As the bus moved slowly moved towards the north end of the stadium where the dressing rooms were, the supporters were going crazy. As we neared the ground, I saw my next-door neighbour Tom Fergus and his mates, who had parked their caravanette just next to the entrance to the dressing rooms. Earlier, I had obtained tickets for them for the game but they had left Scotland early on the Friday morning so they didn't know I was involved. When I walked over to them, they asked me what I was doing at Wembley. You should have seen their faces when I said: "I'm playing." They didn't know whether to believe me or not but I was quick to put them in the picture! They wished me all the best and I headed for the dressing rooms.

The whole changing area at Wembley in those days was a bit of a disappointment, old-fashioned with high ceilings and ordinary fittings. But when we walked out on to the pitch about 1.30pm, the surface was magnificent, flat and true. The atmosphere was electric – there seemed to be more Scots than English supporters – and we soaked up the thunderous applause before returning to the dressing rooms at about 1.45pm. We had to be back on the field by 2.40pm to meet the royal guest, the Duchess of Kent, and although obviously delighted to shake hands with her, I was a shade disappointed as my favourite royals at the time were Princess Alexandra and Princess Margaret.

After the presentations, we broke off to begin the game. It suddenly dawned on me that the manager was not around and there had been no team talk – nothing. In fact, the game had never been mentioned. Then Bobby Brown appeared from nowhere and said: "Have a good result and we will have a great night in London after it." That was it and, after all the preliminaries, I said to Billy Bremner: "What's happening?" He just shrugged his shoulders and replied: "Just play where you've been picked."

I lined up at outside-right against Ray Wilson, the World Cup-winning full-back. The game started with play going from end to end and it was not long before I realised Ray was giving me lots of room. He didn't want to go forward, so that was fine by me. We were keeping possession of the ball just as well as the English players, maybe even a bit better. In one of our attacks, as I drifted into the English box with no sign of the full-back, I received the ball, quickly had it under control and shot. It was heading for the bottom right-hand corner of the net but suddenly their goalkeeper, Gordon Banks, got down to it. Fortunately for us, he couldn't hold it and, as he spilled it in front of him, there was the ever-sharp Dennis Law to put it into the net for our first goal.

That settled us, we played some really good football and were unlucky not to go further ahead. In the second half, we continued to play well. Bobby Lennox scored our second goal and it looked all sewn up but Jack Charlton nicked one back and it was all on again. I was involved in our third goal. Jim McCalliog received the ball outside the English penalty box to the left of the goal and he and I worked a wall pass to put him clear and he touched the ball neatly past Gordon Banks into the net, making the score 3–1. The game should have finished there but back came England to score again. However, it was all too late for them and the game finished 3–2 for Scotland.

When I was a boy, I had dreamt of playing against Billy Wright, Stanley Matthews and my favourite player, Tom Finney, not realising they would all be retired by the time I was old enough to play for Scotland. (In 2008, I had the privilege of meeting Sir Tom Finney at a sports dinner in Preston.) I had already played against England at Hampden in 1966 and we lost on that occasion but my dream as a child about playing for Scotland against England had been fulfilled. Going on to the pitch at Wembley was not as daunting as it had been at Hampden. I was relaxed and ready to go, unlike the year before at Hampden, where I was nervous and took a long time to settle into the game. Maybe I was beginning to get used to the big occasion – due to playing with Celtic – and growing more confident in myself. As you can imagine, the noise inside the stadium was deafening. The supporters invaded the pitch on the final whistle and I was swept off my feet by a huge, burly Scotsman. "How are you, Wongo (my old nickname from school)?" said Alex (Parrot) Kilpatrick, an old friend from school who had moved to London. Alex crushed me, then dropped me. He said "well done" then disappeared into the crowd. Alex's bear hug was actually filmed and is shown on the DVD of the 1967 England–Scotland match at Wembley. I have never seen or heard from Alex since!

The 3–2 scoreline flattered England and I'm proud to say I was part of this great Scottish team. We had played brilliantly and, yes, as Bobby Brown had predicted, we did have a great night in London! We attended a function at the Café Royal and were then invited to a cocktail party at one of London's theatres. The stars of the show were leaving and Cilla Black and Frankie Howerd were taking over. By this time, we had all had a little to drink and our captain Billy Bremner informed Cilla in no uncertain terms that he preferred another singer, Sandy Shaw. Cilla naturally took umbrage to these remarks and we were all asked to leave – which we did! We moved on to the Astor Club, where we met a friend of all the players, a businessman from Edinburgh called Peter Williamson, who organised a few drinks for us away from the bustle of the supporters. I'm afraid I don't remember much after the first hour.

After the excitement of these two great victories, both over excellent opposition, it might come as a surprise that the next couple of matches during my "seventeen glorious days" were both 0–0 draws. Each game, though, in different ways was crucial; one being a league match against Aberdeen and the other the semi-final second leg of the European Cup against Dukla Prague.

By the middle of April, 1967, Celtic had already picked up the League Cup and the Glasgow Cup, were still in contention for the Scottish and European cups and were ahead on the league table, just in front of Rangers. Every game now was a vital one and, only four days after the euphoria of Wembley, we ran out at Parkhead in front of a crowd of 33,000 to face Aberdeen.

The Dons were not only in third place on the table but, in 10 days' time, would be our opponents in the Scottish Cup final. It proved a tense night for everyone, with neither side giving any quarter and defences slightly on top, so a scoreless draw was not an unexpected result. From our point of view, though, a point gained was better than two lost and we were reasonably happy with the 0–0 result. The match was of historical importance for another reason, as it was only the second time the team which would become known as the "Lisbon Lions" had taken to the field, the first having been in the 4–0 league win against St Johnstone at Muirton Park, Perth, on 14 January, 1967. As the Lions only played 11 matches in total, the Aberdeen match has gone into the record books.

Four days later, a very confident Celtic party – comprising directors, management, players and supporters – left Glasgow airport by chartered jet for the return leg of our European semi-final against Dukla in Prague.

Arriving in the Czech capital, I was impressed by its old buildings and quaint streets. In appearance, it certainly lived up to the guidebooks' descriptions of being steeped in history, one of the favourite places of the European royals in the 1700s and 1800s and a home of art and music. Much as we acknowledged the impressive architecture on our trip from the airport into the city, however, we were there on business – serious football business. For once, the laughing and joking were muted, the atmosphere among the players was quite serious, with little messing about. We had grasped the importance of this game, which could take us on to be the first club in the history of British football to appear in a European Cup final. Even around our hotel, a fairly staid establishment, every player seemed to have his thoughts concentrated on the forthcoming match, the conversation at meal times unusually focused on football.

On the day before the match – due to kick-off in the afternoon – we trained at Dukla's stadium and found – much to our annoyance – that the pitch did not exactly have a "Wembley" surface and was quite narrow. It reminded me of Broomfield, the ground of Scottish club Airdrieonians. Those who saw a match there will remember it was not a pitch made for silky football. Unfortunately, the pitch in the Juliska Stadium was along the same lines. This concentrated my mind even more.

On the eve of the game, after dinner, we gathered in one of the hotel rooms for the team talk. This turned out to be one of the most surprising in all my years at Parkhead. The manager Jock Stein, otherwise known as "the Boss", had decided on a dramatic change in our tactics for this game and this was the first time I ever heard him talk defensive. He gave me the task of picking up Dukla's star player and midfielder Josef Masopust, who had been the 1962 European Footballer of the Year. He had also decided to play five in midfield, with only one up front. This was the first time in my career I had to play a defensive role but, on speaking with the Boss, he said he believed I would be up to the task. He told me: Just be where he is all the time and that will make it hard for his team-mates to use him.

Masopust was their main playmaker and was used to playing in space. It didn't take long after the game had started for it to become clear to me that he was unhappy with me being close to him all the time. So, I thought, it's working. After about fifteen minutes, as he received the ball in the middle of the field, I took a chance. I tackled him pretty hard from the side. I wouldn't have called it a foul, of course, but the referee did. He gave me a warning but not a card. But it worked in my favour, as now Masopust was looking for me every time the ball was passed to him and that meant he wasn't concentrating on the play as much as he should have been. The Boss's plan was working.

Our lone striker was Steve Chalmers and he was doing a fantastic job, making it difficult for Dukla to return the ball quickly and accurately. Stevie covered so much ground in that game, he must have felt he had run ten marathons. Meanwhile, I was sticking close to Masopust, trying to keep him out of the game. To be truthful, Dukla could have scored at least once before half-time but for good goalkeeping and defending, plus a little help from Lady Luck. We continued to hold on in the second half and, the longer the game went, the more dejected the Dukla players became. In the last ten minutes, it felt to me like they had almost given up trying to score.

When the final whistle came, I was struck by two, conflicting emotions. There was the obvious delight that we had won our way through to the final. Then there was some disappointment when Josef Masopust refused to shake hands and exchange shirts. He even gave me a slap on the jaw as we walked off. I do recall having given him a few hard tackles during the match but I was stunned and saddened at that. Then I started thinking that I must have done my job well for him to be so upset and joined the rest of the team, who were celebrating on the field. The cheering over, I approached the tunnel to head for the dressing rooms and found Masopust, standing waiting for me. He apologised for his behaviour and then exchanged shirts with me. I was relieved this happened as I had always admired him as a player. I could also understand his disappointment as he was reaching the end of his career and, most likely, this game had been his last chance of making a European Cup final.

As the dejected Czechs walked towards their own dressing room, we gave our small band of travelling supporters a wave. A photograph taken at that moment gives an idea of our feelings – everyone showing their delight – and when we made it back to the dressing room, the euphoria continued with all the boys on a high. The Boss was also well pleased, although one comment showed his cynicism was never very far below the surface: "I see we're now a British club – but if we'd lost we would still be Scottish!" Travelling back to Glasgow on the charter flight, we celebrated a bit more. Enjoyable though the champagne was, however, we still hadn't won anything. The chance to do that would come quickly, though, as at the end of the same week, we had to play Aberdeen in the Scottish Cup final at Hampden Park.

We had just four days between arriving home from Prague and the cup final so it was home for one night only, then off to Seamill to prepare. I often hear today of teams complaining about too many games at the end of the season but if it's handled properly, I think it can be good for them as games are the best way of keeping up fitness and there's no need for the heavy training sessions. This was one area the Boss excelled in; he seemed to know just how much preparation we needed. With just a few days to prepare for the final, we travelled to Seamill by bus and, as usual, there was plenty of banter and a card school (the game was brag and the stakes were very low).

On the subject of cards, I remember playing with Jim Baxter on a train journey from Kirkcaldy to London to watch the England–Scotland game in 1961, that England infamously won 9–3. Charlie Drummond, our goalkeeper at Raith Rovers at the time, was sitting in the corner of the carriage when Jim said: "U, r ye playing cairds?" Charlie said: "Naw". Jim replied: "Well, get oot o that seat. It's fur the caird players". So Charlie gave in and took a hand. By the time the train reached Dunbar, east of Edinburgh, Charlie was rising out of the seat and twenty pounds the poorer. As he vacated the seat, Jim (also known as "Stanley", after a well-known Scottish comedian) said: "At least ye hid a twenty pound view oot the winday tae mak it worthwhile". I digress – but that Saturday proved a disastrous day, having to watch Scotland lose by nine goals to three.

At Seamill, we were allocated our rooms – in pairs – and again I was sharing with big TG. I was becoming used to Seamill; I had now been at Celtic for almost six months and I'd shared with TG most times at the hotel. Over the years, Tommy and I had quite few adventures. One that comes to mind could be put down as a mistake by the Boss – for putting us in a ground-floor room. That meant a ground-floor window which, in turn, meant easy exit and entry. It was always a challenge to beat the curfew and head for the local watering hole to spend an enjoyable extra half-hour or so – but never the night before the game.

Without the need for heavy training after the match with Dukla, everything was done with the ball; short games, shooting and crossing practice, all on the front lawn of the hotel, just a short walk from the beach and the Irish Sea. Most of the squad were fit, except for Joe McBride who was still recovering from his knee operation. There was a quiet air of confidence about the team and every member of the playing pool was up for the cup final at Hampden if selected.

We had been reading in the press about Aberdeen's training camp at Gleneagles and, of course, their manager Eddie Turnbull was talking up their chances. In their squad was Jim Storrie, a player I had grown up with and played alongside in school and juvenile football. We had also played together at Kilsyth Rangers, Jim at inside-right and me on the wing. Jim went on to play at Airdrie and Leeds United before he joined Aberdeen. He had been playing up front in an attacking role for them but I had always thought Jim's best position was just behind the strikers. Anyway, I was looking forward to playing against him. Two Kirkintilloch boys in the cup final: Who would have thought?

After training on the Friday, that day before the big game, the Boss read out the team for the final. I was in the side at No.8, to play up front beside Stevie Chalmers. I can't explain the feeling I had – my first Scottish Cup final. I know it's an old cliché but I really could have "jumped over the moon". Before long, though, my mood switched to one of anxiety, nervousness. Would I play well or not? It took me a while to go to sleep that night.

I was up around 7.30am on the Saturday and down for breakfast at 8.00am. The newspapers were reporting that Eddie Turnbull would not make the trip from Gleneagles to Hampden Park as he had a severe stomach problem. That might have seemed to be something of a blow for Aberdeen but I also thought it just might spur on the Dons' players to try harder for their unwell manager. So there would be no complacency from us, I thought. We had a stroll along the beach before a short team meeting to finalise plans. After a light lunch, we set off for Glasgow, meeting the usual police motorcycle escort at the edge of the city. As we approached the ground, we began to realise the size of the crowd. All the roads to Hampden Park were packed and, after the game, I found out that over 127,000 punters had been there that day. I spoke to Jim Storrie before the game and asked about Eddie Turnbull, for whom I had a lot of respect as a manager. Jim told me he had a stomach problem which had recurred so he was confined to bed. I told Jim it was no wonder he was in bed ill after having to watch his lot play every week. Laughingly, Jim replied: "Well, we'll see out there."

I started to change for the game just after 2.00pm and, like most players, I had my usual routine. I didn't like to change in a hurry but didn't like to be last ready, either. Checking the boots, studs and laces were all in place didn't soothe my nerves, so it was a welcome relief when Bertie Auld piped up with a few words. I can't remember now exactly what he said but the gist of it was that if Eddie Turnbull had been feeling sick before, he would be feeling a lot worse by five o'clock. The nerves eased as I felt the confidence in the room. Team captain Billy McNeill ("Caesar") led us out as usual and what a reception it was as we came out of the tunnel. It was deafening. The excitement surged through my body. This was it, the biggest stage on the domestic front, the Scottish Cup final – and I was playing!

This was another important day in my football career as I scored two more goals that turned out to be crucial. At the time, my impression of the game was that we were always in control, passing the ball around confidently, seldom allowing Aberdeen a chance to show their form. In the press the following day, the journalists' comments were along the same lines.

The goals came either side of half-time. The first was fairly straightforward, when I side-footed the ball into the corner of the net through a crowded goal mouth. The second was much more memorable. After destroying a couple of defenders, "Jinky" Johnstone raced to the goal-line before brilliantly cutting the ball back. Stationed at the far post, I stepped back slightly to let the ball bounce once before volleying it, at about waist height, high into the roof of the net. It was a goal for a big occasion and both of us were delighted. "Great goal, Wispy", the Wee Man shouted as we swung each other around.

"How could I miss with a cross like that?" I said. It may sounds a bit soppy in print but, believe me, at the time, I could have kissed him!

The crowd that day was a record size for the Scottish Cup. It was also very vocal and it was a tremendous buzz to play in the atmosphere they created. To score in any final is a fabulous feeling but, even more than that, this was my first final as a Celtic player and to score the only two goals of the game was a great lift for me with the club's supporters. Taking to the field, I was hoping I would play well and that we would win, so putting two good goals in the net for Celtic was a bonus, as I felt I was repaying some of the outlay made by the club in bringing me to Parkhead.

As we all celebrated that evening at a hotel, I took a few moments to reflect on my own position. I had arrived at Celtic after the winning of the first two trophies of that season, the League Cup and the Glasgow Cup, so the victory that day in the Scottish Cup was my first medal in Celtic's colours. Ordinarily, that would be enough for any player but I was in the fortunate position of being with a side still in contention for the Scottish League title as well as, almost unbelievably, the European Cup, the final of which lay just a few weeks ahead.

Chapter 2

NO GREAT EXPECTATIONS

When people write or talk about the achievements of the team known as the Lisbon Lions, they usually mention the fact we were all born within a thirty-mile (fifty-kilometre) radius of Celtic's home ground in the east end of Glasgow. As the years have gone by, it seems more and more amazing that a group of football players who were, by European standards, practically neighbours should have managed a feat such as winning the continent's most coveted club trophy. And you could safely bet now, in these days of multi-million-dollar teams assembled from all over the world, that the European Cup will never again be lifted by a bunch of players not only from the same country but just one small part of it.

Possibly less well known is that the distance of thirty miles is only needed to include one of our number. Bobby Lennox was brought up – and still lives – in the seaside town of Saltcoats, on the Ayrshire coast. The others all came into the world much closer to the Parkhead district of Glasgow, where the Hoops have played since 1888.

In my own case, I was born in Kirkintilloch, just three miles outside the Glasgow city boundary, on 23 June, 1940. Home was a small farm cottage in the local district of Hillhead and I was the third child in the family; my siblings, James and Margaret, at the time apparently quite taken with the new addition.

My father, Andrew, like my mother a native of Kirkintilloch, was born in 1909. He had been a foundry worker all his life, employed at the local Star Foundry. In his earlier days, he had been a goalkeeper for an amateur team in the area, which I think was called Hillhead Football Club. Dad also had a brother and a sister, my uncle Hugh and aunt Sarah. Uncle Hugh never married and aunt Sarah married Donald Manson, one of my favourite uncles when I was a boy.

My mother, Sarah, was also born in 1909 and came from one of those large families more typical of that era; she was one of eight children, three boys and five girls. Her own father had worked as a barge man on the Forth and Clyde Canal and, later, on the "puffers", small cargo boats that plied the canal and small ports along the western coast of Scotland. Mum had started work at fourteen years of age on the pit-heads at the Waterside coal mine, separating coal from stones. My maternal grandmother died of throat cancer when my mother was just sixteen and mum then had to look after the younger members of the family until she was married. Even while bringing up her own family, my mum took various jobs as a domestic help and continued working until she was in her late sixties. Both my parents are now deceased.

My father wasn't really a football supporter and, although he took an interest in the results of some matches, he didn't support any team. My brother, James, played the game from the age of twelve through the Boys' Brigade and church football but, after serving an apprenticeship, he joined the Army and that was the end of his football career. James was always well respected by his peers as a player and I'm sure he could have played successfully at a higher level than he did, although I do remember him saying he wasn't all that keen on training.

Most of my relatives supported Rangers. As a youngster, I didn't support any particular club but, when I was about thirteen, one of my cousins, Margaret McCulloch, who was about three years older, took me to my first senior match. That was at Ibrox, to see Rangers play a British Army side. My mother only allowed me to go because it wasn't what she felt was a "serious" game; in other words, it wasn't a league or cup game. From then on, I spent much of my free time playing football but, on the odd occasion, I would go to Falkirk, not far from Kirkintilloch, to see Falkirk FC play at their home ground, Brockville. I was permitted to go to these games only if Celtic and Rangers were not involved, my mother being worried about me getting into trouble among the big crowds that followed these two teams. I shudder to think what she thought years later, when I couldn't have been more involved in "Old Firm" occasions.

The farm cottage was a great place for a young boy to grow up. Outside there was plenty of room to play and we had various animals. Across the road from the cottage was another farm – owned by the Lawson family – and I spent many hours helping out around the Lawsons' farm, bringing in the milking cows in the mornings and evenings and helping with the harvests. My favourite dog was a black Labrador, fairly unimaginatively called Rover. More interesting was the cat's name, Adolf. Adolf was a great catcher of mice and rats, had a very white face and dark whiskers and had a habit of raising one paw which, of course, caused him to look not unlike Hitler. Well, whatever Adolf meant by raising his paw, it looked a lot like the Hitler salute – and he certainly took no prisoners!

My bath-time was a real experience. This always happened on the same day as the washing was done in the outside wash-house, in a huge, copper, fire-heated boiler. After the baths, we were carried back into the cottage wrapped up in towels. The toilet was outside, next to the wash-house and it often froze in the winter. As a wee lad, I was never particularly brave at going outside to the toilet in the dark evenings and it was a case of getting out and back in as fast as my feet could carry me. I'm not sure I was the brightest kid in the family but I did have a great imagination. Many a time I charged out of the toilet pulling up my trousers after hearing a funny noise of some sort and imagining werewolves and monsters.

My closest friend in those far-off days was a boy called Willie McFarlane, who lived in an old tenement building across from our cottage. Willie's father was an Irish immigrant and there were nine children in the family, so we always had plenty of company. Another close friend was Jack Telfer. Unfortunately, Jack had contracted polio as a young boy and had a caliper on one of his legs – but that never held him back. Our main playground was the banks of the Forth and

Clyde Canal, at the bottom of the fields leading down from our house. We swam doggy paddle-style in the canal as soon as we were able and when you could swim to the other side, you became a fully initiated gang member.

We lived in that farm cottage from 1940 to 1952. Then we moved further up the same street to 127 Hillhead Road, a brand new, three-bedroom council house with fitted kitchen and bathroom. The luxury of an inside toilet was indescribable; well-lit, warm and – most important – no werewolves. We were still living in that cottage when I started school at Lairdsland Primary. It was a good school and, right from the beginning, I was happy there, although over a lengthy period leading up to Christmas in my first term, heavy snowfalls covered the area and we were completely snowed in; it must have been three or four feet deep.

One of my first teachers at Lairdsland was Mrs Jarvie, a tall lady with perfectly permed hair. She was a very caring person but also extremely strict. Two other lady teachers were Miss Laurie and Miss Hardie. It isn't too hard to guess that we soon had their nicknames sorted out: Laurel and Hardie! Miss Laurie was extremely small and came to school every day on a bicycle. Her head only reached its saddle when she stood next to it. When she was actually on the bike, she was known as the "pea on the drum". Obviously dedicated to their profession, she and Miss Hardie taught well into their sixties.

When I was around eleven years old, a new headmaster came to our school, Mr Davidson. He was as wide as he was tall and quickly gained the nickname of "The Bull". At 4pm every day when the bell rang, there was always a race downstairs to see who could get out of the building first and, on Mr Davidson's very first day, I ran smack into him at the front door. Running was against the school rules, so I had to be punished and the new headmaster took me back to his room and delivered the punishment of two cross-handers with a leather belt. That was our first encounter and, over the following twelve months, there were to be a few more.

Even during these early days, football was a major part of my life. It was our main form of play and, as you can imagine, while the fields all around gave plenty of space for the game, the quality of pitches left a lot to be desired. I would have been about six when I saw my first football match at junior level. Junior football in Scotland doesn't have anything to do with age – you can be eighteen or thirty-eight and play junior football, just as you can be either of those ages and play senior football. It is just a level of football and many towns and suburbs of the bigger cities are home to teams that play at "junior" level. I was taken by some older cousins to watch the local junior team, Kirkintilloch Rob Roy, in action, although I can't remember who was the opposition. By the time I was eight or nine, my school friends and I were making our own way to Adamslie Park to see the Rob Roy play. In those days, Glasgow was a long way off for a "wee lad frae Kirkie", so we never attended any of the big matches in the city. That had to wait another four or five years.

During these years when I was watching Rob Roy, the centre-half was Des Connor. While playing for Celtic, I met Des's brother Jackie Connor, an ardent Celtic supporter who was a friend of The Boss, Jock Stein. Jackie travelled throughout Europe with the Celtic team during the years I played with them. In 2007, at the 40th anniversary celebrations in Las Vegas, USA, of Celtic winning the European Cup, I was lucky enough to meet up again with Des Connor, who now lives in San Francisco. He was amazed that I could remember watching him play in many games for Kirkintilloch Rob Roy back in the late 1940s and here he was helping me celebrate winning a European Cup medal.

Around 1950, if you lived in Kirkie, you were fortunate indeed, as this was the town in which you could buy the best ice cream in Scotland. Ice cream shops and cafes had been established in the town by the Italian Ghiloni family, who had settled in Kirkintilloch in the late 1800s. As luck would have it, on my way home from school I had to pass one of the shops, on the corner of Main and Victoria streets. It was run by one of the Ghiloni brothers called Victor and his wife Concetta. They had a daughter, Nancy, who was blessed with lovely, long black hair and exceptionally good looks.

As I hailed from the district pronounced locally as "Hullheed" (or Hillhead, to the toffs), I wasn't always welcome in Victor and Concetta's shop as I was usually trying to get ice cream for nothing. Mrs Ghiloni would shout: "That's that Hillhead boy again, get oot o ma shop". I would know then to take off quickly. Victor also had an ice cream van and Hillhead was part of his rounds so I'm pleased to be able to say we always got our ice cream – when we could afford to, we bought it and, when we couldn't, Victor would give us a "freebie". He would park near the football pitch and watch us playing and I'm sure he made a few sales while he was there. I grew up at the same time as Nancy in Kirkintilloch but I never got to know her all that well, just in case she thought like her mother and told me to "get oot"! Olive and I were to meet Nancy again later in life, when introduced to her by Olive's sister Hazel, who worked alongside Nancy. We socialised a lot when we lived in Scotland and became very close friends. Since Olive and I have been living in Australia, we have spent many happy times with Nancy and her husband Steve Andersen when we have been holidaying back in Scotland.

My first competitive game of football was for the school team at Lairdsland Primary School in 1951, at the age of eleven. Normally, you had to wait until you were in Primary 7 to get a game but I managed it in Primary 6. We were selected to play for the team by the school janitor Mr Archie Miller and his method of selection was simplicity itself. Each boy took a penalty kick: if you scored, you were in; miss it and you were out. You won't find Archie Miller's method in any coaching manuals but they worked for our team – we lost only one game during the whole year.

I seem to remember that the goalkeeper tried his best to get all his pals in the team but, as he was as small as the rest of us, it was very difficult for him to influence the selections by saving any penalties. Mr Miller actually moved the penalty spot in towards the goal by a couple of paces so most of us could reach the net with our kicks – and that made the 'keeper's plan even harder to achieve. In fact, there were few complaints over team selection, as Mr Miller had a pair of size 13 boots, large enough to settle any argument. Of course, there was no such thing as political correctness in those days, when a good boot up the rear end was the norm. You daren't even mention it to your parents, as they would automatically take the side of whichever staff member was involved and you could well be on the wrong end of another "boot" for your trouble.

I played at right-back then, because I could kick the ball further than most of the other boys. We played our home matches at Rob Roy's ground Adamslie Park, mainly on Saturday mornings. If that wasn't available, we would use a field called Old Mill Kelvinside, also in Kirkintilloch. Our opponents were mainly teams from other schools in

East Dunbartonshire, our main rivals being near neighbours St Ninian's. We also played against teams from some of the surrounding towns such as Bishopbriggs, Chryston, Croy, Condorrat and Cumbernauld. The only time I can remember playing against a Glasgow side was in the West of Scotland Schools' Cup, when we met Springburn Public School. They beat us 2–0 on a red ash surface – my first experience of it – and it was not an enjoyable outing. I was glad to get back to Kirkie, where all the pitches were grass.

If I've given the impression that these early years of my life were almost idyllic, then I've succeeded in my mission. These were wonderful, happy times. The only real worrying moment in my life came at the age of five, when my father contracted tuberculosis through his work at the foundry. He was hospitalised in Helensburgh and I would travel there with my mother to visit him every second Sunday. Like many people, we didn't have a car and that made the journey a long one. First, we caught a bus from Kirkintilloch to Glasgow and then another from the city to Helensburgh, a trip which took three hours. We visited from 11am to 3 pm and then made the three-hour trip home again. My dad was in hospital for almost a year and, as you might imagine, things weren't easy for my mum and the family. Fortunately, my dad recovered and was finally able to come home and go back to work. He seemed to have reasonably good health for the rest of his life and didn't appear to be troubled by any lasting effects from the tuberculosis.

The other problem in my primary school days came right at the end, when all of us had to sit the Qualifying Examination, usually known as the "Qualie". How we fared in this would determine which school we would attend for our secondary education and, we were always being reminded, was an important moment in our education. For once, football had to take second place.

When the results of the "Qualie" were published, I found I had done well enough to have earned the choice of attending Lenzie Academy or the local Townhead Secondary School. The former had a reputation as an academic institution, where teaching of languages was given particular importance, while Townhead concentrated its efforts on technical subjects. Even as an eleven-year-old, I saw my future as being in a trade of some sort, so Townhead was my choice. Its reputation for having a pretty good football team might also have had something to do with it.

Most of my classmates moved to Townhead as well, such as Jim Baillie (nicknamed "Bunty"), Walter Dobbie ("Doeball") and Willie Reid, who tragically died at the age of sixteen after an accident at a heap of coal mine waste – or coal "bing", as they were called. He had been gathering lumps of coal and selling it to neighbours when the hole he was in collapsed and he suffered fatal head injuries. A guy called John Breton spent a lot of time in my home as he was from a one-parent family and there was company to be had. One of my best mates at that time was Kenny Knox, who lived in the same area as I did; Kenny went on to play for Hibernian. Jim Storrie joined my class from Townhead Primary School. Jim's stepfather was Willie Hewitt, who had played for Partick Thistle at left-half; Jim went on to have a successful career with Airdrie, Leeds United, Aberdeen and several other clubs.

The school team was organised by the physical education teacher Mr Wilson. He also coached us, as he had earned a Level Two coaching qualification from the Scottish Football Association coaching centre at Largs, south-west of Glasgow, in Ayrshire. Mr Wilson helped improve our heading, passing and ball control skills but didn't know a lot about playing the game as he had never played himself. The best thing about him was that he never had a bad word to say about our play and all he ever did was encourage us to do our best. Thanks to him I learned, even at this early stage, that it's better not to criticise players when a word of encouragement goes ten times further. Mr Wilson also got me involved in basketball – I played for the school against others in the area – and springboard diving, for which I had to travel to Springburn public baths in the north of Glasgow, as there was no pool at Kirkintilloch.

In my first year at Townhead Secondary, we went through the season undefeated but, as there was no league, the fixtures were all friendlies. It was the same in my second year. By third year, though, we played in an organised league, in which we finished fourth out of ten teams. By this time, I was also playing for the Boys' Brigade in the East Dunbartonshire/Stirlingshire league.

My mother attended church every Sunday and encouraged her family to do the same. Hillhead Parish Church was fairly new and the minister was an ex-police superintendent called Mr Borthwick, who was also captain of the Boys' Brigade company, the 4th Kirkintilloch BB. Most of my friends joined this new company, whose ethos encouraged us to behave well and have respect for others and their property, irrespective of religion or race. I enjoyed the religious side of the Boys' Brigade and attended Bible classes, followed by the church services.

However, when it came to football, the BB had some disadvantages. There was only one level and, as long as you were not over eighteen, you could play. If you were good enough at fourteen, therefore, you could be playing against guys four years older than you. Our pitch was at Hillhead, about 300 yards from the church. Unfortunately, it was just an open field which sloped to one side and, when it rained, the water was channelled off to that side, creating ruts in the pitch. It was used so much and had so little maintenance that, in the centre from goal to goal, the surface was quite bare; grass managed to grow only out on either wing.

We played against other BB teams from the northern suburbs or small villages around Glasgow, such as Bishopbriggs, Kilsyth (which had three BB companies) and Chryston (two), plus the other three in Kirkintilloch. In our league, there would have been up to 20 teams. For the most part, I played at outside-right, a small, fairly slight figure out on the wing. I soon learned to get away from full-backs and find space to receive the ball but I think that was more an instinct for survival, as the backs were normally much bigger than me and none too particular about how they tackled. The referees were normally one of the officers from either company and were not always up with the rules – if they knew many at all! During one season with the team, when I was around sixteen, I fancied a bit of a change and played in goal for a few games. I did fairly well in the first few matches – until we met the 1st Bishopbriggs BB, who beat us 14–0! Suddenly and painfully, I realised I might not have a future between the sticks.

It all sounds a bit disorganised, yet I look back on that time as a great learning period. You quickly had to learn how to look after yourself on the field and, apart from playing football with the school and BB teams, I spent many, many hours kicking a ball with mates. Throughout the summer, we would still be out at 10.30pm, seven days a week. This was where, unknowingly, we improved our techniques and became fairly skilful – proving the old adage that the more you practise, the better you become. As a group, playing football was all we had to do. We had no TVs, computers or video games, so playing on and on in the slowly fading light of the late summer evenings was common. We would play for hours, swapping positions from goalkeeper to fullback, wing-half to winger; all positions were covered, which gave us a good understanding of the game.

During my BB years between eleven and seventeen, I attended the Boys' Brigade camp at Stonehaven, in Scotland's north-east, just south of Aberdeen. Mr Borthwick's number one lieutenant was Mr Hugh Brownlee, recently discharged from the Army in which he had been an officer. Naturally, the camps were run military-style. There were groups of six boys in each tent, with inspections every morning at 7am, so wake-up was at 6am. Then it was a mad rush to wash, dress and get the tent, bedding and kit all organised ready for inspection.

Each tent group had a day of fatigue duty starting at 7am. For those on fatigues, the call to rise was at 5.30am, which gave them a chance to have everything prepared for inspection and still be on time reporting to the cook. The boys would have breakfast at 8am and then were called to parade by 9.30am, when checks were made on numbers and any points of dispute sorted out. During the morning, there would be activities for each group, such as wayfaring, fishing and swimming off the rocks, head tennis, cricket, baseball and five-a-side football; all designed to keep everyone occupied.

Lunch was at 12.30pm and 1.30pm and those who were not on duty were allowed to go into town, five miles from the camp. The camp was set up in a field belonging to Gallaton Farm, south of Stonehaven on the coast road to Montrose. The farm was owned by the Begg family, who supplied milk, potatoes and vegetables to the camp. When I was eleven and one of the youngest at the camp, I became friendly with the Beggs' elder son Duncan. I remember that Duncan had a younger brother and sister and his mum was a primary school teacher. Mrs Begg would read stories at night for her younger children but she was such a good storyteller that I loved to sit in with the family for the tales. She read Robinson Crusoe, Long John Silver and Tales of Robin Hood, to name a few. My favourite was Rob Roy McGregor. Mrs Begg was expert in making the characters come alive by adding her own interpretations of them and the stories in which they played their part.

Stonehaven at that time was one of the few towns in Scotland which boasted an outdoor swimming pool of Olympic dimensions and also diving boards and a slide. During the summer, we often watched competitions where promising swimmers and divers tried to qualify for the Scottish national, Commonwealth Games and Olympic teams. On our first day at camp, a priority was to buy a fortnightly ticket for the Stonehaven swimming pool.

Once the officers found out which other Boys' Brigade companies, Scouts or other youth organisations were in the area, they set about organising football matches. Around 1955, Stonehaven Juniors, who played at Cowie Park in the northern part of the town near the swimming pool, began organising tournaments for five-a-side and eleven-a-side teams; they also entered a local team in both competitions. The eleven-a-side team was restricted to under-eighteens and the five-a-side tournament was open to all ages. The prize for the eleven-a-side winners was £10, with £5 going to the successful five-a-side team. One of those In the Stonehaven team in 1957 was a goalkeeper called John "Jack" Reilly, later to join Hibernian before emigrating to Australia in 1970 and representing them against West Germany, East Germany and Chile in the 1974 World Cup in Germany.

Near the campsite – about a mile-and-a-half away - was Dunnottar Castle, one of the best-known and most spectacular castles in Scotland. While at camp back in 1951 or '52, the story went around that the castle was haunted by the "White Lady", who had apparently been imprisoned with a group of Covenanters in a tiny dungeon with just one small window. In the year that followed, one by one, they died. Nowadays, the "White Lady" was said to appear at the castle's gate around midnight.

There was midnight bathing at the Stonehaven pool on Friday and Saturday nights and we were allowed to go once we had reached the age of fourteen. With no buses to take us back to the camp, it was a lengthy walk which, as fate would have it, led us past the gates of Dunnottar Castle. Our group would approach the castle keeping perfectly silent then, about twenty yards from the gate, we would take off, running as fast as we could without a word being said, for at least another 200 yards. Of course, with a bunch of excitable young boys, there was always someone who would say "I saw her!" I have to be honest, however, and admit that, for all the years I was there, I never laid eyes on the ghostly "White Lady". And, to be equally honest, I'm quite happy I didn't.

In my junior years, I had no great expectations. I had a thoroughly enjoyable childhood – surrounded by many cousins and friends – and lived each day as it came. We always played together and in the summer went hiking in the nearby Campsie Fells and swimming in Campsie Glen. I always enjoyed kicking a ball around but I had no grand dreams of becoming a professional footballer or anything like that. I just wanted to get through school and had no plans and no ideas about what the future might hold.

Chapter 3

WILLIAM WALLACE MEETS ROB ROY: THE JOURNEY TOWARDS BECOMING A PROFESSIONAL FOOTBALLER

I left school at the age of 16 and followed most of my relatives into work at the Forth and Clyde Steel Foundry in Kirkintilloch, where I became an apprentice moulder. At the same time, I also joined a local juvenile football club called Kelvinside Thistle, which played in the Glasgow and District Under–21 League. They played at Old Mill Kelvinside Park in Kilsyth Road, Kirkintilloch, a good pitch with a fair covering of grass on it all year round. Two old railway carriages had been converted into dressing-rooms and the committee had put in running water but only of the cold variety. Unless we were really muddy after a match, most players preferred to go home for a bath.

This was a very well run and successful team and I collected a few medals over the 45-match season. During that campaign of 1956–57, we won our league and league cup – the Andy Roberts Cup and West of Scotland Cup. We lost in the semi-final of the Scottish Cup, beaten 1–0 by Westrigg Bluebell at the Armadale Juniors' ground. Playing for Westrigg Bluebell at this time was Alex Hamilton, who later played for Dundee and Scotland. Alex and I went on to play for Scotland in the same team, although at that first meeting we were just two young boys finding our way in the game; I don't think we actually spoke to each other.

At this stage of my life I was still involved with the Boys' Brigade and was even thinking of becoming an officer. In 1957, as usual, I went to the BB summer camp at Stonehaven and, once again, took part in the tournaments organised by the local junior club at Cowie Park. Then fate took a hand. After one match, an older gentleman approached me and asked if I would like to have a trial for Benburb Juniors in Glasgow. This gentleman was Mr Shields, a member of Benburb's committee, who was on holiday with his family in the town. I was more than happy to accept his offer and, in the first week of August, played the trial at Benburb's ground –Tinto Park – just along the road from Rangers' stadium at Ibrox. There were two remarkable things about this trial game: In a twist of irony, it was against Rob Roy of Kirkintilloch, my home town team; and, almost unbelievably, playing for Rob Roy that day was a centre forward called Steve Chalmers, one of the men with whom I would later share many of the greatest moments in my career.

Benburb won the game 3–2 and afterwards the committee asked me if I would sign for them. I told them I would like some time to think it over and, without any ulterior motive, accepted the offer of a lift home in the Rob Roy team bus. During the journey home, Rob Roy's manager asked me to play for them on the following Saturday against Blantyre Celtic at Adamslie Park, their home ground in Kirkintilloch. I agreed and a week later helped Rob Roy to a 10–3 win, in which I scored two goals and Steve Chalmers three. Curiously enough, we weren't rivals for the same position at that time, as I usually played in the outside-right role.

Things then became more complicated as, while I was still thinking about Benburb's offer, the Rob Roy committee decided to ask me to sign for them. However, on the advice of one of my uncles, I turned down Rob Roy's offer. Jim Brown was my mother's brother and a man of sound ideas. He told me that if I played for a local team while I was living in the town, we would cop it all week if we lost. He felt the reception I might receive when I went into work at the foundry on a Monday could well depend on the result of Rob Roy's game on the Saturday before and he thought I could do without that. It was sound advice, which I was happy to take on board. On the following Monday

I met good friend Jim Storrie, who had played with me at Kelvinside Thistle. Jim was signed and playing for Kilsyth Rangers and asked me if I would travel to their training with him on the next night, Tuesday, to have talks with that club's committee as they, too, were interested in signing me. I agreed and, after successful discussions I signed up with Kilsyth Rangers Football Club. Kilsyth were in the same league as both Benburb and Rob Roy.

All round, it turned out to be a good decision. Although Kilsyth is only five miles from Kirkintilloch, that small distance made a big difference, as there were very few Kilsyth Rangers' fans working at the foundry at the time. Fitting in to the team was easy, too, as I was again playing with my friend Jim Storrie, with whom I had played in schools' and juvenile football. And I was joining a good side, as Kilsyth had won the Scottish Cup the season before and there was plenty of competition for places. Opponents raised their game to match us, which became clear in one of my first matches when we met Duntocher Hibs. At right-half was Patrick "Paddy" Crerand, another player whose great career saw him enjoy six years with Celtic. Paddy was a commanding figure on the field, even in his early days at Duntocher Hibs. Always a team player, he was an excellent passer of the ball and a vigorous competitor who encouraged everyone around him. He hated to lose.

Rob Roy were disappointed I had signed for Kilsyth Rangers, partly because they liked to have a high percentage of local players in their team. The Rob Roy club president was also the owner-manager of the Forth and Clyde Steel Foundry where I was employed, so I copped a lot of flack as there was a strong rivalry between Rob Roy and Kilsyth Rangers. Around the late '50s, these teams competed for the Coronation Cup each year, the game attracting a large crowd, and winning the cup gave the winners "bragging rights" for the following year. Fortunately, I only played for Kilsyth for six months, so I didn't play in the Coronation Cup competition. In fact, I didn't stay long in junior football, playing about twenty-eight league and four cup games before joining Stenhousemuir in the Second Division of the Scottish Football League.

I signed on 28 January, 1958, and the connection with Stenhousemuir — or the "Warriors", to use their nickname — came through their one and only scout. Unfortunately, I never did meet the man who gave my career this significant boost and I don't even know his name. Anyway, after he had recommended me, I was approached by Mr Alan Johnston, secretary of Kilsyth Rangers, who asked me if I would be interested in a trial match with the Warriors. I accepted the invitation and travelled on the appointed day for the game at Stenhousemuir's home ground Ochilview, which was against East Fife. The Kilsyth Rangers' committee man who accompanied me had a fine day; he was well looked after in the boardroom, enjoyed a few whiskies and earned a £5 note for his expenses. John Macaulay and I got on very well that day and, as it happened, in the days and years ahead, too, when he became my father-in-law!

I was also well looked after that day, especially at the end when I was handed a brown envelope. Not being used to such things, I waited until I got home before I opened it and, to my delight, found inside a crisp £10 note. I don't think I'd ever seen one before. Needless to say, I soon signed on the dotted line for more, making my debut for Stenhousemuir against Dumbarton at Ochilview on 22 March, 1958.

It wasn't an auspicious start — we lost 6–1! Playing in the second division was even tougher than in the Scottish Junior League although, in those days, the Junior League was really senior football. Most of the players at Stenhousemuir were over 30 years old; only a lad called John Kilgannon and I were under 25 – and I was 17.

Around this time, flu injections were introduced and Stenhousemuir was one of the first clubs to take advantage of them. I was chosen to visit the treatment room for my needle along with a chap called Rab Quinn, a former Hamilton Academical and Celtic player. Rab had red hair and quite a young face but I knew he was well over 30 years of age. The doctor was busy filling in our forms and innocently enough asked Rab how old he was. In response, an embarrassed Rab told the doc to look after me first and that he would tell him how old he was after I had left the room. Being a youngster, I was a bit surprised at all this but, as my career continued, I discovered that most footballers are touchy about their age – especially in their later years!

We had a goalkeeper at that time called Archie McFeat and everyone reckoned Archie was close to 45. He was injured against Inverness Clachnacuddin in a Scottish Cup game at Inverness in that season of 1957–58, the damage effectively finishing his career. After Archie came a "young" 'keeper called Stan Gullen, who arrived from

Preston North End. At 43, Stan was two years younger than Archie and his inclusion lowered the average age of the team to 37! I felt like a baby and that season I was the youngest player playing in the Scottish Cup.

I remember that game against Clachnacuddin for a very unusual incident in which the referee awarded a penalty from the other end of the field. We were mounting an attack on the Highlanders' goal when the whistle blew and the referee ran all the way up the pitch towards the goal at our end. The linesman had apparently seen our goalkeeper kick one of the opposing forwards and signalled the referee. We were all astonished by the decision, although it only contributed a little towards our 5–2 defeat.

Back then, most second division clubs were run by a committee and Stenhousemuir was no different, although a human dynamo called Jimmy Weir called just about all the shots. We only had one trainer/physiotherapist – one person combining both jobs – and the senior players would take training so he could attend to any injured players. That trainer/physio was Bill Williamson, who had joined the club from Bo'ness United. He was the first trainer I ever knew to have music on while we trained, the tannoy blasting away all through the session.

The physical side of the preparation was excellent but, on the coaching side, we did very little. Training facilities were also very good, as we used Ochilview and the pitch was always in superb condition. Our training gear was also first-class; always clean, with warm tracksuits for winter. The only item players had to provide themselves was a jockstrap. Boots were supplied, cleaned and kept at the ground, although we did train and play in the same ones. It felt like I was in a new world and I just loved being involved. I was still working in the foundry while, on the social side, I had started going out with a lovely young lady called Olive, whose dad had accompanied me to Ochilview when I transferred from Kilsyth Rangers.

Towards the end of that season, we met the league leaders Arbroath at Ochilview. Much to my delight, we beat the "Red Lichties" 7-0 and pulled up to within a few points of them, with Greenock Morton one point behind. Promotion seemed very much on the cards and I was excited. Strangely, however, things did not work out in our favour in the final few games of the season, during which there were a lot of mysterious team changes. Of course, promotion could have been a financial disaster for the club, which would have found it very difficult to maintain a first division place. The ground would have required considerable upgrading and the support base was only small. Anyway, for whatever reasons, we played some very unusual team combinations in those remaining games of the season, results didn't go our way and the promotion that had seemed more than likely only a few weeks earlier didn't come about.

The other thing I'll always remember about Stenhousemuir was that the ground was next door to McCowan's toffee factory. At Christmas and whenever we had a good result in the Scottish Cup, we would receive a big box of toffees. I loved the old "penny caramels" and a box of them was just up my street.

The chairman at the time was Alex Cummins, the secretary Jimmy Weir was the backbone of the club – as most secretaries of small clubs were at that time – and my first full season at Stenhousemuir was very enjoyable. I travelled by bus for training on Tuesday and Thursday nights, getting a lift on the way home from left-back Bobby Kennedy, who had played earlier in his career for Third Lanark. He would drop me off at Kilsyth, where I would meet Olive for half-an-hour at the café before catching the last bus for the night from Kilsyth to Kirkintilloch.

I was still playing at outside-right but was knocking in a few goals and receiving some publicity in the press. After a holiday with some pals, I reported for pre-season training. This went well and, as the season got under way, things seemed to be much the same as in my first season. Unknown to me, though, someone was monitoring my progress.

On Friday, 23 October, 1959, my night-before-the-game ritual had been as normal. I had gone along to our local cinema that evening with a couple of pals and, after the movie, visited the local fish and chip shop, got my usual order and walked home. When I reached the house, I was surprised to find Jimmy Weir and some officials of Raith Rovers sitting in the living room. My parents did not have a telephone, so they had just had to wait until I arrived home.

I was introduced to the Raith Rovers' manager Bert Herdman and another man, who was one of the directors. I asked my mum and dad to stay in the room and the negotiations started. The two clubs had apparently agreed on a transfer fee of £2,500 and now they needed my agreement to the move. That didn't take long. About an hour after arriving home, I had signed as a full-time player on a wage of £18 per week, plus bonuses. To say I was delighted was an understatement. First of all, to be a full-time footballer was the dream of all the boys I went to school with; and secondly, I would be bringing in more money. Between my apprenticeship wage and my earnings from Stenhousemuir, I had been averaging around £7 a week. Now I would get £18, with the possibility of more if we won. No wonder I was happy!

Then, just to add the icing on the cake, I received a signing-on fee of £200 and I thought I was a rich man. The money was paid in two instalments, the first after my debut game with Raith the following Saturday and the second one month later. I bought a new car, an Austin A30, which cost me £190 – £60 down and a bank loan for the rest – and travelled all over the central belt of Scotland to show it off. By the time I changed it for a newer model, it had covered over 200,000 miles. What a great little servant.

STENHOUSEMUIR: FACTS AND FIGURES

1 February 1958 – October 1959

First senior match, first senior goal and first senior hat-trick

UNDER the heading "New Ochilview Winger", The Falkirk Herald of Saturday, 1 February, 1958, noted that: "On Tuesday (28 January) Stenhousemuir signed William Wallace, 17-year-old outside-right from Kilsyth Rangers. The player had a run with the 'Warriors' during the (Christmas and New Year) holiday games and created a good impression. He travels with the team to Arbroath this afternoon." On the same page was news he had been selected to play in that league match at Arbroath.

On the following Saturday, 8 February, 1958, the Herald carried a match report. It said: "It was only some lucky saves by Williamson, the Arbroath 'keeper, that deprived Tom Elder's boys from a deserved interval lead." Williamson was in defiant mood, with fine saves from Kilgannon in particular, including "a spectacular one-handed effort." However, 'Muir defender Neillands sustained a foot injury halfway through the first half and went to outside-left. He did not re-appear after half-time, leaving the visitors with only ten men – this was eight years before substitutes were allowed in Scottish football. 'Muir were down to nine men when Sutherland fell heavily and had to retire fifteen minutes from full-time. It was no surprise, then, that a heavily-handicapped Stenhousemuir – then a mid-table side – lost 2–0 to an Arbroath side challenging at the top of the table but eventually beaten for promotion by Stirling Albion and Dunfermline Athletic.

Teams:
Arbroath: Williamson, Sinclair, Young, Beveridge, Archibald, McLevy, Kirkwood, Shireffs, Anderson, Fernie, Sharp.

Stenhousemuir: Dodds, Sutherland, Kennedy, Neillands, Silcock, 'Junior', Wallace, Kilgannon, Stewart, Campbell, Keilt.

Referee: JB Barclay (Kirkcaldy).

Venue: Gayfield, Arbroath.

Stenhousemuir's problem appears to have been a leaky defence, eg conceding seven goals to Hamilton Academical and six to Dumbarton, Stranraer, Dundee United and Albion Rovers during that league season. Stenhousemuir finished the season fourth from bottom. Willie Wallace played regularly at outside-right during his time at Stenhousemuir, although he did play at outside-left in a 2–0 home defeat by Dunfermline on 29 March, 1958, with Stewart moving to outside-right.

Wallace's first goal in senior football came in the 4–2 league defeat by East Stirlingshire away at Firs Park on 5 April, 1958. The Saturday "pink" edition of the Edinburgh Evening News stated that, in the 25th minute, "Wallace scored from close in" to reduce East Stirlingshire's lead to 2–1. He scored his first hat-trick in senior football during a 7–0 home league victory over Arbroath – who were promoted that season – on 20 April, 1959. The goals came in the 20th, 27th and 68th minutes.

The "Warriors" finished the 1957–58 season in third place, five points behind second-placed Arbroath, in the process earning around £160 in "talent money". The Stenhousemuir team in those days was picked by five members of the committee, itself chosen on a three-yearly basis by the season ticket-holders. It was one of the few remaining senior clubs in Britain to have this arrangement, according to a Glasgow Evening Times report on 11 February, 1959, previewing the forthcoming Scottish Cup home tie against Partick Thistle, which Thistle won 3–1. The Larbert club has few claims to fame but it became the first Scottish club to host a floodlit match – as distinct from earlier, experimental forms of artificial lighting – when Hibernian played a friendly at Ochilview on 8 November, 1951.

Pat Woods

"... He used to comment that the favourite pastime in that town on Saturday night was going down to the Co-operative store to watch the new ham machine working. I guess nothing much happened in Cardenden on a Saturday night!"

Chapter 4

IF YOUR RELATIVES WON'T PAY TO SEE YOU, WHO WILL?

My team-mates at Raith Rovers were mostly seasoned professionals, like Alfie Conn, John Urquhart, Andy Young, Willie McNaught, Andy Leigh and Bernie Kelly. Alfie Conn had spent the earlier part of his career at Hearts, where he played in one of the best teams in the club's history with stars like Dave McKay, Jimmy Wardhaugh, Freddie Glidden, Alex Young and John Cumming. By then, Alfie was in his twilight years, as was another former Tynecastle man John Urquhart. Still, they were both very good players; indeed, John Urquhart was one of the best left-wingers in the league. Willie McNaught was one of the most talented left-footed players I have ever seen yet he received only five international caps, which was a huge injustice to a great left-back or centre- half. At that time, however, your selection for the national side often depended on which club you played for rather than your ability.

There was also a group of good young players coming through, like Willie Polland – who would later be transferred to Hearts, along with yours truly – Dennis Mochan, brother of Celtic trainer Neil and the one and only Jim ("Stanley") Baxter. Even today, most football followers will have heard of the ability of Jim Baxter. Back then, he was only 18 or 19 but he had the confidence of a seasoned player, no respect for reputations and loved to play football. I can remember going to Ibrox and elsewhere and Jimmy saying: "Don't worry about the game today. There's only one ball … and I'll have it". We played Rangers on 21 November, 1959, the Saturday after they had returned from playing Red Star Bratislava, where they had secured their place in the next round of the European Cup. Much to everyone's surprise, we beat them 3–2. Jim Baxter scored one of the goals, had a fabulous game and, just as he'd promised, kept the ball all day! Not long afterwards, Rangers signed Jim. I think it was to get the ball back! Like me, Dennis Mochan was on the young side. After a spell with Raith, he moved to Nottingham Forest and had a successful career in England.

Dennis, Jim, Andy Leigh and I played golf together at Burntisland, Kirkcaldy or Pitreavie golf courses. Jim and Dennis would share a set of clubs as they were both left-handed. The idea was that whoever was carrying the clubs would give the other one the club he wanted. However, if Dennis asked for a seven iron, he would be given a three iron, so you can imagine the scores. If Andy's wife was going shopping, Andy would bring his little boy with him but so he wouldn't wander off or be in any danger, Andy would strap him to a golf buggy and stick a lollipop in his mouth. We had many a hilarious afternoon at the golf – although sometimes it was a bit more serious!

As might be expected from a team in a higher division – Stenhousemuir were in the second division at the time – the facilities at first division Raith Rovers were a big improvement on those of the Warriors. We trained at the local council parks in Kirkcaldy, which had three or four excellent pitches, there was a good atmosphere at the club and it was always enjoyable at training. Our coach – the first I ever had – was Jacky Stewart, who had played for Raith before going to Birmingham City. We also had a trainer – I suppose today they would call him a conditioner or fitness coach – called Willie Hunter, who had been a very good sprinter in his day and ran under the name of "Willie Black" in the professional Powderhall sprints in Edinburgh. He was an excellent trainer and a strong disciplinarian. On Fridays, we had sprints at Raith's ground Starks Park and if you finished last in your group once or twice in the morning session, you were given the job of rolling the pitch in preparation for Saturday's game. I'm sure that roller weighed two tons, not that I pushed it very often. Jim Baxter, however, was a regular. Jim hated training.

Jacky Stewart would work more with the younger players and, in the afternoons, we would spend time taking corners, crossing balls or in passing drills, anything to improve our game. He concentrated on areas suited to each individual player. For example, I would take corners and practise crossing on the run, while Jim and Dennis would concentrate on passing and target practice.

Willie Hunter took all the main training sessions but, as he also doubled as the physio, Jacky or one of the senior players would fill in for him. I remember one day the older players played a trick on Willie, who was often making statements that he should be the Scottish national team trainer and that every other trainer was useless. After training, one or two of the players went to the press telephones in the stand, phoned the office and asked to speak to "Mr Hunter". When Willie came to the phone, they told him they were calling from the Scottish Football Association (SFA) and that he had been selected as trainer for the Scottish team to play against Wales in two weeks' time. Of course, Willie took it to be true and went straight to the manager's office to tell him the news.

Bert Herdman had been manager of Raith Rovers for many years and was a great character with a keen sense of humour. Unfortunately, when he became excited, he started to stutter. When Willie told Bert the news, he laughed and said: "Willie, ha..hav..have y..ye gone aff.. faff..aff y..y..yer he..he..heid? The fo..folk in Gla..Glasgow are n..no tha..that da..daf..daft!" He then picked up the phone and called the SFA, who confirmed Willie would not be the trainer for the Scottish team for the match against Wales. Needless to say, Willie was more than a little disappointed and, when he found out what had transpired, he let us all know it in no uncertain terms. Of course, he got his own back at training sessions over the next few months.

Bert was like most managers of that era, in that we never saw him during training. In fact, he didn't even have team talks. The side chosen would just be posted on the board. Before a match, the captain Willie McNaught would have a few words to say before we went out on to the pitch. In those days, like every other club, we were still playing the old W/M formation well-known to all of us – two full-backs, centre-half, two wing-halves, two wingers, two inside-forwards and a centre-forward and, of course, a goalkeeper. So we were all aware of how the system worked, our own roles in it and who we should pick up. I suppose the manager felt there was little left for him to contribute. But Bert was right up to speed with all the other aspects of the game – like the provision of tickets.

Just before my first game for the club, I had received my allocation of two complimentary tickets, which my brother and father would use. My uncle and cousin had also travelled up to the game with my father and asked if I could obtain tickets for them, too, so I went to Bert's office and asked him if I could have two extra tickets. Well, you would have thought I had asked for a rise of £100 pounds a week. He said: "Wh..wh..who a..are th..they f..fur?" I replied: "My uncle and my cousin". His voice rose and he stuttered back: "If..fif y..your rel..rela.. relations w..will no p..pay t..tae se..see y..ye pl..play, who w..will? No extra tickets!" I didn't buy any extra tickets for my relatives, as most of them followed Rangers and all the teams I played for in Scotland played against Rangers. Therefore, any tickets I got were at the wrong end of the ground for my relatives, even the two complimentary tickets. It always seems the most important people at clubs receive most of the complimentary tickets. Who are they? Certainly not the players!

The funniest incident I can remember about Bert was when the club decided to have a Christmas dinner-dance at the Station Hotel in Kirkcaldy. All the town's dignitaries were invited, including the Lord Provost – who was the club chairman – and his wife. The first bloomer came when the players came to book into their rooms on the afternoon of the dance. The married couples had all been allocated to single rooms and all the single blokes and their girlfriends allocated to double rooms, a bungle of even greater magnitude given the public morals of that period. Once that was all sorted out, things went well, until the band set up ready to start and Bert went to the microphone to introduce the first dance. He said: "Th..th..the fir..first da..da..da..dance w..will b..b..be a w..wal..waltz". The band leader asked if it was to be an old-time waltz or a modern waltz. Bert replied, with the microphone still on: "Y..you jus..just pl..pl..play th..the fu.. fu..fu****** mu..music an..and we..we'll d..d..dae th..the fu..fu.. fu****** da..dan..dancin'!

Raith were a good team to play with as there was always a word of encouragement from the older players and, of course, there was the added benefit of playing with Jim Baxter. Even in those early days, you could tell that Jim was going to be a world-class player. He had the confidence of a veteran and was extremely positive about his own ability. In saying that, he was quite a shy person, both on and off the field. Indeed, Willie McNaught once made the comment that Jim "could not get a 'bird' in an aviary". Jim was later to prove him wrong!

At Starks Park, Jim was always in trouble as his time-keeping was not the greatest. He drove an old ex-army motorbike and made a remarkable sight as he rode along with a leather helmet, pair of jeans and a singlet in the middle of winter. The bike broke down more often than it went, so he would often be late for training. Yet that shyness came to the fore when Rangers came in to buy Jim and he didn't want to go. Willie McNaught talked to Jim and convinced him it was the right thing to do. He also added a few other words to Jim, as he did to me when I left to go to Hearts: "To continue to train and work hard and to stay away from the 'bevvy'." Jim was never keen on training but he was made to put the effort in while at Raith and he didn't drink alcohol at that time. I only wish Jim had listened to the last part of Willie's talk. Not only would we have seen Jim at his best for a lot longer but we would still be able to enjoy his company today.

At Raith, we had some silly results in a few games near the end of the season. I remember one match against Third Lanark, who, unfortunately, went out of existence in 1967. The game was at Kirkcaldy and until half-time we were playing very well and were 2–0 up. As the second half progressed, we went from bad to terrible, hardly crossed the halfway line and lost the match 3–2. There were a few senior players in our side who didn't seem too worried about the loss. I had no idea then what was really going on but it was a game I thought we should never have lost.

My game had improved immensely during my time with Kilsyth, Stenhousemuir and Raith. It was at Starks Park that I made the biggest change in my football career, the move to centre-forward. It proved to be an inspired move as, after the switch, I was fortunate enough to score goals on a regular basis – and there were some memorable games.

In the Scottish Cup of 1960, I recall the third-round tie was played in front of 20,000 people at Starks Park against Celtic. We hadn't been playing all that well in the league but neither had Celtic. Stevie Chalmers opened the scoring for Celtic after seven minutes but I managed to equalise six minutes later. An unfortunate own goal by Andy Leigh within a minute of me scoring put Celtic ahead 2–1. Celtic scored another two goals through Willie Fernie and John Hughes and we lost the match 4–1, although the newspapers said we had given a good account of ourselves. This was my first experience of the "Old Firm".

Raith had signed me to replace Jimmy McEwan, who had been transferred to Aston Villa, and part of the transfer deal was a game for Raith Rovers against Aston Villa at Villa Park, Birmingham. At the time, Villa were one of the prominent teams in England and it was a fantastic experience for me playing at their home ground. Their left-winger, a Northern Irishman called Peter McParland, was one of the best players in England and performed exceptionally well against us. We played well enough in the match but lost to a very good side.

Aston Villa visited Starks Park on Tuesday, 27 September, 1960, for the official opening of the floodlights. I remember this game as we wore our third-choice strip to allow Aston Villa to wear their normal colours, white with two blue hoops. Villa was managed by Joe Mercer, one of England's best-known players who became a distinguished manager. The score finished 2–1 in our favour, with Bernie Kelly scoring the first goal and yours truly the second. I played at outside-right that night as I was just making the transition from winger to centre-forward and could play in both positions.

Raith Rovers made the trip to Wembley in May, 1961, to watch Scotland play England in that disastrous 9–3 defeat, forever remembered – however unfairly – as "Frank Haffey's game". In my opinion, it was a very ordinary performance on the day by all the Scottish players but, as usual, the goalkeeper shouldered the blame. Returning from London through Yorkshire, we played Leeds United on the Monday night in a game organised to help cover the cost of the Wembley trip. The Yorkshire club had been promoted back into the English first division thanks to stars such as Jackie Charlton, Billy Bremner, Johnny Giles, Norman Hunter, Gary Sprake and Eddie Gray. They might have had a reputation for rough play but they were also a great side. We lost 2–0 but I have always put that result down to the weekend in London – not the ideal preparation!

Leeds United played a return game at Kirkcaldy on 10 October, 1961. Don Revie brought his young Leeds side to Starks Park and, on this occasion, we beat them 4–1. Yes, they did have their first team out on the pitch and it was a great result for Raith, although I can't remember whether I scored or not. Just three weeks before that match against Leeds, Raith played an Israeli touring team, Petach Tikva, and won 4–1. Again, I can't recollect scoring in that game but I do remember a comment made by Bert Herdman as the Israelis came through the main entrance carrying five or six huge suitcases: "A..a th..th..think th..they..they've come fae th..th Gle..Glesca Ba..Barras t..tae sell us s..s..some s..s..suits." This thought apparently came to Bert because our team usually carried all our boots and strips in two large hampers.

I enjoyed my time living in Kirkcaldy with a family called Roseweir, whose home was just two minutes from the ground. Ma and Pa Roseweir were a fantastic couple. Pa had been gassed during the Second World War and never left the house; Ma was a great lady who looked after him and was also like a second mother to me. They had two sons who were both coal miners, the elder of whom lived in Cardenden, a small town a few miles north-west of Kirkcaldy. I only remember that because he used to comment that the favourite pastime in that town on Saturday night was going down to the Co-operative store to watch the new ham machine working. I guess nothing much happened in Cardenden on a Saturday night!

If my memory serves me, I only paid about £3 and 10 shillings a week in rent and, knowing the importance of a good home life for a football player, I was happy and content. It did not matter where I was going or what I was doing, I always left Mrs Roseweir's house wearing a clean shirt. Even if the one I had taken off had only been put on to go across to training in the morning, I would have to have a clean one in the afternoon.

Their semi-detached council house was extremely homely inside, while outside there were front and back gardens, both of them always spotless. I often used their back garden as a shortcut to Starks Park via the churchyard, which was immediately behind the house. My bedroom was fairly large with a double bed and Mrs Roseweir kept the room as fastidiously clean as if it were a hotel room, clean towels always at the ready. They placed no restrictions on me regarding times of coming and going, either, as I was the only person lodging at the time and they had given me my own key to the house. I had full board with the Roseweirs and the meals were always first-class; home baking, baked dinners, scones, pancakes – you name it, I ate it!

The only drawback for me was that I missed seeing my girlfriend, Olive, who lived at Kilsyth on the western side of Scotland. Olive would give me some grief about not phoning often enough but it was difficult. I could only reach her at work as the family did not have a phone at home and, with my busy timetable, 5pm would come around too quickly and I would realise she had already left her office for home. Things weren't too bad, though, as I was able to see her most weekends.

Five other young Raith Rovers' players were housed opposite Starks Park in a three-bedroom tenement apartment. They were helped by a lady who came to their apartment each morning at 7am and left each night at 6pm and who cooked and cleaned for them. I can remember four of the five: Jimmy Stevenson and Jim Peebles, both from Paisley; Pat Connolly, from Coatbridge, who later became a policeman; and Billy Watson, from the Alloa area. During the two years I spent in Kirkcaldy, there was a different story every day. On one occasion, Jim Peebles met a girl at the dancing on a Wednesday night and he invited her to come to the movies with us on the Friday night. He had organised to pick her up from her work but he didn't realise she worked at a fishmonger. When we picked her up in my car, she was still wearing her little white Wellington boots and the clothes she had worked in all day. Unfortunately, the smell of the fish was still strong when we settled into our seats at the cinema and within a very short time we had three empty rows in front of us and another three behind us. In the end, poor Jim sat by himself with the girl as we all deserted them for an area where the aroma was more pleasant. She was a lovely girl – but that was the first and last date.

Raith's goalkeeper at this time was Jim Thorburn, who had joined the club from Douglasdale Amateurs in 1956 and was sold to Ipswich Town in May, 1963. After a spell in England, Jim returned to Scotland to play for St Mirren. Occasionally, he used to stay over at Mrs Roseweir's after a midweek fixture, as there was an extra bedroom. He and I would go into town after a match, usually to the dancing –

although it was always a rush because if you weren't in the ballroom by 10pm, you wouldn't be allowed in. After one evening match, it was almost 9.30 by the time we made our way up through the churchyard and the back garden to Mrs Roseweir's. I rushed in through the back doorway, said a quick "hello" to Ma and Pa sitting in the lounge and headed for my room to change. When I came down again, I looked for Jim but he was nowhere to be seen. I stuck my head into the lounge to ask whether Jim had come in through the back door. Mrs Roseweir said: "No, son, the door's still open". I went out into the back garden to call for Jim and saw him … flat on his back on the grass. I could hear him moaning so I ran to where he was, bent over him and said: "What's wrong?" He gargled: "I ran into the clothes-rope"! Being much taller than I was, Jim had obviously not seen the line and the rope caught him fair and square around the neck. He was lucky not to have "hung" himself! By this time, Ma Roseweir had come to the back door to see what had happened and, when I told her, she couldn't stop laughing at Jim's misfortune. All the same, with Jim still rolling around on the grass moaning, we decided we should call an ambulance but Jim managed to reassure us both when he muttered: "Don't bother, I'm sure I'll be OK".

So our original priorities were restored, we both jumped into the car and, by a few short minutes, just made it to the dancing in time. Needless to say, Jim's chances of meeting a young lady that evening were not helped by the fact that he hadn't had a chance to pick up a clean shirt and, perhaps more important, his neck was bright red, like someone had recently tried to strangle him! It didn't matter much, anyway, as we were both engaged lads and really only at the dancing to listen to the music!

RAITH ROVERS: FACTS AND FIGURES

October 1959 – April 1961

IN the Fife Free Press of 24 October, 1959, "Novar" reported that Willie Wallace had been signed for Raith Rovers on Thursday evening, 22 October, along with Ian Spence, an inside-forward who had been a prolific goal-scorer during the past four years at Stirling Albion. The fees were not disclosed. Stenhousemuir secretary Jim Weir had told the Glasgow Evening Times that the fee was "moderate but sufficient to keep the wolf from the door." "Novar" added that Wallace was regarded as one of the most promising young wingers in the Second Division and both players had been signed because the Raith management needed to strengthen a side which had lost six matches in a row, three of them at home. Both players made their debut against Clyde at Stark's Park on 24 October, a match Raith won 3–1.

Teams:
Raith Rovers: Drummond, Polland, Mochan, Young, McNaught, Baxter, Wallace, Leishman, Kerray, Spence, Urquhart.

Clyde: Thompson, Walters, Haddock, White, Sim, McPhail, Wilson, Herd, Meek, Robertson, Ring.

Referee: WD Massie (Dundee).

Venue: Stark's Park, Kirkcaldy.

Attendance: 5000.

Clyde opened the scoring in the 47th minute through Robertson. Two minutes later, Jim Baxter equalised from the 18-yard line after Kerray side-footed the ball to the inrushing left-half, who walloped it high into the net. Kerray scored the other two. "Novar", commenting in the 31 October edition of the Free Press, said both Spence and Wallace had added "some much-needed running power" to the Raith attack.

Wallace's first goal for Raith came in his second match for club, against Third Lanark at Cathkin Park on 31 October, 1959. According to the Scottish Daily Express report the following day, Raith centre-forward Kerray "slipped down the wing and crossed to Wallace, in the centre position, to side-foot the ball home." Raith won the match 3–1.

Wallace's right-wing partners in his debut season at Raith were Leishman, Conn and French. With Wallace in the side, Raith had a sensational 3–2 League victory against reigning champions Rangers at Ibrox on 21 November, 1959. Rangers were two up inside thirteen minutes but, four minutes later, Raith were level through Kerray and a Baxter 20-yarder. Kerray scored the winner ten minutes after the interval. This was the match in which Baxter's performance made Rangers' manager Scot Symon determined to sign the player, which he did eight months later. A year earlier, a back-page snippet in the sports edition of the Glasgow Evening Times of 8 November, 1958, had noted that Baxter, one of the young players involved in a "coaching spell" with Scottish team manager Matt Busby before a recent international match against Northern Ireland, "was not considered to have the strength and build for a top-class wing-half when he joined Raith but is now considered among the best."

Willie Wallace's first match against Celtic took place on 9 January, 1960, a 1–0 defeat at Parkhead. Only two players in the home side that day would go on to partner Wallace in the Celtic European Cup-winning side over seven years later, namely Bertie Auld and Billy McNeill, who was playing at right-half in a half-back line of McNeill, Evans and Peacock. The only goal in this match was scored by Neil Mochan, later the trainer of the Lisbon Lions.

Three weeks after that Celtic defeat, Wallace was a member of a Raith side which suffered an embarrassing Scottish Cup exit at the first hurdle, a 2–0 away defeat at the hands of Second Division Queen's Park on 30 January. Before the match, Raith chairman Jimmy Gourlay had remarked that Raith would be the only team to get a practice match at Hampden before the final, a comment that backfired as the home side's Charlie Church "roasted" the usually reliable Raith pivot Willie McNaught.

Wallace went into goal ten minutes from the end at Motherwell on 16 April, 1960, after Raith keeper Jim Thorburn was stretchered off with concussion following an accidental clash with Ian St John. The Sunday Post match report remarked: "Willie Wallace donned the (yellow) sweater and showed he, too, knows a thing or two about goal-tending." He kept a clean sheet during his short spell in goal, with the score remaining as it was before he went into goal, 2–1 for Motherwell.

In the 1960–61 season, Wallace's right-wing partners were Kelly, Spence and Easson. However, Wallace was fielded at centre-forward for the first time on 17 December 17, 1960, when Raith defeated Airdrieonians 2–0 at home. This re-positioning took place after the regular centre-forward Jim French was dropped – from both the first and reserve teams – after he and Denis Mochan, brother of Neil, failed to report at a Glasgow hotel at the appointed time before the match against Ayr United the previous Saturday. Although they arrived at the ground in time, the decision had been made not to field them. Raith chairman James Gourlay denied that the further dropping of French for the Airdrie match was a disciplinary action, telling the Fife Free Press that an opportunity was being taken to experiment with Willie Wallace at centre-forward in an attempt to add some "punch" to the attack. Ironically, Wallace himself had been dropped for the Ayr match, possibly a reflection of criticism he had received for his performance in the 3–1 home defeat by Partick Thistle on 3 December. There was an early sign of the experiment proving successful in the 2–0 away victory at St Johnstone on 24 December when, according to the Fife Free Press match report, the "terrier-like" approach of Wallace "often had Saints' defence in a dither." He scored in that match after Little, the opposing centre-half, failed to control the ball and "the nippy little centre" gained possession, eluded two defenders and slammed the ball past the 'keeper.

Wallace's last game for Raith was in a 1-0 defeat at Airdrie on 22 April, 1961, before an estimated crowd of only 2000 at Broomfield. Wallace had been regularly commended in match reports for his tenacity in a side which struggled to avoid relegation in the latter stages of the season, reaching safety but finishing third from bottom. Raith had been in decline since the departure of Baxter to Rangers during the previous close season for a fee of £17,500 – then a record between Scottish clubs – and had been suffering financially in recent seasons, rarely enjoying five-figure gates outwith visits from the Old Firm. Wallace's transfer to Hearts only three days after that Airdrie match was probably down to – or at least was clinched by – the impression he made in Raith's 1–1 home draw with the Edinburgh side three weeks earlier. The Sunday Post match report on that game described Wallace as "full of fire – the most dangerous forward afield."

SUMMARY OF GOALS AND APPEARANCES

Joined 22 October, 1959

NUMBER OF APPEARANCES (GOALS SCORED IN BRACKETS)

	L	LC	SC	TOTAL
1959-60	26 (12)	-	1	27(12)
1960-61	30 (12)	4 (2)	2 (3)	36 (17)
	56 (24)	4 (2)	3 (3)	63 (29)

Abbreviations: L = League; LC = League Cup; SC = Scottish Cup.

Pat Woods

"At Hearts, we were always fit and ready to go at the start of the season. This was the start of my sixth season at Tynecastle and, apart from the money disputes with the club, I enjoyed every moment playing there."

Chapter 5

AFFAIRS OF THE HEARTS

My next move was as unexpected as it was welcome. It was near the end of the 1960–61 season and, as usual, I had gone to training at Stark's Park in the morning. It seemed like a perfectly normal day when I made my way back to the Roseweirs for lunch. Not long afterwards, though, the groundsman called in and told me I had to go back to the ground by 1.30pm and be dressed to travel to Edinburgh on the train at 2pm. "Dressed" meant collar, tie and club blazer.

When I arrived at the ground the manager, Bert Herdman, told me we were going to Edinburgh, more specifically Tynecastle, the home of Heart of Midlothian FC, as they were interested in signing me and Willie Polland, our centre-half. Bert continued by saying in his own, unmistakable way that I shouldn't ask for too much money as I was going into the deal as "an extra pair of trousers for the suit"! "Mind you," he said, "you must be the 'short pair'." I think he meant my stature, not my playing ability, because when I was talking with him a year or two later, he told me he had let me go too cheaply and, if he had the chance again, he would have charged for a "waistcoat" as well. Bert might not have known very much about the technical side of football but he sure had a sense of humour.

Bert Herdman was one of those old-fashioned managers – similar to Scott Simon, Jimmy McGrory and Tommy Walker – who never had much to do with the playing side of the team or the individual players. But he was very good in one sense; he was straightforward. There were no hidden thoughts with Bert and what he thought, he said. He had firm grasp of what was required of a decent player and possessed a good head scout at Stark's Park at that time. They seemed always to buy cheaply but successfully. We were never regarded as a classy side, even though we had players such as Jim Baxter, Willie McNaught, Andy Young, Johnny Urquhart, Benny Kelly, Willie Polland and Charlie Drummond, who was the goalkeeper for many years. In the second team, we also had quite a few promising young players coming through so Bert must have been doing something right as he had kept the Rovers in the top league from 1947 to 1961. After Bert was sacked, it only took one season for Raith to be relegated.

Anyway, in this case, he did a good deal for Raith, as they received the sum of £15,000 for Willie Polland and me. I don't know what percentage I was of the £15,000 but a pair of trousers certainly wouldn't have cost much! Considering they earned this amount of money for two players and £20,000 for Jim Baxter's transfer to Rangers, it seems bargains were to be found when buying players from Raith Rovers as we were all playing in the top league in Scotland. Also, two of us went on to earn international selection and Willie Polland certainly had the ability, in my opinion, to play international football. By comparison, transfer fees between clubs in England at that time had reached up to £100,000 per player. Of course, today's transfer business is an entirely different matter.

My move to Tynecastle came just at the right time in my career. Hearts had done very well from 1955–60, then sold half of their team to English clubs. Dave Mackay had gone to Spurs, Alec Young and George Thompson to Everton, Bobby Blackwood went to Ipswich and all of them did really well in England. Jimmy Murray had also moved on, joining Falkirk. Still at Tynecastle were Willie Bauld, Gordon Smith, John Cumming, John Hamilton, Gordon Marshall and Bobby Kirk and the Hearts' management brought in six new players from other Scottish clubs – from Queen's Park came goalkeeper Jim Cruickshank and left-back David Holt, from Queen of the South inside-forward

Maurice Elliott, from St Johnstone another inside-forward John Docherty and from Brechin City wing-half Jimmy Sandeman, plus Willie Polland and me from Raith Rovers.

Later they bought a player from Aston Villa named Willie Hamilton, who was one of the best footballers I ever played with. Jock Stein, as manager of Hibernian in 1964, obviously agreed as he took Willie to Easter Road that season. If Willie's character had been as good as his play, maybe he would also have gone to Celtic when the "Boss" made his move west in 1965. I felt Willie Hamilton was every bit as good a player as Jim Baxter; in fact, Willie could use both feet and Jim was all left (although still better than most players who could play with both). Willie was always complaining of a stomach ulcer, which he blamed on the army food he was given during his compulsory period of national service. Eventually, he had obtained a medical discharge from the army. Willie's family lived at Airdrie but I don't think he went home very often; he drove a little A30 van and seemed to keep his belongings in it. He had not been doing too well with Villa and was sold very cheaply to Hearts. By this time, unfortunately, he was also beginning to have his fair share of problems off the park and these were affecting his play. Willie and Norman Davidson were good mates and socialised a lot in Edinburgh. Norman was from Kintore, just outside Aberdeen, and both were single so they had no need to account for anything they did away from the club. I could probably write another book with the stories that circulated about Willie but how do you separate fact from fiction? What I will do is repeat that Willie Hamilton was one of the most talented football players I had the privilege to play alongside – as good as Jim Baxter and I played many times with each of them. I know I would select both in my team, even in today's football. Sadly, both had the same hectic and ultimately self-destructive social lives.

My debut at Hearts was actually in the 1960–61 season, although I played only in the final two games of the league campaign. As these matches were not important either to the championship race or the fight against relegation, Willie Polland and I received permission from the Scottish League to play in them. My first match was against Dundee FC at Tynecastle, which we won 2–1. My first goal for Hearts was against Celtic in the following week at Parkhead, where we won 3–1. I remember that Celtic recorded one of the lowest crowds ever at Parkhead for that game, reported as 7,000. Our outside-right that night was a young player who had been released by Celtic; his name was Tommy Henderson. The Celtic team contained a few unfamiliar names, players trying to push their way into the first team. They included Frank Haffey, John Curran, Willie O'Neill, John G Kelly, John Kurila, John Clark, Bobby Carroll, John Divers, John Hughes, Steve Chalmers and Alec Byrne. Once again, the names Chalmers and Wallace appeared in the same match – although this time on opposite sides.

In the following season of 1961–62, we began to blend into a reasonable team and finished eighth in the league. We also reached the League Cup final against Rangers but, after a 1–1 draw in the first game, Rangers proved too strong in the replay and we lost it 3–1. I was selected in the team for the first game but injury prevented me taking part in the second. I also sampled European football for the first time, as Hearts had qualified for the Inter-Cities Fairs Cup, generally referred to as the Fair Cities' Cup. This was one of three European trophies at the time: The winner of the Scottish league played in the Champions Cup; the winner of the Scottish Cup played in the European Cup Winners' Cup; and the second- and third-placed teams in the league would play in the Fair Cities' Cup. Our opening Fair Cities match was against Union Saint-Gilloise, of Belgium, whom we defeated in both legs, 3–1 away and 2–0 at home, for a comfortable aggregate win. My first competitive goal in Europe came in the 70th minute of that second, home leg on 4 October, 1961. However, in the second round, we came up against an as-always very talented Inter Milan side and went down 5–0 on aggregate.

A real thrill for me in the early part of this season was to be in the same forward line as Gordon Smith. Gordon moved to Dundee shortly after I arrived at Tynecastle and was by then in the veteran stage but his skills were still there for all to see. He was a great example to all young players and the perfect gentleman on and off the pitch – except on one occasion I was aware of. Just outside the main door at Tynecastle, Gordon became involved in an altercation with a sports writer called Willie Ross, who wrote a derogatory article about him the previous week. Gordon just walked straight up to him and, without any conversation, smacked him in the mouth and walked through the front door into Tynecastle. I'm sure it gave Gordon some satisfaction and, fortunately, the reporter didn't take it any further. I felt Gordon should have had a lot more Scottish caps; he had great ball control, was very quick and crossed an accurate ball. In short, he was a typical Scottish winger of his day.

At this time, Hearts were using me in three or four positions and I was finding it difficult to change between them all the time. It turned out well, though, because during the final two months of the season I found a role playing just off the front striker which seemed to suit me perfectly, as I had a bit more freedom. Early in that season, Jimmy Cowie, of the Edinburgh press, wrote an article that said: "Twinkle-toed Willie Wallace is rapidly becoming a favourite of the Tynecastle fans after the match mid-week against Union St-Gilloise and could find himself established as Tynecastle's top football prospect". I still like to think Jimmy Cowie had been looking into a crystal ball when he wrote that!

After the disappointment of losing to Rangers in the 1961 League Cup final, all the boys in the side were determined to reach another final as soon as they could. To the delight of everyone in the team and the fans, that occurred in the following year when, in front of a crowd of over 51,000, we ran out at Hampden against Kilmarnock. It was a tough match with one goal settling it and, for the fourth time in the club's history, we took the League Cup back to Tynecastle. In the early part of the game, I was forced to do more defending than attacking as we were under fairly constant pressure. Relieving the defence with a long ball I managed to find Willie Hamilton, who controlled the ball, beat a couple of defenders and drew the centre-half with a glorious pass to Norrie Davidson, who promptly dispatched the ball into the net. The game was fairly even up to the last five minutes, when the ball was crossed into our box and Frank Beattie headed the ball home. From my position, I thought it was a goal and was extremely disappointed to lose an equaliser so late in the game. However, to my surprise and delight, the referee awarded a free kick for handball, the score remained at 1–0 until the end of the 90 minutes and we had won the League Cup. The League Cup win against Kilmarnock was my first experience of winning any silverware and playing at Hampden and winning the cup final both felt unbelievable. There was a fantastic crowd from Edinburgh to support the club and walking up to receive the winner's medal was very special. After the match, we travelled by bus back to Edinburgh, where we had a celebration night in the Charlotte Rooms in Charlotte Square.

I had another unforgettable victory in 1962. Olive and I were married on 2 April, which was a Monday. This date and day were chosen for two reasons, one being that the end of the tax year was on 5 April each year and, if you were married before that date, you could recover most of your tax paid during that year. The other was that Hearts had kindly given me three days off – I had to be back on the Thursday of that week for training. Our wedding was in the Anderson Parish Church, Kilsyth, with the Reverend James McDonald officiating. The day was cold and wet and the photographs were taken just inside the front entrance to the church as all of us tried to keep out of the rain. The reception was just across the road in the Masonic Hall and our local baker Harry Wilson gave us our wedding cake as a present and my friend Jim Baillie ran the bar for us. After a good reception with plenty of dancing, we enjoyed a rousing send-off in our A30 as some of the male guests shook it for all they were worth. We spent three days at The Covenanters Hotel in Aberfoyle, where it rained without even looking like stopping. I took one picture from the bedroom window and ventured out of the hotel only once, to visit the chemist. No, it wasn't to buy anything honeymoon-related – I had managed to acquire an extremely sore throat and, as I don't speak loudly at the best of times, nobody could hear a word I was saying. I also managed to fall over a stool in the bedroom. All in all, our three-day honeymoon could have been better.

In 1963–64, we were back in the Fair Cities' Cup but Lausanne, of Switzerland, proved difficult opponents and knocked us out in the first round. After 2–2 draws at Tynecastle and in Switzerland, the tie went to a third match which Lausanne, with home advantage, won 3–2. In the following season in the same competition, once we had disposed of Valerengens IF, of Norway, 4–1, we were drawn against Spain's Real Zaragoza in the second round. A 3–3 result at home was followed by a 2–2 result away. Then came the toss of a coin in the middle of the field to determine whether the third game would be played in Spain or Scotland. The timing was perfect: just as the coin landed on the grass, the floodlights went out. So everyone – players and officials – went back to their respective dressing rooms. UEFA officials quickly arrived to inform us that our captain John Cumming had guessed wrongly – but to this day I still have absolutely no idea how that was decided! We duly played the third game in Spain and lost 1–0. During my time at Tynecastle, we also had an Edinburgh Select team playing charity games, including matches against Chelsea and Tottenham. I played in a few of these and, despite the strong rivalry between Hearts and Hibs, the players always blended well and provided strong opposition for the English clubs.

As fate would have it, although Kilmarnock were involved in my very first "high" in football when we won the 1962 League Cup, they were also the cause of my first major "low" – losing the league championship on the final day of the 1964–65 season. On 24 April, 1965, we lost the league title to them in a dramatic game at Tynecastle. We could have afforded to lose 1–0 and still have been champions. Instead, we went down 2–0 and, once the mathematics was worked out, we lost out on the league title by 0.04 of a goal. In those days, of course, goal average (goals scored divided by goals conceded) determined the winners rather than simple goal difference. Hearts had scored 90 goals and conceded 49 throughout the season, a goal average of 1.83, while Kilmarnock had scored 62 and conceded 33, an average of 1.87. If today's system of goal difference had been in place, Hearts would have won comfortably by 41 to 29.

In terms of personnel, the Hearts team during the period 1961–64 was consistent. We had a squad of 20 players: Gordon Marshall was a fine goalkeeper; Bobby Kirk and Davie Holt were two capable full-backs; the trio of Willie Polland at centre-half plus wing-halves John Cumming and Billy Higgins made up the half-back line; Tommy Henderson, Johnny Hamilton and Bobby Blackwood shared the wing positions; Willie Hamilton, Alan Gordon and I parcelled out the inside-forward positions; while Norrie Davidson and Tom White shared the striker's role. Other players who joined the club during these seasons were full-back Chris Shevlane and centre-half Alan Anderson, while Roy Barry, Robin Stenhouse, Eddie Thomson and Tommy Traynor were pushing through from the second team. Mixed fortunes awaited the latter two in later years Down Under. After his playing days were over, Eddie Thomson went on to become the national coach of the Australian team, while, tragically, Tommy Traynor took his own life in Melbourne while still of a relatively young age.

The manager of Hearts at the time I joined the club was a gentleman called Tommy Walker. He was one of the famous "Wembley Wizards", a Scottish team which crushed England 5–1 at Wembley in March, 1928. Mr Walker never came to the training ground – except on a Friday lunch-time with the wages. He was also a lay preacher. Mr Walker looked after himself in every way; if we went into a training camp, he would stay in a luxury, five-star hotel close by but mainly would go sightseeing with his wife. John Harvey was the first team's trainer and coach, assisted by a chap called Donald McLeod, who doubled as the masseur.

At this time, I was enjoying some pretty good form and scoring goals on a regular basis. I scored more than 100 during my career with Hearts and, of all of them, it's the 100th goal that sticks in my mind more than any other. I hadn't hit the back of the net for almost five weeks and we were at home playing Falkirk, whose goalkeeper was a big lad named Willie Whigham, who was a more than competent shot-stopper. A cross from the wing eventually came my way and I swung my right foot at the ball. I completely mistimed the kick, whereupon the ball proceeded to hit my knee and shot into the roof of the net. Well, as everyone knows, "it doesn't matter how they get there, they still count" – and that was certainly the case with this particular effort, although I celebrated like I'd actually meant it and had just won the World Cup with it.

In 1964, I asked Hearts for a transfer. I felt I was due a bigger basic wage; I had been one of the top scorers for the club for four years but I was still on the wage I had agreed to when I signed from Raith Rovers. The wages at Hearts hadn't varied throughout those four years. They were £28 basic, £10 a win and £5 a draw – no appearance money and I don't remember ever receiving any signing-on fees for renewing my contract each season. I raised the topic of a wage increase with Tommy Walker at the end of the season but he refused to consider it, then I received a letter in mid-June to tell me training would start in early July and I would have to play for the same money, without a new contract. As the old retention system was still legal, I had no choice. Despite all this, it was to prove an eventful season; I was top scorer again and received my first international cap.

On Thursday, 12 November, 1964, I played for Scotland for the first time in a representative game against Tottenham Hotspur, a testimonial match for John White who had died on a golf course after being struck by lightning. We won the match 6–2 and Tommy White – my Hearts' team-mate – actually played for Spurs that evening. I had an exceptionally good second half playing at outside-right and scored a goal. The press reported on the following day that the team had created a problem for the Scotland selectors as everyone had played well. The players in blue that night were: Cruickshank, McCreadie, Kennedy, Greig, Yeats, Baxter, Wallace, Martin, St John, Gilzean and Wilson. The press also agreed that Jim Baxter – without his old buddy Dennis Law, an absentee that night – had played his finest international for Scotland thus far. His best was yet to come, though. "Stanley" was in great form that night but, in my opinion, his display against England at Wembley in 1967 was his greatest. Thirteen days later, on 25 November, I received my first full Scottish cap against Northern Ireland at Hampden Park. Jim Baxter captained Scotland that day and George Best earned one of his early caps for Northern Ireland. Scotland won the match 3–2 with Davie Wilson scoring twice and Alan Gilzean the other. I also played in a couple of Scottish League Select matches in season 1965–66, one against an English League Select at Newcastle and the other against a Northern Ireland Select at Ibrox.

At the beginning of that season, the rest of the Hearts' players decided to ask for a meeting with the manager to ask for a £5-a-week rise. I hadn't discussed my situation with anyone but Mr Walker and John Harvey, who agreed I should have had my increase 12 months earlier. The chairman of the club at the time was Bill Lindsay and the vice-chairman a Mr Strachan, both of whom attended a meeting in the boardroom at Tynecastle. They indicated to the rest of the board that they had no knowledge of any discontent expressed by any player for over two years. You can imagine how I felt. When the chance came – at our pre-season training camp at Dalguise House – to speak with the chairman, Bill indicated to me then that the board had no idea I had been unhappy for two years. At that time – and even today – I took that with "a little pinch of salt". I found it difficult to believe that, after two years and with the subject broached by the media from time to time and the number of occasions on which I had spoken directly to Mr Walker, the board would have no inkling of what was going on. Almost unbelievably, they also claimed they didn't know I had played out of contract for a year.

Anyway, before the start of that 1965–66 season, the board agreed to give everyone an increase of £5. In turn, I agreed to accept this as long as the club left me on the transfer market. Mr Walker was to remain as manager of the club, so nothing had really changed on that front. It may seem strange to modern players but I didn't know Mr Walker all that well; as I said earlier, he didn't attend training at any time during my six years at Hearts and we saw him only at Friday lunch-times when he gracefully handed out the wages. He spoke very briefly before our games and didn't mingle with the players at all. Personally, I think he could have been a lot fairer in his dealings with me. Almost a year later, towards the end of the season, I again went to see Mr Walker to discuss my contract. This time he accused me of being greedy, claimed I was a bad influence on the rest of the squad and left me out of the group who travelled to Norway for some pre-season matches. My thoughts at the time amounted to "nothing changes".

But things did change. At the end of season 1965–66, the SFA brought in a new contract in which the retention clause became an optional one, so all players had to sign these new contracts. To explain, I had played my early career under the retention system that I felt was unfair, as a player could not leave a club even if he did not agree to the conditions of the contract. The retention system proved to be illegal and was then altered to a system whereby, as long as a club did not pay a player any less than the previous season, that player remained the property of the club. This system was called an "optional contract". If a player did not agree to sign, he could still be sold on the transfer market. Not until 30 years later, with the Bosman Rule of December, 1995, was a player able to move to another club free of any fee. Until then, everything had benefited the club, not the player. Unfortunately, due to a mistake by Mr Walker's secretary, all the Hearts' players signed the old contracts, which were forwarded to the SFA. The governing body was quick to realise the wrong contracts were signed and, presumably, didn't spare their words in telling the Hearts officials to make the players do it all again – and as quickly as possible.

It was early July, 1966, and the playing staff had gone to a training camp at Dalguise House, outside Dunkeld on the road to Aberfeldy. This was an old country house that had been converted into a hotel for wayfaring and cross-country training. It was not a place for the faint-hearted. We arrived on Monday morning after travelling in our own transport and my travel companions were Tommy Traynor, Jim Murphy and George Miller. We stopped at a nursery near Bankfoot, off the Perth–Inverness road, where we picked up some fruit for the two weeks we would be in camp. Unfortunately, about half of it was eaten before we arrived at Dalguise House. When the four of us arrived, Mr Walker, John Harvey and the training staff were already there. Although Tommy Walker was nominally in charge, John Harvey was manager in all but name. He was an excellent coach, a very honest man, extremely approachable and always concerned if we wanted to discuss any team matters. He was also quite capable of dealing with individual problems you might have as a player. In my opinion, John should have had much more credit than he received for any successes that came Hearts' way over the years he was with the club.

We settled in and each of us was allocated two sets of training kit that became our responsibility. There were laundries in the main building, with washing powder supplied, dryers were available and, after training every day, we washed and dried our own gear. We also had to make our own beds, serve ourselves at meal times and then clean up. At the evening meal on the first night, I asked John Harvey if I could speak to Mr Walker, as he had promised my position would be discussed at the most recent board meeting, particularly the fee the club would need if I were to be transferred. John told me I would have to wait until lunch on Wednesday; Mr and Mrs Walker were staying in a five-star hotel at Pitlochry and had planned some touring on Tuesday so they would not be back at Dalguise House until Wednesday lunch-time. In the meantime, John said that if Mr Walker telephoned, he would let him know I wanted to speak to him.

All through this time, the Walker–Wallace relationship was a non-event. We seldom saw the man and in order to request a meeting with him, it was necessary to go through his secretary for an appointment. He was never at training and most days when we returned to the ground, he would already have left. To make communications even more difficult, we had dressing-room facilities at our training ground so we were not always at Tynecastle during the week. In any meetings or conversations I had with Mr Walker, he always assured me he would take any dispute to the board, then he would inform me later that the board had made a negative decision. Subsequently, however, I had found out that the board claimed to be unaware of any disputes! It sounds odd but that is how things were at Tynecastle – no one seemed to want to rock the boat and there was absolutely no way players were allowed to approach any of the board members.

Mr Walker had not been at Dalguise House since Monday but apparently had spoken with John Harvey a couple of times on the phone. On the Thursday morning, we had just finished breakfast and were relaxing on the lawn when the chairman's car pulled up. Naturally, we were all surprised to see Bill Lindsay at the camp and even more astonished when the vice-chairman Mr Strachan also emerged from the car. John Harvey walked out of the building to greet them. All three seemed sombre and quiet and they disappeared into the main building. After about 15 minutes, the team captain John Cumming and I were summoned to the dining room. At this time, I was vice-president of the Players' Union and Alex Ferguson – now Sir Alex, the manager of Manchester United FC – was on the committee. John Cumming and I were asked to sit at a table with the chairman and vice-chairman.

Bill Lindsay started by telling us the club was in a very bad position concerning the players' contracts and they wanted to discuss it with the captain, me as the players' representative and the manager Mr Walker. However, they had been unable to contact Mr Walker as he had left his hotel that morning to go sightseeing. Mr Lindsay was furious, as he thought the manager was in camp with us, not playing the tourist. They asked John Cumming and me to talk to the players about the situation and convince them to sign the new contracts they had brought with them. They ended by saying we would reconvene when the manager turned up.

John and I met with the players out on the lawn and the guys' first reaction was "Great! We're free agents". At that time, you had to re-register with the SFA by the end of April and, as all the players had been re-registered by the club – albeit on old contracts – they were technically out of contract. From past experience, however, we felt that the SFA would not be backing the players but was much more likely to give its full support to the club. I suggested we might ask for an increase in the basic wage and not create any fuss. I knew – and I think Bill Lindsay did, too – that to have the administrative mistake made public would have been terrible for the club's reputation. The press, as they say, would have had a field day!

At around 12.30pm, Tommy Walker arrived and within half an hour his contract was terminated and he was gone. That was the last time I saw him until some years later when I was playing for Celtic against my old club Raith Rovers, with whom, through John Urquhart, he had found a job. Amazingly enough, after the game he came up to me as if I was his long-lost son, shook my hand and wished me all the best!

After Mr Walker's departure from Dalguise House, Bill Lindsay had a meeting with John Cumming and me which lasted just 15 minutes. Mr Lindsay said that if the players agreed to sign the new contracts, the club would increase the basic wage by £10. Now as £10 was about two-thirds of the national basic wage, we had no problems convincing the players to agree to the deal, which brought a difficult situation to a satisfactory conclusion for all concerned. Yet, I've always wondered what might have happened if the Hearts' players had decided not to sign; I think it's quite possible that something similar to the Bosman Rule may have come in much earlier. In the end, of course, it was an awful lot of trouble for £10 – today a player pays that just to park his car for an hour!

In my role with the Players' Union, I knew the SFA wouldn't support the players if they didn't sign the proper contract, as union dealings with the SFA on behalf of players were never easy. For example, the union had been trying for many years to acquire part of the football pools' money to set up a fund to help part-time players after serious injury. If I remember correctly, I think the sum was £250,000 out of something like £3 million. The SFA's financial committee – made up of club directors – claimed this money was instead to be used to give players appearance money. Throughout my time in the union, we were unsuccessful in creating any type of insurance for the benefit of injured part-time players, the reason being that the SFA would not allocate even a small portion of the money it earned through the football pools towards any scheme to benefit players.

Despite the tumultuous events of the first few days at Dalguise House, the focus of our two-week summer camp remained on fitness for the coming season. Our training sessions consisted of three sessions a day, each lasting three hours. After a light breakfast, the morning session included a cross-country run over an army-type course, plus some circuit work on the field after the run. The after-lunch session would be mainly running exercises with a ball and, for the evening session, we would again run the cross-country course but without the circuit training at the end. This pattern continued; it was hard but well planned, as John Harvey was a master at making players fit and well prepared. At Hearts, we were always fit and ready to go at the start of the season. This was the start of my sixth season at Tynecastle and, apart from the money disputes with the club, I enjoyed every moment playing there.

I loved my time at Hearts. It was a great club to play for. The only thing that upset me came near the end of my time at Tynecastle, when some of the club's supporters accused me of not trying. The accusation came in a letter from a representative of the Hearts Supporters' Association after a home defeat. I chose to ignore the complaint as I knew within myself I had always done my best for the club and that, if I was successful, my family would reap the benefits. All the same, I was hurt by it. I have always prided myself in giving my all in every game. Like all players, I had my good days and bad but I'm proud enough to believe most of them were good.

My transfer request – which I had forwarded to the club over two seasons before – had never been withdrawn. I had been informed by John Harvey that some clubs, including Newcastle United and Stoke City, had made enquiries. The rumoured fee was around £80,000. Never for a moment, though, did I think a move to another Scottish club would raise my playing career to such a different level. Joining Celtic was to change my life forever. Within seven months, I had won everything I could win in Scotland – the Scottish First Division championship, the Glasgow Cup, the Scottish League Cup, the Scottish Cup and, of course, the European Cup.

HEART OF MIDLOTHIAN: FACTS AND FIGURES

April 1961 – December 1966

THE Scotsman of 26 April, 1961, reporting the previous day's transfers of 20-year-old Willie Wallace and the 25-year-old defender Willie Polland from Raith Rovers to Hearts for a combined fee of £15,000, noted that Raith fans were stunned and shocked. Although the Polland move was less of a surprise since he had asked for a transfer, the report added that "by letting Wallace, the most promising player on the Raith Rovers' payroll, go, the Stark's Park faithful are wondering where it is all going to end. The economic situation has, however, forced the hands of the Kirkcaldy management. During the past season they themselves have spent £15,000 on their successful struggle to avoid relegation (including £7000 to Hibs for Fox and Buchanan). Locals are concerned that the club's future has been sold. But, on the credit side, Raith will not be in the red at the start of next season."

As for Hearts, it was seen as a drastic move to remedy the mediocrity of a club which had recently – 1958 and 1960 – been Scottish champions but for whose followers 1960–61 had been "a long dreary season", the team ending in mid-table with 34 points from 34 matches.

Wallace's debut for Hearts was in the last home league match of the season at Tynecastle on 29 April, 1961, against Dundee (who would become Scottish champions the following season). Hearts won 2–1 through goals by Hamilton and Henderson, with Wishart scoring for Dundee. The Sunday Post reported that Wallace was "always cool, calm and extremely mobile and scarcely put a foot wrong. A most pleasing debut."

Teams:

Hearts: Marshall, Kirk, Holt, Higgins, Polland, Cumming, Henderson, Docherty, Wallace, Elliot, Hamilton.

Dundee: Liney, Hamilton, Cox, Seith, Ure, Wishart, Penman, Crichton, Waddell, Cousin, Robertson.

Referee: WM Syme (Glasgow).

Venue: Tynecastle.

Attendance: 14,000.

Wallace's first goal for Hearts came a few days later, on 2 May, 1961, at Parkhead against a Celtic team which had lost the Scottish Cup final replay the previous midweek to a Dunfermline Athletic side managed by Jock Stein. According to The Scotsman's report of Hearts' 3–1 win, Wallace's 15th-minute goal came when he "flashed the ball first time into the net from a Henderson cross." Wallace's direct opponent was John Kurila. The other scorer for Hearts was Davidson, who netted twice, while John Divers scored for Celtic.

Two of most memorable matches – for different reasons – of Willie Wallace's time at Hearts were the 1–0 League Cup final win over Kilmarnock at Hampden on 27 October, 1962, and the day a few years later when Kilmarnock claimed their revenge, defeating Hearts 2–0 at Tynecastle on the last Saturday of the season to take the league title on goal average.

In the first of these, the move leading to the 26th-minute goal was started by Wallace, back helping his defenders while Hearts were under constant pressure. According to the account in Scottish Football No.9 (edited by Hugh Taylor), "Wallace slung a long ball from the heart of his defensive area. The ball landed at Hamilton's feet. Almost casually, the inside-man took it under control. Off he meandered. Away on the left, he lured centre-half Jackie McGrory, beat him and cut back a glorious pass across goal. Norrie Davidson was storming in and he smartly whipped the ball into the back of the net from close range." The final had a controversial ending when, in the closing seconds, Frank Beattie seemed to have headed a dramatic equaliser from a Richmond free-kick. However, referee "Tiny" Wharton had apparently spotted an infringement – rumoured to be a handling offence on the part of Beattie – signalling for a free-kick to Hearts. The Kilmarnock players surrounded the referee, who then consulted a linesman. The decision was not changed. The Scottish Football account noted that: "Pictures and television films studied after the match failed to produce conclusive evidence. It is true that Beattie's hand was up. But it is also true that no Hearts player protested, the linesman's flag was not raised and there did not appear to be anyone else who saw what the referee saw."

Teams:

Hearts: Marshall, Polland, Holt, Cumming, Barry, Higgins, Wallace, Paton, Davidson, W Hamilton, J Hamilton.

Kilmarnock: McLaughlan, Richmond, Watson, O'Connor, McGrory, Beattie, Brown, Black, Kerr, McInally, McIlroy.

Referee: T Wharton (Glasgow).

Venue: Hampden Park.

Attendance: 51,280.

Kilmarnock earned their revenge on 24 April, 1965, when they defeated Hearts 2–0 at Tynecastle to snatch the league title from the Edinburgh club on goal average, the system then in operation for deciding the destination of the title when teams finished level on points. Two first-half goals by Davie Sneddon and Brian McIlroy took the title to Kilmarnock by the decimal margin of 0.04 of a goal. No club other than the Old Firm pair would win the title again until Aberdeen broke the Glasgow giants' duopoly in 1980. The other historic dimension of 24 April was provided by Celtic – now under the guidance of Jock Stein – who ended a major trophy famine of almost eight years by beating Dunfermline Athletic in the Scottish Cup final, a victory which Jock Stein always maintained was the keystone of the fabulous era at home and abroad in which Wallace, as a Celtic player, was to participate.

Teams:

Hearts: Cruickshank, Ferguson, Holt, Polland, Anderson, Higgins, Jensen, Barry, Wallace, Gordon, J Hamilton.

Kilmarnock: Ferguson, King, Watson, Murray, McGrory, Beattie, McLean, McInally, Black, Sneddon, McIlroy.

Referee: RK Wilson (Glasgow).

Venue: Tynecastle.

Attendance: 37,275.

Roald Jensen could have put Hearts on the road to the title in the fifth minute when he jinked past two defenders and drew the 'keeper from his goal but his shot hit the post. Kilmarnock struck twice as the half-hour approached, Davie Sneddon heading the first goal in the 27th minute from a Tommy McLean cross then, two minutes later, Brian McIlroy scored the second from a Bertie Black centre. In the closing minutes, Alan Gordon almost rescued the situation for Hearts with a shot from around fifteen yards which looked to be goal-bound, before Bobby Ferguson, the young Killie 'keeper, threw himself at the right-hand post and turned the ball away. Allan Herron, covering the match for the Sunday Mail, said on 25 April, 1965: "The cold facts are that Hearts just didn't have it when the chips were down. While Killie snarled their defiance and fought like tigers for every ball, Hearts wobbled." Hearts have only once come close since then to winning the title, Celtic edging them out on goal difference in 1986.

The dispute with Hearts that led to Willie Wallace joining Celtic came into focus around the start of season 1966–67 when John Hughes, the Scottish Professional Footballers' Association boss, publicly criticised the Edinburgh club. He said: "With regard to Wallace and Anderson, the committee and players are unhappy about the publicity given out by manager Walker regarding the contracts position. Both are under contract until June 1967 and the agreement between the Scottish League and the PFA does not specify a new contract be signed until the expiry of the old one." (Reprinted in Jim Craig's "The Story of Lisbon", part 6, Celtic View, 16 August, 2006)

Wallace's value to Hearts can be appreciated by the fact that, after joining the club towards the end of the 1960–61 season – when only two games remained to be played – he was their top-scorer in the seasons that followed until he left the club in December, 1966, nearly halfway through the 1966–67 season. Incredibly, he still finished that final season as Hearts top-scorer, with nine goals to runner-up Jim Murphy's seven. Hearts scored only 49 goals in their 41 competitive matches that season. Only 39 were scored in their 34 league matches, 10 in their six League Cup matches and none in the Scottish Cup, where they fell at the first hurdle to Dundee United. Contrast those 39 League goals – at the time, Hearts' worst haul in a 34-match season since the end of World War II, with their totals of 132 in winning the title in 1958 and 102 in 1960. Hearts scored barely one-third of the 111 scored by League champions Celtic in 1966–67. Wallace contributed 14 goals in his 21 league appearances during that unforgettable "clean sweep" season. It all underlines what an astute piece of business was done by Jock Stein.

SUMMARY OF GOALS AND APPEARANCES

Joined 25 April, 1961

NUMBER OF APPEARANCES (GOALS SCORED IN BRACKETS):

	L	LC	SC	EU	TOTAL
1960-61	2 (1)	–	–	–	2 (1)
1961–62	26 (6)	9 (5)	2	3 (1)	40 (12)
1962–63	34 (17)	10 (6)	2 (2)	–	46 (25)
1963–64	34 (23)	6 (3)	3 (1)	3 (1)	46 (28)
1964–65	34 (21)	4 (3)	4 (1)	–	42 (25)
1965–66	33 (19)	5 (3)	4 (2)	5 (3)	47 (27)
1966–67	10 (4)	6 (5)	–	–	16 (9)
	173 (91)	40 (25)	15 (6)	11 (5)	239 (127)

Abbreviations:

L = League; LC = League Cup; SC = Scottish Cup; EU = European competitions.

Wallace had the following record in the Summer Cup:
      1963–64: 6 (2)
      1964–65: 3 (1)
Hearts did not reach the final in either season.

He was in the Hearts team which won the League Cup in season 1962–63.

Pat Woods

"I had never had any problems with my family over which clubs I played for. However, some of my "friends" proved less loyal. I realised I'd lost some of these – mostly Rangers' supporters – on the first Tuesday night after I'd signed for Celtic."
(Signing for Celtic, November, 1966)

Chapter 6

LIFE CHANGES FOREVER: JOINING CELTIC

It all happened on a December day in 1966. It was a Tuesday, a day that invariably meant a slog at training – and this particular Tuesday was no different. After the hard work, we usually had lunch at the pub at Haymarket Station, mainly the first team players from the West of Scotland who travelled by train. I had travelled by car via Bonnybridge and Falkirk to pick up a couple of the younger players. I did my usual thing on the drive home, calling in at the bookies in Falkirk to give them my daily donation, then travelling on to arrive about 3pm. I hadn't been there long when the phone rang. It was the Hearts manager John Harvey, who asked me if I would be interested in talking to Celtic about signing for them.

John said Jock Stein had called him and would contact me if I were interested. He also told me both clubs had agreed terms and it was now up to me if the transfer went any further. As my wife Olive and baby daughter Lynn were out shopping and mobile phones were a thing of the future, I couldn't talk to Olive about it all. Only minutes after John's call, Mr Stein telephoned. He asked me if I would be interested in joining Celtic. I said I would and he invited me to go to Parkhead at 4.30pm that same afternoon. He told me the Hearts party wouldn't be there until 5.30pm and I asked him if it would be alright for me to be there without the Hearts' director and manager. He said he had sorted that out with John Harvey.

As I lived at Cumbernauld, only 30 minutes from Parkhead. I waited until 3.50pm before I left, hoping Olive might arrive and I could let her know what was going on. But there was no sign of her by the time I had to go, so I left for the meeting as the only person in my family knowing that anything was happening that afternoon, let alone that what might occur could well be the biggest move in my football career.

On the road, my mind was in turmoil thinking about all the practicalities. What terms should I ask for? What length of contract would be best? Was I really up to the move? These and many other thoughts kept me fully occupied during the drive into the east end of Glasgow. Then another thought struck me: what would the rest of the family think? They were all Rangers' supporters, like my uncle Jim Brown – my mother's brother – who was president of the Kirkintilloch Rangers Supporters' Club. Then I thought to myself that Uncle Jim had taken an interest throughout my career so far and his advice had always been the same: "Do what you feel is best for you and your immediate family". So I took comfort from that as I pulled into the car park next to the stadium they called "Paradise".

There was no one at the door when I approached the main entrance but I noticed a little, square window, so I knocked on it. A young girl opened the window and asked who I was looking for. I said "Mr Stein" and the gentleman behind her, with his back to us, turned and said: "Wispy – come in. The Boss will be with you in a few minutes". This man was Sean Fallon, assistant manager to Jock Stein. Sean took me through the front door and into the main entrance hall, where I sat down on a bench, beneath a picture of John Thomson, to wait for Mr Stein. John Thomson, as everyone who follows Celtic knows, was a famous Celtic goalkeeper, sometimes known as "the prince of goalkeepers", who died tragically in an on-field accident during a match against Rangers at Parkhead in 1931.

As I sat there, I reflected on what I knew of the man who, in a few minutes, might be my new boss. He had been a player with Celtic before his career came to a halt through injury, then moved into a coaching role with the Parkhead reserves. He had become manager of Dunfermline Athletic at the start of the 1960s and led them to a Scottish Cup win in 1961, plus the bonus of European competition. He then switched to Hibs in 1964, his new team soon winning the newly-introduced Summer Cup. It had been a good start to a managerial career.

I was also aware that he had joined John Harvey and, I think, Willie Waddell to visit Inter's training grounds at Milan, Italy, to study the methods of Helenio Herrera. Incidentally, after that trip Hearts had become the first Scottish club to use the 4–2–4 system in Scotland, although a well-known local journalist observed that it wouldn't be possible to play this system as only 10 players were involved. This journalist was also a boxing commentator for Scottish Television and, about this time, during a broadcast from the Kelvin Hall of a fight between a black American and a white English boxer, he tried to assist viewers by telling them the fighters were easily distinguished as one of them had a white stripe down his shorts!

After 10 minutes or so on the bench, I saw Mr Stein emerge from another room. He came over to me, introduced himself and took me into the boardroom (which I was to visit a few times over the next six years). Seated at the table waiting for us was the Celtic chairman, Bob Kelly. I sat on the opposite side of the table from both of them. Mr Stein did most of the talking, telling me that the terms would be £65 basic appearance money, plus bonuses for the League and the Cup. This was a great start for me, as my basic wage at Hearts was £35 a week, no appearance money and bonuses were nothing like as regular as they would be at Celtic. I was very happy with everything I had heard up to this point. Then Mr Stein said the signing-on fee would be £1,000 and they would sign me until the end of the season. As this was all happening in December, that meant I would only have a six-month contract. I asked Mr Stein why the signing-on fee was so low and whether he was signing me only as a stop-gap until other players were fit. He said that the signing-on fee was low as the transfer fee was only £20,000 and, as the season was already halfway through, I could sign for six months and renegotiate a new contract at the end of the season.

I was quite taken aback by the size of the transfer fee. I knew that, at the start of that season, Hearts had been offered over £80,000 by

Newcastle United and Stoke City. I couldn't understand then – and don't understand now – what exactly went on and why the transfer fee was set so low. I also said to Mr Stein that I didn't understand the £1,000 signing-on fee, either. It was the normal expectation at that time that a signing-on fee would be a minimum of 10 per cent of the transfer fee. His reply was quite curt: "Oh. That's in England, not here." He had the transfer papers all ready and asked if I would sign them as, apparently, John Harvey had said it would be alright to complete the deal before the Hearts' representatives arrived.

However, it now seemed to me that it wasn't quite as rosy a deal as I'd expected. Apart from the low signing-on fee, it also meant that, if I agreed, I would receive nothing from Hearts for the six years' service I had given them and I would be on only a six-month contract with Celtic. So I said "no" and was standing up ready to leave the boardroom when Mr Stein suggested I should wait until the Hearts' party arrived. I agreed, left the room and went back to my seat on the bench under John Thomson's picture.

When the Hearts people arrived, they simply said "hello" to me before going into the boardroom. John Harvey was the only one of the party who knew I had been at Parkhead since 4.30pm; the others thought that, like them, I had just arrived. After a few minutes, John Harvey and Jock Stein came out of the boardroom, had a short chat just outside the door and then Mr Stein went back inside. John walked over and asked me what the problem was. I explained exactly what had happened since I had been there. He also appeared to be disappointed with the offer. "Leave it with me," he said and he walked back into the boardroom. I waited for about 10 minutes before John emerged again. He told me Hearts would give me £2,000 as their part of the deal. That was fine with me, so now the only remaining problem was the six-month contract. John advised me to take the offer now and, if things didn't work out, they would have me back. Knowing and trusting John Harvey – I always found him to be an honest man – I decided I would sign for Celtic.

I phoned Olive to tell her the news. She seemed happy with the outcome but a little confused over the details. I said to her that rather than go into it all over the phone, I would explain everything when I saw her at home. When I arrived, she had dinner ready so I opened a bottle of wine and, as we ate, we discussed how it would affect us

– more than that, how it would change our lives. This was especially important as many members of my family supported Rangers and the rivalry between the Old Firm clubs – and their huge supporter groups – could sometimes become pretty intense. I explained to her how much bigger Celtic was as a club than Hearts, that the team was full of top-class players, that I would benefit as a footballer and, of course, that we would benefit financially. The discussion probably became a bit less focused as we finished both dinner and a second bottle of wine but at least I must have managed to convey part of the story effectively enough, as she summed it up by saying: "Good – and you won't have to drive through to Edinburgh every day!"

Some members of the family were clearly disappointed I had signed for Celtic and not Rangers. I told them Rangers hadn't asked me to sign and had never expressed an interest in me. I had never had any problems with my family over which clubs I played for. However, some of my "friends" proved less loyal. I realised I'd lost some of these – mostly Rangers' supporters – on the first Tuesday night after I'd signed for Celtic. I went down to the pub in a village called Torrance, three miles from Kirkintilloch, as I'd been doing for many years, to play cards and have a pint or two. As I walked through the doorway, I was quickly challenged with: "What do you want?" The question came from the pub's owner, who was also the barmaid. When I said I wanted a pint and to play cards with my mates, she replied: "There's none o' them here and we don't serve turncoats in this bar – so get oot!" As I turned to leave, I glanced over at the corner table where we usually played cards. There was no one there. It didn't take long for me to realise things had changed.

Unlike today, when a player can be transferred and then perhaps not play for his new club for two or three weeks or more, my first game for Celtic came just four days after signing. The match was against Motherwell at Parkhead and it was quite an experience to be greeted by a crowd of around 40,000 for an ordinary league game. I was fairly nervous before the game and just sat quietly in the dressing room – a big change from the noisy times in the dressing room at Hearts. I remember trainer Neil Mochan coming over and telling me I was to wear the No.8 shirt. He pointed to a peg on the other side of the room; this was to be the spot I would use during my years at Parkhead. I was getting ready at my own pace when the Boss, Jock Stein, came over to me and sat down. He said: "Just to go out and enjoy it today – do as you would normally do. You'll be up front with Stevie (Chalmers) but when necessary drop off". I replied with something like: "OK, I'll do my best". In truth, those simple instructions came as a great relief, as I had been doing the same thing for five years at Hearts. Over the 90 minutes I had a steady game, while Stevie scored a hat-trick in our 4–2 win. During the game Motherwell's centre-forward, a certain John "Dixie" Deans, was sent off; was he trying too hard to catch the eye of our Boss?

A few days afterwards, I was in Glasgow – in Sauchiehall Street, to be exact. I was feeling great after Saturday's result and, as I was walking past the Marks and Spencer store, a young lad approached me and said: "You're Willie Wallace, aren't you?" He must be a fan, I thought, so I replied: "Yes. What can I do for you?" Before I could utter another word, he said: "You can play f**k all!" Then he sprinted away. Everyone close to us heard it all and many started laughing, so I raced away as well – into the nearest shop and buried myself among the clothes' racks. After a while, though, I enjoyed a giggle about it and thought: "Back to earth, where my feet should be!"

I scored my first goal for Celtic one week later. The goal was against Partick Thistle and came within the first two minutes of the game. As it happened, it was also the 50th league goal of the season for Celtic and I scored a second in the match as we won 6–2. It hadn't taken me long to settle in at Celtic, as I had played alongside Tommy Gemmell, Billy McNeill, Bobby Murdoch and Jimmy Johnstone when I played for Scotland. As well, Neilly Mochan's brother Dennis played at Raith Rovers at the same time as I did and I used to give him a lift in my A30 from his mother's house in Falkirk to Kirkcaldy, so I also knew the Mochan family quite well.

The question has been asked many times as to whether I was bought by Celtic to replace Joe McBride. All I know is that when I arrived at Celtic in November, 1966, Joe McBride was fit and my being a "replacement" for him was never suggested to me by anyone. Jock Stein had said I was joining the club to strengthen the squad. If there was anything else behind my move, I know nothing about it. I actually played alongside Joe in at least one game before his serious knee injury.

As a group, we spent a lot of our time at the Seamill Hydro Hotel in West Kilbride on the Ayrshire coast, our home away from home. It was a change from my Hearts days, where we would only go into camp for pre-season training or before cup finals. I grew to like our time at Seamill and, thanks to some "unofficial" activities in and around the hotel, was destined to have a few run-ins with the "big man", as we all referred to Mr Stein. The hotel itself was centred around an old, large house in its own grounds and, during my time at Celtic, an annexe to the hotel was built. There were many places to hide, as "secret passages" ran through the building and just beyond the retaining wall at the bottom of the lawn – where we did some light workouts – lay a sandy beach and the Irish Sea.

While we were at Seamill, we would play a lot of golf at the West Kilbride course. Naturally, we hoped we didn't have to play against the Boss and Neil Mochan, as the Boss always had to win. Ronnie Simpson and Steve Chalmers were the top two golfers in the club but I don't remember playing much in their group. The others in my playing foursome were "Big Tam" (Tommy Gemmell), "Ten Thirty" (Bertie Auld) and "Caesar" (Billy McNeill). On one of the short holes at Seamill, Big Tam managed a hole in one; I don't think any of us equalled this spectacular shot in any of our other golf matches. The "Three Amigos" of that era – Jimmy Johnstone, Bobby Lennox and Willie O'Neill – were the only non-golfing members of the squad. They would hide in the bunkers or bushes around the course and steal or throw away any balls that went close to them. But it's strange how things turn out: "Lemon" (Bobby Lennox) is now a 14-handicap golfer and a shark at that handicap; and "Pumper" (Willie O'Neill) reckoned he was a "scratch" player – he used to walk the round with us but never hit a ball. I remember playing against Willie after he had moved to Carlisle, in northern England. Willie reckoned I kicked him during the game and that, when he asked me why I did it, I replied: "You don't play for us (Celtic) now, son". Well, I know that couldn't have been true, because well as I might have kicked him, I'd never have called him "son". We had a laugh about this at the Lisbon Lions' 40th anniversary celebrations in Las Vegas, when Willie brought up the subject by saying: "Do you remember the 'tour'?" This "tour" was when Celtic went to Carlisle – we didn't even stay overnight! Willie O'Neill died in May, 2011, and he is sorely missed.

I remember Tom Callaghan's first trip to Seamill. Tom lived in Fife and, as he would be passing through Condorrat and Kirkintilloch on his way to the Ayrshire coast, he suggested he would pick me up first, then Tommy Gemmell and Bertie Auld on the way. We had to be at Seamill at 12 noon for lunch so he said he would be at my place by 10am. When he arrived, I invited him in for a cup of tea and a bacon sandwich. "Do we have time?" he asked. I tried to put him at ease: "Course we do – plenty". We got to Big Tam's home at 10.45am and, as he wasn't quite ready, he invited us in for a cup of tea. Tom Callaghan, nicknamed "Tid", asked him if we had time and Big Tam said: "Aye, nae bother". So by the time we reached Bertie Auld's home at Giffnock it was 11.20am and – you guessed it – yes, of course, we had time for a cup of tea. By now, Tom was becoming more than a little worried. Bertie reassured him: "Don't worry, Tid. We've plenty of time. The Boss will be OK." We left with just enough time left to reach Seamill in time for lunch. About halfway to Seamill, though, there was a pub called The Copper Lam. Bertie said to Tid: "Turn in here for a couple of minutes and we'll have a quick cup of coffee". Tid, beginning to look extremely worried, said: "We'll be late." But he was overruled: "No, we won't – lunch isn't until 12.30." So we left the pub at 11.50am with absolutely no chance of making it to Seamill on time. When we did arrive in the hotel car park, Big Tam, Ten Thirty and I grabbed our room keys and were halfway up the stairs when Tid came in through the front doorway. At precisely that moment, the Boss came out of his bedroom, which was right at the main door, and caught Tid. "Where have you been? It's twenty past twelve?" he said. Tid replied: "I'm sorry I'm late, Boss, but the guys weren't ready when I went to pick them up." The Boss asked whose car we'd been travelling in. "Mine," said Tid. "Well, you're responsible. You should just have left them if they weren't ready. What a start for your first time to Seamill. Let that be a lesson to you on who not to pick up in the future!" Tid never offered us a lift again – but he did go on to serve Celtic well and I'm happy to say he's still a friend.

I shared a room with George Connelly just before we played Rangers in the 1969 Scottish Cup Final. This was the game in which George frequently dispossessed Rangers' defender John Greig, on one occasion sticking the ball into the net after doing so for a well-remembered goal. We had gone to bed quite early on the night before the game and I was just settling and half-asleep. Then, out of nowhere, George said: "Wispy, do you think if we win tomorrow, we'll get enough bonus for me to buy a bathroom suite for the house I'm doing up?" "George," I said, "Go to sleep". Five minutes later, his voice sounded again: "Wispy, if I don't get enough for a bathroom suite, I'll buy new carpets". "George," I said, "Go to sleep!" Then, another five minutes later came: "Wispy, how much is a new fridge?" Stupidly, I told him sleepily that it depends on the size of the fridge you buy. It was clearly the wrong thing to say, as it only encouraged him. "Oh. Do you get different sizes? What's the best kind to get?" "George," I barked, "Go to sleep!" It seemed like that had worked. Ten minutes passed, then he started on a different track. "Wispy, can you buy just one chair in a three-piece suite?" Well, how do you answer that? By this time, I was convinced he was winding me up. "George," I said, "Don't ask me another question. Go to sleep!" It was almost midnight and things had been quiet for a while. Finally, I thought, he must have gone to sleep. Then suddenly he sat up and said: "I've made up my mind. I'll buy a new bed because I don't have one." He then lay down and within minutes was snoring his head off! The following day, he played a great game and scored a fine goal as we won 4–0 in front of 133,000 fans at Hampden. I still don't know what he bought with his bonus. I only wish he had played a lot longer than he did. He was quite a talent.

Some games are memorable for all the right reasons; a few just stay in your mind. Among the latter was the night I was sent off against Dundee United at Parkhead. Jim Craig went off injured and the Boss put me to right-back. Davie Wilson was playing at outside-left for Dundee United and had a little dig at me from behind a couple of times. The referee did nothing about it so, on the third occasion it happened, I threw a punch at him and Davie, the football super-diver, was on the deck before I was halfway to his chin. You would have thought he'd been hit by Sonny Liston. All the referee saw was my fist up so he ran over and sent me off. I protested that I hadn't touched him but the referee had another look at Davie – who by this time looked unconscious – and said: "Off!" By the time I left the field, the thing that was worrying me was passing the dug-out, which contained the Boss. As I headed for the tunnel entrance, I heard him say: "You deserved getting sent off – you missed him!" So I copped a two-week suspension for a "fresh air punch".

Playing at Parkhead was a great experience as, no matter who provided the opposition, the crowd always created a terrific atmosphere, singing all their songs and calling out to their favourite players. They loved it when "wee" Jimmy Johnstone and "big" John Hughes ("Yogi") went on their typical runs – you could feel the excitement emanating from the crowd down on to the field. It was easy to play with players like Jimmy and Yogi, as the Boss would tell you to leave them the space, get yourself into the penalty box and give them something to hit. I have mentioned Jimmy Johnstone and John Hughes as they were tremendously exciting, attacking players but, overall, what a squad of players was present at Parkhead throughout the '60s. There were so many combinations to choose from and none of them would ever let you down.

My team-mate Tommy Gemmell was another player who generated great excitement. He became a very close friend and we shared many happy times away from football. Golf, shooting and fishing were our main activities away from the game and our families were close when the children were young. Tommy and his family lived in Kirkintilloch and we were not too far away in Condorrat. We were both members of Dullatur Golf Club and played friendly games with the priests of Croy Parish. It could become quite embarrassing – sometimes if TG sank a long putt, he would shout "God's a Proddie" – but the Fathers always took the remarks in good spirit and they seemed to win more games than we did. Maybe they really were receiving a little more "help from above".

I had played against Ronnie Simpson when he was goalkeeper at Hibernian and always found it difficult to score against him. He had an uncanny knack of reading everything in front of him and stopping the ball with all parts of his body. You would always find Ronnie the same way, up for a laugh on every occasion. When I met him at the ground on one particular training day, he said: "Hi Wispy, what have you been up to?" I asked him why and he replied: "Oh, the Boss has been looking for you and he didn't look all that happy." I then spent all morning at training working very hard, keeping my head down and staying well out of the way of the Boss. Of course, I only found out afterwards that he hadn't said anything at all. Ronnie was one of the true gentlemen of the game and a tear comes to my eye when I think of "Faither"; a better human being you couldn't meet.

Then I think of a player like John Clark. "Mr Reliable" made the game look so easy, yet the selectors of the Scottish national team didn't seem to know he was around. Mind you, I had seen this type of thing happen at Raith Rovers and at Hearts, with players like Willie McNaught and John Cumming also being overlooked. I only roomed once with John Clark, as he was usually "Caesar's" room-mate. In 1968, Celtic played in the US and Canada in a two-game tournament. The first game was in New York against AC Milan, where we drew 1–1 and I scored the goal. The second was played in Toronto in front of a record crowd of 30,000 and we defeated AC Milan 2–0. After the game in New York, John and I were in our room getting ready for bed when he said: "I think I'll give Irene a ring". Back in the '60s, long-distance calls had to be connected by an operator and I heard John say to the one in the hotel exchange that he wanted a number in Holytown, Scotland. He hung up and sat waiting for the call to be connected. Three or four minutes later, the phone rang, John picked it up and a voice said: "Jerusalem here." All I heard was "I don't want f****** Jerusalem! I want f****** Holytown, Scotland" and he slammed down the receiver. He turned to me and was about to say something but his little outburst was so unlike the normal, friendly, courteous Clarkie that I had burst out laughing. That set him off even more: "It might be the Holy City but they're no' even near each other." And that started me laughing again, unable to stop, the tears streaming down my face.

"Looking at replays of the game, it was a "dead cert" penalty and if the referee or his linesman couldn't have seen that, then white sticks should have been issued as part of their gear."
(On being pulled down by Inter goalkeeper Giuliano Sarti in the second half of the European Cup final)

Chapter 7

25 MAY, 1967: THE BIRTH OF THE LISBON LIONS

CELTIC 2–1 INTERNAZIONALE,
Estadio Nacional, Lisbon, 25 May 1967.
Scorers: Mazzola 7 pen, Gemmell 63, Chalmers 84.
Referee: Kurt Tschenscher (West Germany).

CELTIC: Ronnie Simpson, Jim Craig, Tommy Gemmell,
Bobby Murdoch, Billy McNeill (c), John Clark, Jimmy Johnstone,
Willie Wallace, Steve Chalmers, Bertie Auld, Bobbie Lennox.
Squad also included: Jim Brogan, John Fallon, Charlie Gallacher,
John Hughes, Joe McBride, Willie O'Neill.
Manager: Jock Stein; Assistant Manager: Sean Fallon;
Trainer: Neil Mochan.

INTERNAZIONALE: Giuliano Sarti, Armando Picchi (c),
Tarcisio Burgnich, Aristide Guarneri, Giacinto Facchetti,
Gianfranco Bedin, Mauro Bicicli, Mario Corso, Angelo Domenghini,
Alessandro Mazzola, Renato Cappellini.
Manager: Helenio Herrera.

The atmosphere was so relaxed that you could have been forgiven for thinking we were preparing for a friendly game, not one against Inter Milan in the European Cup final. The week before we left for Lisbon, where the final would be played, was spent at the Seamill Hydro Hotel, our second home. It was May, 1967 and, in the six months I had been a Celtic player, I had spent a lot of time with the team in camp at the Hydro. We were there before the Scottish Cup final against Aberdeen and now here we were back again, preparing for a match that could make us the first British side to win the European Cup.

We played our golf as usual at West Kilbride golf course. I normally teamed with Tommy Gemmell, Bertie Auld and Billy McNeill while hiding behind bushes and in bunkers were Jimmy Johnstone, Bobby Lennox and Willie O'Neill, whose aim was to disrupt the game as much as possible by throwing balls into the bunkers or the rough or talking just as you were about to play your shot. Today Bobby Lennox, or "Lemon", is an excellent golfer and actually becomes annoyed if anyone puts him off his shot. Changed days! As an aside, Bobby earned his nickname due to a misprint of his name in a newspaper, I think when we were in Serbia for the Vojvodina match. The others all had their nicknames by the time I first arrived at Parkhead.

The weather that May was very pleasant and we trained at the local amateur club's facilities at West Kilbride. The surface wasn't fantastic, there were no markings and just a set of goalposts. We worked hard without over-training and spent time on a few things the Boss wanted us to do in Lisbon. The Boss had a very clear picture of how he wanted the team to play. We knew Inter would be more defensive but were very good on the break, with Alessandro Mazzola up front. However, the Boss stressed that if we performed at our best, we were in with a chance of defeating the European champions. All that week and for the first couple of days in Lisbon, no one but the Boss had any idea of the selection of the team. The goalkeepers were Ronnie Simpson and John Fallon, full-backs Jim Craig, Tommy Gemmell, and Willie O'Neill, the two central positions were set with Billy McNeil and John Clark, midfielders were Bobby Murdoch, Bertie Auld and Charlie Gallagher and up front were Jimmy Johnstone, Steve Chalmers, Bobby Lennox, John Hughes and yours truly. What a squad it was for the Boss to choose from, as a combination of any of these players would have made a great team in any match against any competition. This had been proved many times during the season and was underlined again two weeks after the Lisbon final, when we played Real Madrid with two or three changes and won 1–0 at the Bernabéu stadium in Madrid.

The week at Seamill before leaving for Lisbon was relaxing but the four days in Lisbon before the game were also quite laid back, until the day of the match. That was when nervous thoughts started entering my head and butterflies took hold of my stomach. Trying to stay calm proved impossible – until the nerves disappeared in an instant when I was walking down the tunnel leading to the field and heard the singing. We came out to tumultuous applause from the thousands of Celtic supporters who had followed us to Lisbon. It was an unbelievable sight and an indescribably welcome one!

I felt the team were very relaxed and confident during our warm-up before the kick-off. When the referee called together Armando Picchi and Billy McNeill, the team captains, for the coin toss, I experienced a bit of nervous tension but was ready to go. Then I had my first touch of the ball and the tensions disappeared – no fumbles or mistakes – and, along with the rest of the team, I settled down quickly. What did surprise me was the apparent lack of real urgency from the opposition. Inter Milan appeared to be waiting for something to happen.

We were playing well and mounted a few good attacks on the Inter goal. Jinky Johnstone headed the ball at goal, which was unusual for him, and TG had a strong shot which just cleared the crossbar. I had what I thought was a good, strong shot but Inter's goalkeeper Sarti plucked it from just below the bar as if it was a back-pass. In the first few minutes, we had most of the play and were creating chances but, in one of the few attacks by Inter, Jim Craig brought down Renato Cappellini. Inter were awarded a penalty kick and Sandri Mazzola scored. This was gut-wrenching but the team pulled together strongly and were soon attacking again, in the fashion which was Celtic's trademark at that time. However, Inter's goal kept them in front right up to half-time.

The half-time team talk from the Boss was short and simple: Keep playing as we were and we would certainly score. Our plan up front was to push Inter's back four into their own box and create chances from outside the box for Bertie Auld and Bobby "Chopper" Murdoch. The longer the second half went, the Inter players seemed to be tiring and they were finding it difficult to cross the halfway line or even get out of their own penalty box. There was one incident midway through the second half where I chased the ball to just outside the goalpost, almost on the dead ball line, beat Sarti and another Inter defender and slipped the ball between them. I was just about to roll the ball into the net when Sarti grabbed both of my legs and held on to them, pulling me down. To my amazement, the referee waved "play on"". I questioned his decision and he replied that he hadn't had a clear view so he couldn't give a penalty! Looking at replays of the game, it was a "dead cert" penalty and if the referee or his linesman couldn't have seen that, then white sticks should have been issued as part of their gear. The incident was extremely disheartening – but I realised there and then that we would have to score goals that couldn't possibly be disputed.

As things turned out, it wasn't long until we scored a goal that was not only indisputable but was one of the best goals I saw throughout my career. Tommy Gemmell ran on to a good cut-back from Jim Craig just outside the box and hit it hard and sweetly into the top right-hand corner of Sarti's net. What a feeling! Now we had them and the Inter players were looking dejected and their heads had dropped. Not long after TG's goal, Stevie Chalmers glided home a shot and made the score 2–1 in our favour. His shot was from outside the box, so the Boss's tactics worked to a tee. After that, we went on to change the play a bit by keeping the ball as much as possible. The minutes dragged out like hours until, finally, the referee blew the full-time whistle.

What a fantastic feeling – exultation and relief. We had just won the European Champions' Cup. We tried to congratulate each other but the field was suddenly invaded by supporters and it was just about impossible to find each other. A couple of unusual things happened then. Firstly, still on the pitch, I was mobbed by a group of people who, to begin with, I thought were Celtic supporters who had jumped the moat around the playing area. Unfortunately, I realised pretty quickly they were mostly Portuguese and were ripping my jersey and shorts off. I was becoming concerned as I couldn't free myself when a couple of Celtic supporters came to my rescue and helped me out of the fray.

I was left with my jockstrap, socks and boots, so I took off as quickly as I could for the safety of the tunnel and the dressing room. As I reached the tunnel, I met Neil Mochan, who said: "What happened to you?" I didn't stop to answer; I just kept going down the tunnel! Then, just before I reached the dressing room, I met a couple of my friends, who had travelled from Kirkintilloch for the game; in fact, I had actually obtained tickets for them. Their names were Ian "Budgy" Martin and James "Doc" Docherty, who had extremely bandy legs. Ian told me they'd been robbed during the game and they'd lost their passports and all their cash. Could I help them?

There was I, having just won the European Cup, standing in a jockstrap, socks and boots feeling not a little conspicuous and someone asks me that! My immediate thought was: "Where does he think I keep my money?" However, just at that point, Jock Stein arrived and asked me what the problem was. I explained everything to him as quickly as I could and he took some money from his pocket and said: "Fix me up when we get back home". I gave the cash to the boys and hurried off to the dressing room. To the lads' credit, they repaid the money a few days after we returned.

Once back in the dressing room, away from the celebrations and confusion on the playing field, I was able to sit quietly – for once – and I gave thanks to my Maker for the good fortune he had bestowed on me. In my mind, I raised a glass in tribute to the many people who had helped me in my life, which, similar to most of my Celtic team-mates, had begun in fairly humble circumstances in a small town just outside the Glasgow city boundary.

After the game in Lisbon, we attended a UEFA presentation dinner. I don't really remember much about it except for one thing. We received a wall plaque as a commemorative gift and I put mine on my seat. I then went to the toilet, came back and sat on it. It broke into a hundred pieces, much to the amusement of my team-mates. After the dinner, we joined our wives at the Folklore dance club somewhere in Lisbon and, after a short time there, accompanied them to the airport, as they were flying back to Glasgow in the early hours of the morning. It was a bad idea – the airport was in chaos and the arrival of the European Cup-winners didn't help the noise level. We quickly left our wives there and made our way back to Estoril and our hotel.

I was rooming with Bertie Auld and, when we arrived at the hotel,

Bert's brother Ian was sitting there, looking the worse for wear. Bert went over, had a chat for a couple of minutes, then came back over to me and said: "Ian's been thrown out of his hotel. Is it alright if he shares our room?" I agreed without a thought but Bertie went on: "He'll be nae bother. He can sleep in the wardrobe (we had a large, walk-in wardrobe in the room) and if the Boss or Neilly comes into the room, they won't be able to see him". The plan went well, we put Ian in the wardrobe and settled down for the rest of the night. Only a few minutes later, we found out the wives were coming back from the airport as their flight had been cancelled. They would be sharing our rooms. Bert said: "Wispy, don't say a word to Liz (Bert's wife) about Ian being in the wardrobe. You know how families are!" I agreed I wouldn't even tell Olive. The ladies duly arrived at the hotel and we asked them what they wanted to do. Olive said she wanted to lie down, having been on her feet for 24 hours, so up to the room we went. I went ahead to make sure Ian was still in the wardrobe and, as I entered the room, Ian was coming out of the toilet. I grabbed him, quickly explained what was going on and put him back in the wardrobe. He said: "OK. Is Liz here?" When I said she was, he went as white as a sheet. "God, Bert'll kill me if Liz finds out I'm in here," he said. I replied: "Just get into the wardrobe. I'll make sure they don't find you." He went in, I closed the wardrobe door and put a chair in front of it.

Moments later, Bert and the girls arrived at the room. We sat on the beds and were having a chat but Ian must have fallen asleep and the noise of his snoring was unbelievable. Olive said: "What's that?" I responded: "That's Caesar and Luggy (John Clark) next door. Luggy's got bad sinus and always snores like that." The women asked how Billy could sleep through the noise and I said: "He snores as well. That's why the Boss puts them in the same room. "Poor Liz and Irene," Olive said. "How do they manage to sleep with those two snoring like that!" From then on, Ian never let up. It was a good job the women were only there for a couple of hours before they returned to the airport. I don't know to this day if Bert ever told Liz about Ian being in the wardrobe. I've told Olive but she doesn't believe me; she still thinks it was Luggy's sinuses causing the problem.

The next day, when we arrived back in Scotland, will always remain bright in my memory as one of the greatest days of my life. Returning to Glasgow as champions of Europe was simply a once-in-a-lifetime experience. Who would have believed it – 17 Scots winning the European Cup? I've always believed every competition starts from the first round, so every player in the squad deserves a share of the credit for the winning of the cup that season. The crowds on the streets and inside Parkhead were fantastic; they gave us such a tremendous welcome home. Only a week later, I signed a new, three-year contract with Celtic.

After the 1966–67 season ended, Olive and I enjoyed a holiday at Palma Nova, on the island of Majorca in Spain, where we stayed at the Delfin Playa. Also staying at the hotel were Bobby Moore, of England, and Rangers' John Greig and Davy White, all with their respective wives and families. I had no idea of this when I booked the holiday and when I arrived and saw them I wondered if it might be a bit embarrassing for everyone. However, there was no need to worry and we all had a fantastic holiday. The manager of the hotel, Luis, was both a gentleman and a football fanatic and organised a game between the hotel staff and guests, to be played on Real Mallorca's training pitch. Everyone was taken by bus to the ground for the game and the guests won by four or five goals to nil. Afterwards, Luis threw a party for the winners at his villa, next door to the hotel. He even had a cake specially made as a trophy for us. John and Dave particularly enjoyed the cake, as it was the only "trophy" they had won that season!

We also visited Billy McNeill and Joe McBride and their families, who were on holiday on Majorca at the same time. They were staying in the mountains, in a villa at Banyalbufar belonging to Joe Beltrami, a well-known Glasgow lawyer. A crew from a Spanish TV station came to the villa to interview us but, as we had had a good lunch and a few drinks before they arrived, I'm afraid my memories of the interview are not as sharp as they might have been. However, I do remember that afterwards we went down to the local hotel for a swim in their pool. The three of us – Billy, Joe and myself – were capering around with a ball in the pool and, as always happens, it was knocked out of the water. In this case, though, it also went over the fence and off down the mountainside, as the hotel and all the buildings at that particular site were on extremely steep terraces. Bravely, Joe decided he would go and retrieve the ball. He had been gone for about 20 minutes when he returned, bleeding from several parts of his body. It turned out he had slipped down one of the terraces and, in fact, had been very lucky not to have fallen all the way down to the ocean. Billy and I were, of course, full of sympathy – but both of us agreed the really good news was that we finally had our ball back!

One of the funniest days of my time at Celtic was when Neil Mochan took Tommy Gemmell and me to Larbert Hospital to visit a couple of Celtic supporters who were there drying out from alcohol. While we were at their bedsides, one of the nurses approached and asked if we would call the hospital bingo session in the dining room at 3.30pm, as it would be nice for the patients to meet us. She didn't mention that the patients who would be playing were from the section of the hospital that housed the mentally ill. When we arrived at the dining room, Tommy, Neilly and I sat at a table facing the bingo players, who were mostly women. We shook up the bingo balls ready to go when I heard Neilly make one of his characteristic, funny little giggles. At the same time, he was trying to say to both of us: "Don't look". Of course, I glanced up to see what was going on and noticed that – well, there's no other way of saying it – the women facing us along the front row had no knickers on. The nursing sister had her back to them and a puzzled look on her face, wondering why the three of us were laughing. When she turned round and saw what was happening, she almost fainted. That was the end of the bingo session and the ladies were back in their wards in no time. I wonder if they ever got to play bingo again?

As a footnote to the European Cup final, we played Peñarol, of Uruguay, in a friendly game at Parkhead in early September of 1967. The game was designed to give us some experience of South American football, as winning the European Cup had earned us the right to play Racing Club of Buenos Aires in that year's FIFA Intercontinental Cup, more often called the World Club Championship. Jock Stein decided to play all-out attack against them and it worked a treat. We dominated play throughout and won 2–1. My goals weren't bad ones, either, and looking back on them always gives me a good feeling, considering Peñarol were the Intercontinental Cup-holders – or world club champions – at the time.

Nothing, however, could have prepared us for what was to come in October and November, when we played three times against Racing

Club in a series of matches that has gone down in football history, for all the wrong reasons.

The first game was the roughest game of football I had ever experienced – and this type of play was to continue throughout the following two. This first meeting was at Hampden Park, where we tried to play the normal, attacking style that had brought us so much success. But it quickly became clear that Racing were going to stop us from doing that by any means, fair or foul. This was the only experience in my career of players nipping, spitting and putting their fingers in strange, unwelcome places. The referee on the night of the first game was a Spaniard, who spoke Racing Club's language and appeared very friendly – and not a little lenient – towards them. The game was not allowed to flow, with the referee blowing for stoppages every 30 seconds or so and the Racing players deliberately time-wasting and using every tactic they could to prevent Celtic from playing our normal style of football. The Celtic supporters were brilliant that night – encouraging us all through the game – and Billy McNeill scored, giving us a 1–0 advantage when we travelled to play in Argentina.

The flight to South America was my first extremely long flight (little knowing then that later in life I would make many more, even longer journeys). Arriving at Buenos Aires, we were transported from the airport to an exclusive club that apparently provided a safe haven for politicians and army personnel. Around the perimeter were military buildings housing tanks and other heavy weapons. Our accommodation was excellent; we had use of the swimming pool, gym, 18-hole golf course and we were well away from the Argentinian supporters. We were treated very well but, as things turned out, the hospitality did not extend to the football game. Travelling to El Cilindro stadium at Avellaneda, just south of the city centre, was a less than pleasant experience as, when we approached it, the Racing Club supporters were loud and threatening, battering the sides of the bus with their fists, spitting at the windows and conveying the strong impression that they really would harm us – if they could get their hands on us. Once safely inside a very ordinary dressing room, at last we started to get our minds on the game. We then found out the officials for the match were all South American. As we had a Spanish trio at Hampden, I suppose FIFA thought it fair we should have three

South Americans for this one. Joe McBride had travelled with us but did not play and, as I had brought my cine-camera with me, he took it with him into the stand. The Celtic party's seats were so high in the stadium, they could almost have waved to the passengers in the passing aircraft as they approached the nearby Buenos Aires airport.

The noise was deafening as we walked on to the field, flares and fireworks exploding and police marching around carrying machine guns and accompanied by their huge Rottweiler dogs. As both teams took to the playing field, the noise was unbelievable and the dogs were going wild, barking and straining on their leads. Wee Jimmy Johnstone was petrified: "Wispy," he said, "I hope they don't let them aff the lead during the game." It was certainly an entirely different atmosphere to playing in Europe.

Ronnie Simpson was in goal as we did our usual warm-up routines. We were crossing a few balls and hitting shots at him when he went down on one knee, holding his head with both hands. He had been struck on the head by something thrown from the crowd and had a gash on the back of his head. Ronnie left the field there and, as things turned out, didn't return. John Fallon took over in goal for the full game.

Despite everything, we were playing well enough and took the lead when Tommy Gemmell converted a penalty kick awarded for a foul tackle on Jimmy Johnstone. Racing then equalised with a good goal and the game was played out pretty much evenly until the final few minutes, when they scored a second from what was clearly an offside position. Not long after that, the referee blew the whistle to end the match. Under today's rules, we would have won the trophy on the "away goals" rule but, of course, that didn't apply in those days and the 2–1 result meant we would have to play a third and deciding game.

The decider was set down for "neutral" Montevideo, Uruguay, three days later. Rumours were circulating that Celtic's chairman Robert Kelly didn't want to play the third game after the problems of the first two. He felt we should fly home to Glasgow but, instead, we made the much shorter flight across the River Plate to Montevideo. We received a great reception from the Uruguayan public, who seemed to have a fairly strong dislike of the Argentinians. Reaching the hotel, the Boss told us he had some information that the Argentinians might have organised for women to be in our rooms. I think this was the quickest I ever saw the players register at reception! Of course, when we got there, there were no women – just the Boss and Neilly Mochan on patrol with the Boss saying: "Now you're in your rooms, just stay there!"

Unfortunately, the same three officials who had controlled the Buenos Aires game were put in charge of the play-off, with the linesman who had allowed the "offside goal" against us to stand now promoted to referee! The game at the Estadio Centenario was to become the biggest fiasco in the history of football, the "battle of Montevideo" as some have labelled it. There were players being sent off at the referee's whim, police on the field and escorting players off, players fighting, tackles by the Argentinians that were closer to assaults designed to cause bodily harm – it was absolute mayhem. A goal was scored in the game but, because of the chaos, I don't recall exactly how it came about. Anyway, by this time we had realised we had no chance of winning this particular trophy. I think the selection of the officials and our having a home game as the first game were both in favour of the South Americans.

Returning to Glasgow, we had to endure a punishment issued by Celtic for our behaviour during the game in Montevideo. We were fined the bonus we had earned by defeating Dundee in the League Cup before we left for South America, apparently because the club feared we would be disciplined and fined by FIFA. This came as a complete shock, as I couldn't recall anything being mentioned in the press about any FIFA decision and I also believed that, if FIFA were to punish anyone for their behaviour in the Montevideo match, it would have been both teams. Losing that bonus, together with not receiving any bonuses I can remember for these matches, was more than harsh. Whatever happened to the old saying "it takes two to tango"? The Racing Club players went on to be praised loudly by their country and they received all their bonuses, which included new cars. The Celtic players had a chat amongst ourselves and, despite everything, we decided we wouldn't challenge the decision made by the club and would just get on with the season.

"It was a wonderful night for the club and our supporters, made even more special with the announcement of an attendance of 133,061 ... Apart from the win in Lisbon, I think the game in Leeds and the second leg at Hampden Park were two of the best Celtic performances of my era."

(After the European Cup semi-final second leg against Leeds United, 1970)

Chapter 8

ALL GOOD THINGS . . .

I have always been proud to say I was part of the squad that achieved so much for Celtic in Europe. To play in two European Cup finals alone was a fantastic achievement and if anyone had foretold that when I was a young boy, I would probably have thought they should be committed to the well-known Woodilee Asylum in in my home town of Kirkintilloch. The year after we defeated Inter Milan in the final was the only disappointment and I still say we were robbed in Russia. We scored three good goals that night against Dinamo Kiev but only one was allowed to stand for a 1–1 draw. Except for that episode, we always progressed into the later stages of the European Cup and played against all the top clubs in Europe. We held our own against all of them and I managed to score a few goals along the way.

One memorable game was a League Cup tie against Rangers at Parkhead on 30 August, 1967. We were one down with 15 minutes to go and seemed destined to go even further behind when Rangers were awarded a penalty. Kai Johansen smashed his shot against the bar and, when it re-bounded back to him, he instinctively knocked it into the net. Unfortunately for the Light Blues – fortunately for us

– that was a foul, as to make it legal another player has to touch the rebound before the penalty-taker touches it again. So a free-kick was awarded to us, we took it quickly and raced upfield, where I knocked in the equaliser in 78 minutes. In the 83rd minute, Bobby Murdoch made it 2–1 and right on the whistle, Bobby Lennox scored a third. The Celtic fans in the crowd of some 75,000 had a night to remember and celebrated accordingly.

The championship in 1967¬–68 was very tight, with Rangers right on our tail. We actually won our last 16 league fixtures to finish top, five points ahead of Rangers, and I'm happy to say I scored 15 goals during those games. Playing against Rangers, the "old enemy", was always exciting but I never really treated games against them any differently from other games. I also seemed to be able to score quite regularly against Rangers, particularly in cup matches. I netted a couple of goals against them at the start of the 1968–69 season in the League Cup group section in front of 80,000 at Ibrox and, two weeks later, I got the winner in the return fixture at Parkhead.

My luckiest goal for Celtic was against Greenock Morton at Hampden in the League Cup. The ball was crossed from the right wing into the Morton box and I jumped with the centre-half, just got above him and the ball hit me on the shoulder and looped over the keeper's head into the net. In the press the next day, it was reported to be a well-directed header into the net by Wallace. It was late in the game when I scored, though, and the reporter might have been watching proceedings through "Johnnie Walker" eyes.

One of my most memorable League matches was a 6–0 win against Kilmarnock at Rugby Park, played on 2 March, 1968. I scored four goals in that game, playing in midfield! The four goals were all good ones but the fourth was one of the best I would score in my whole career. Starting inside our eighteen-yard box, several of my team-mates and I worked the ball down our right flank. After a couple of touches in our half, I made my way forward through the inside-right channel – for the younger reader, that would be between the winger and the striker – and just outside the Kilmarnock box, I was given a fairly poor pass, the ball bouncing badly. Just as it rose up, I flicked it over one defender's head with my right foot, beat another by switching the ball on to my left foot before clipping it, again with my left foot, back across the goal, totally wrong-footing the goalkeeper. It was some goal, one of four goodies! On that day, Jimmy Quinn played one of his early games for Celtic. Jimmy died very young from a heart attack. He was one of the "Quality Street" gang, as the young reserve Celtic team became known.

One of my most pleasant experiences when playing for Celtic was the game against West Ham – the Bobby Moore testimonial match – at Upton Park, London, in 1970. As I mentioned in the previous chapter, I had met Bobby and his family when they were on holiday at the Delfin Playa Hotel on Majorca at the end of the 1966–67 season at the same time as me, my wife Olive and our eldest daughter Lynn. I found Bobby to be one of the nicest guys I had met and, in my opinion, one of the best players I have seen play in his position. To play in the testimonial match for Bobby was a great honour for me. Celtic put on a great display that evening and thoroughly outplayed the Hammers. But, as sometimes happens in football, although we scored three goals – none of which would remain in the memory – West Ham scored three wonderful efforts to tie the match!

Later that year, while on tour in North America, the club arranged an extra match in Boston, Massachusetts, against a New England Select XI. We played at a college ground with no proper floodlighting, so portable lights had been installed around the field. The game had been going for about five minutes when Jinky Johnstone had a ball played to him wide on the right. He beat the full-back and took off up the line, ran a few steps and tripped with no one within five yards of him. The wee man thought he had been deliberately tripped by the full-back and got up to have a go at him but the full-back was 10 yards away. Jinky then looked just behind him and there was the culprit, a steel peg and guy rope inside the touchline by two feet, holding up the lights. The wee man turned to me and said: "Wispy, ah wis gonna banjo him when ah got up – but look at whit ah fell over!" He couldn't stop laughing as the ground staff came and took the peg out of the ground and away from where it could cause any damage to anyone.

We played two very important matches against Leeds United at their Elland Road ground and at Hampden Park in the semi-final of the European Cup of 1970. Although I had been involved in friendly games against Aston Villa, Tottenham Hotspur, Leeds United, Blackburn Rovers and Manchester United, this was my first match against a top English club side in a highly competitive game. And despite all our recent achievements, the English press, of course, didn't rate our chances at all.

We stayed north of Leeds in Harrogate, a lovely Yorkshire town just south of the Dales and about 45 minutes from Elland Road. The hotel was old-fashioned and very comfortable, without being too "posh". It was just an ideal spot to prepare for this type of match. Once again, the Boss had chosen a place away from the hype and bustle so we had two days' preparation, with one training session on the ground the night before the game, no press interference and not many supporters around. By contrast, the Leeds' fans were never out of the newspapers, radio or TV, their confidence – maybe even a touch of arrogance – plain for everyone to see.

Leeds were managed at this time by one of their ex-players, Don Revie, and their trainer was a little guy called Les Cocker. The Leeds players were very fit and hard to beat and their team was full of internationals, Scottish, Irish, Welsh and, of course, English. You might note – in contrast to today – no overseas players. Leeds had won the English First Division Championship in the previous season, setting a record points total of 67 with only two defeats all season in their 42 league games. There were three Scots in their team, Peter Lorimer, Billy Bremner and Eddie Gray, all internationalists.

On the night of the game when we arrived at the ground, the crowd was unbelievable and the majority, it seemed, were Celtic supporters. I thought to myself: "How the hell are they all going to get in?" I found out later that most of them did – over walls or broken-down gates – so that whatever the official crowd was that night, you could easily add on another 25 per cent. I can remember being in the changing rooms before the game; the atmosphere was great, we had prepared well and everyone looked to be full of confidence. We had four changes from the Lisbon team: Evan Williams was in goal; David Hay was at left-back; Jim Brogan was playing sweeper; and George Connelly was in midfield. I played as the main striker, with big George sitting just behind me. The Boss said to me that Leeds' defender Norman Hunter liked to throw his weight about so if you gave him a "wee dig" early on, things might be different. I did and Norman soon realised that what he wanted to give out was exactly what he would get back. Norman was six feet tall, quick, gave no quarter and expected none; he always let you know he was going to be around to compete for every ball. Some people at the time felt he was a dirty player but I don't think he was any different from many defenders in the game at that time. With Celtic, we had experienced really dirty players in the World Club Championship games against Racing Club of Argentina. Norman was a gentleman compared with those guys.

Johnstone and Lennox both sat wide, with Auld and Murdoch in midfield. Our back four were Hay, McNeill, Brogan and Gemmell. Everyone played their part with David Hay and George Connelly outstanding and we won the game 1–0, with young George scoring the only goal. Even this seemed to do little to dampen the confidence of the Leeds team, their supporters and the English newspapers before the second game at Hampden. Apparently that result had just been a temporary setback and, according to the English press, they were still going to wipe the floor with us!

I was on the bench for the return game at Hampden. The Boss changed the team around and one of the changes he made up front was playing John Hughes in my place. This worked a treat and, despite Leeds scoring first through Billy Bremner, we went on to win 2–1 on the night, 3–1 over the two games. John Hughes scored one and Bobby Murdoch the other. It was a wonderful night for the club and our supporters, made even more special with the announcement of an attendance of 133,061. This outnumbered the previous largest crowd for a European tie. Apart from the win in Lisbon, I think the game in Leeds and the second leg at Hampden Park were two of the best Celtic performances of my era.

After the first game at Leeds had finished, we travelled back to Harrogate, had supper and a couple of beers when I remembered that my wife Olive, who had travelled down to the game and was staying with her cousin at a small town called Hemsworth, was about an hour's drive south of Leeds and two hours from us. I talked "Big Tam" Gemmell and "Ten Thirty" Bertie Auld into going with me for a visit and we caught a cab at 1.30am. You can imagine the cab driver's face when I told him we wanted to go to Hemsworth. He said: "Do you know where it is and how far?" I said: "Yes, how much to take us there and back?" His first reply was a slightly confused "What?" then, after a minute or two, he announced "forty pounds". I said: "Done." We arrived about 3am, waking up everyone in the house and probably most people in the neighbourhood. At first Peter, Olive's cousin, could only muster: "What the hell are you doing here at this time of the morning?" I said: "I came to say hello to Olive." So we went into the kitchen and soon Olive and Peter's wife Betty came downstairs. We all had a cup of tea and a glass of wine and, half an hour later, we were on our way back to Harrogate. We returned to the hotel just in time to have breakfast, pack our bags and leave for Scotland.

We had long been friends with Olive's cousin Peter Castle and his wife Betty. The four of us had been overseas on holiday together and we had visited each other many times over the years. After Olive and I moved to Australia, Peter and Betty visited us two or three times. On their last visit, Betty had complained of a sore leg which kept letting her down when she was walking. After about two years of visits to chiropractors, physios and doctors, she was eventually diagnosed with motor neurone disease (MND). This was the first time I had experienced this terrible disease so later, when I heard about Jimmy Johnstone having it, I felt completely devastated. Having visited Betty when I had been back in Britain, I had seen first-hand how slow and merciless this disease was as it took its toll. I visited Jinky many times during his fight against MND and every time I left his home, I was humbled by the attitude of the wee man and his enormous spirit. He never let go of his hope and desire to live and hung on to his wonderful sense of humour. I look at both Peter Castle and Jimmy Johnstone's wife Agnes with so much admiration for the way they each looked after their partner with so much care and love, right up to the end. I often wonder whether I would have that strength.

**AN UNHAPPY DAY: THE EUROPEAN CUP FINAL,
1970 – CELTIC V FEYENOORD
CELTIC 1–2 FEYENOORD (after extra time),
San Siro, Milan; Italy, 6 May 1970.
Scorers: Gemmell 30, Israel 32, Kindvall 116.
Referee: Concetto Lo Bello (Italy).**

**CELTIC: Evan Williams, David Hay, Tommy Gemmell,
Bobby Murdoch, Billy McNeill (c), Jim Brogan, Jimmy Johnstone,
John Hughes, Willie Wallace, Bertie Auld, Bobby Lennox.
Substitute: George Connelly.
Manager: Jock Stein; Assistant Manager: Sean Fallon;
Trainer: Neil Mochan.**

**FEYENOORD: Eddy Pieters Graafland, Pete Romeijn, Theo Laseroms,
Rinus Israel, Theo van Duivenbode, Franz Hasil, Wim Jansen,
Willem van Hanegem, Henk Wery, Ove Kindvall, Coen Moulijn.
Substitute: Guus Haak.
Manager: Ernst Happel**

EVERYONE connected with Celtic had been delighted by the results against Leeds and just like the players and management team, were looking forward eagerly to the final against Feyenoord, of Rotterdam. Unfortunately, that match turned out to be something of a disaster; it was certainly the worst experience of my time at Celtic.

Our preparation for such a crucial occasion had been abysmal. Before going to Italy to play in the final, we had gone on a trip to Peterhead to play in a benefit match to raise money for the families of lifesavers lost at sea. I won't go into details about certain incidents over the two days we were in Peterhead but let's just say they weren't related to the field of play and did little to maintain a good relationship between the players and the Boss. When we left to come home, he made his feelings clear about it all by not travelling back in the bus with us.

We flew to Italy two or three days before the game and stayed about 90 minutes' drive north-west of Milan, in the town of Varese. The hotel was an old, former monastery on top of a mountain, very scenic but miles from the San Siro, as we had found out when playing against AC Milan at the same venue the year before. A round trip of three hours on the night before the vital match – merely to see the ground – was something we could all have well done without. On top of that, I think all of us were aware the atmosphere in the camp was not as relaxed as it had been in Lisbon. Not surprisingly, then, we didn't play as well as we could have during the 90 minutes of the match in the San Siro and the scoreline was level at one goal each after normal playing time. Tommy Gemmell scored the first goal after about half an hour but Feyenoord equalised quickly. The game went to extra time but, in the end, Feyenoord finished stronger than we did and their Swedish centre-forward Ove Kindvall scored the winner not long before the end.

It was bitterly disappointing to lose and, when I think of the night, I can still hear the blaring of the Dutch horns as the Feyenoord supporters celebrated. After the match, we went to the hotel in Milan where our wives had been staying but after having a little too much of the amber fluid, I must have been in another world that night as I don't recall much at all until I woke up the next morning. As I emerged from sleep, I remember noticing the bed covers seemed to be extremely high above my head and as I rolled to my right-hand side to climb out, I was blocked by someone else who, after just a few moments, I realised was one of the other players' wives. Now waking up fast and already fearful, I rolled over to the other side – my mind frantically trying to recall all at once where I might be, why I might be there and what I might have been doing there – when I struck another body! This time it was Olive's, which only multiplied the confusion flying around in my mind. Thankfully, both ladies were fully clothed and then I found out why the sheets were so high, both were pregnant and very much soon-to-be mothers. After what seemed like minutes of panic, the two of them relieved all my early morning worries. They explained that I had taken off from where we had been drinking in the hotel to go to bed and apparently had just wandered into the first available room and collapsed in the middle of the bed. I don't know to this day whose room I was in; the girls added that the only room available for them that night had been the one I had fallen into and, since I was out for the count, they just parked themselves each side of me on the king-size bed!

In 1971, Celtic went on a one-match post-season tour to Israel. We arrived at Tel Aviv airport in the early afternoon and all the way into the city on both sides of the road were rows and rows of armoured military tanks, jeeps and troop carriers, all with Egyptian flags on them and obviously captured. There had been conflict between Israel on the one hand and several Arab countries, especially Egypt, since the Six Day War a few years before and there was clearly still a lot of tension around. We were OK, though, insulated from it all by staying in the five-star Tel Aviv Hilton, on a superb site right on the beach.

Unfortunately, because of the fighting, there was a fence all along the beach with gates for access; these were open during the day and closed at night. Late one evening, when most of the tour party was in the hotel quietly playing cards, reading or talking, we heard a bit of a disturbance outside, with horns blaring loudly and floodlights bursting into bright light. Suddenly, two red-faced players – who had better stay nameless – raced into the main lounge. They had decided to go for a walk on the beach and were in the act of climbing the fence when an army patrol spotted them. Frankly, they were lucky not to be shot! Still, as in most football clubs, the other players politely refrained from giving them a hard time about it or trying to embarrass them – I don't think!

In our only match on that tour, we played an Israeli national XI organised by the club side Hapoel Tel Aviv, a first-half goal by Harry Hood being enough for the score to finish 1–0 to Celtic. I came on as a substitute for Lou Macari at half-time. The game at the Ramat Gan Stadium in Tel Aviv on 26 May was the first time Celtic had played in Israel but, looking back, the trip was really much more memorable than the game.

We went to see most of the religious sites in Jerusalem, Nazareth and elsewhere. One afternoon we were at the Wailing Wall, all of us impressed by the size of the blocks of stone and what had been achieved in earlier times with simple tools and no sophisticated machinery. We had two guides – one Jewish, one Arab – with us everywhere we went and when I noticed the old wall had a modern brick wall on top of it, I asked the Jewish guide why it was there. He told me there was an Islamic mosque at the back of the wall that Jewish worshippers did not want to see while praying at the wall. He then walked away. I looked at the little Arab guide, who had a smile on his face, so I asked him for his version. He said the new wall had been built to stop Arabs on the other side defecating in buckets and emptying them over the wall on to the people praying. I never found out which, if either, really was the truth.

From there we visited the Mount of Olives, where we came across an Arab gentleman who had some camels and donkeys that visitors could ride. Wee Jimmy Johnstone fancied a ride on one of the donkeys – well, it was like a big horse to him. He jumped on this poor little donkey and it took off down the road, with the "wee man" hanging on for dear life. At the bottom of the hill, he fell off – luckily without injuring himself – and the donkey ran off, bucking wildly, the Arab frantically trying to catch him. This finally proved to Jimmy that even though he was the right height, he was no jockey! From there, our tour party travelled on to the Sea of Galilee. Again, it was time for a ride – Billy McNeill and I spotted a little boat and asked the owner if we could sail over to the other side. The owner told us we certainly could but it would cost us £20 each. "What?" we said together. "Did you know Jesus walked across these waters?" he said. I replied: "At twenty quid a head tae sail, nae wonder He walked."

My last game for Celtic in European competition was against Boldklubben 1903 of Copenhagen at Parkhead on 29 September, 1971, in the European Cup. Two weeks earlier, we'd lost the first leg away from home 2–1 in a very ordinary display in front of just 6000 fans. The Boss reckoned Jimmy Johnstone – and he wasn't alone – was having such a poor game that he put me on as a substitute for him at half-time. Fortunately, one newspaper writer thought I'd been unlucky with a couple of attempts in the second half. In the return leg, though, I managed to score the first and third goals in the 3–0 victory that took us through to the next round. These were the final two goals I scored in European football.

My last game for Celtic in Scotland was not at Parkhead but at our "second home", Hampden Park. I came on as substitute for Tommy Callaghan in the League Cup semi-final against St Mirren on 6 October, 1971. It was a match the management expected us to win and the supporters obviously thought the same, as only 29,488 turned out for it. And win we did, 3–0. As a result, I thought I might be going to play in another final.

But it was not to be. One week before the final against Partick Thistle, I was transferred to Crystal Palace.

CELTIC: FACTS AND FIGURES

December 1966 – October 1971

WILLIE Wallace signed for Celtic from Heart of Midlothian on Tuesday, 6 December, 1966, for a fee estimated at £30,000. He made his debut in a League match four days later against Motherwell at Parkhead for a side which had previously gone unbeaten in 30 competitive matches that season.

According to Peter Hendry in the Evening Times of 12 December, 1966, he had "a quiet but sound debut." Two days earlier, in his match report for the sports edition, he had described Wallace's part in the second goal of Chalmers' hat-trick: "Wallace began the scoring move with a great pass to Lennox, who hit the upright with his close-range effort. The ball rebounded to Chalmers, who slipped it neatly into the net." Bobby Murdoch got the other goal in Celtic's 4–2 victory with a 30-yarder. Murray and Lindsay scored for the visitors. A notable incident in the match was the sending-off midway through the second half of Motherwell forward John "Dixie" Deans for a foul on Jimmy Johnstone. Ironically, Deans would join Celtic in October, 1971, twelve days after Wallace had departed, together with John Hughes, to Crystal Palace.

Teams:

Celtic: Simpson, Gemmell, O'Neill, Murdoch, McNeill, Clark, Johnstone, Wallace, Chalmers, Lennox, Auld.

Motherwell: McCloy, Whiteford, R.McCallum, W. McCallum, Martis, Campbell, Lindsay, Cairney, Deans, Murray, Hunter.

Referee: R Crockett (Dundee).

Venue: Parkhead.

Attendance: 40,000.

Wallace scored his first goals for Celtic a week later in a 6–2 League victory over Partick Thistle on a wet and windy afternoon at the same venue. It took him only two minutes to open his Celtic account, scoring Celtic's 50th League goal of the season in the process. The ever-alert Joe McBride stretched to head a high cross from Bertie Auld across the goalmouth, where Wallace stooped to head the ball past Thistle 'keeper McFedries in the 24th minute. He scored his second when, as the Glasgow Herald match report of 19 December noted, McFedries could only stand and stare as the ball whizzed past him as a result of

Wallace "belting home on the volley a high crossfield lob from O'Neill." Chalmers (2), Murdoch and McBride scored the other Celtic goals, while Duncan and Gibb scored for Thistle.

Together with Bertie Auld and Steve Chalmers, Wallace was one of three Lisbon Lions who had already experienced playing against clubs they would face in Celtic's 1966–67 European Cup campaign. Wallace and Auld had already played against Inter and, in both cases, Helenio Herrera was coach. On May 3, 1961, only two days after joining Birmingham City from Celtic, Auld played for his new club in the second (home) leg of their Fair Cities Cup semi-final against Inter and, according to the Scottish Daily Mail, the £15,000 signing from Celtic made a fine debut for his new club and played a major part in taking them through to the final. In a match in which Auld faced two players he would line up against in Lisbon– Guarneri and Facchetti, the latter making his Inter debut as an 18-year-old – Birmingham won 2–1, a repeat of the first-leg score. Auld played in the first leg of the final against AS Roma, which finished a 2–2 home draw. Roma won the return leg 2–0 to win the cup 4–2 on aggregate.

In November, 1961, Hearts were outclassed by Inter in the same competition, losing 5–0 on aggregate. On the eve of the first leg, within half-an-hour of their arrival in Edinburgh, the Italian club staged a walk-out from their hotel, with Herrera claiming their rooms were too cold and there were not enough bathrooms. In the first leg at Tynecastle, which Hearts lost 1–0 with Wallace playing at inside-left, there were four Inter players who would play against Celtic in Lisbon in 1967 – Picchi, Guarneri, Bicicli and Facchetti. In the return leg at the San Siro stadium, only Facchetti of Inter's "Lisbon side" played in their 4–0 win, in which Englishman Gerry Hitchens scored twice and made the other two. Wallace played at centre-forward in this match.

Four years later, on 6 December, 1965, Steve Chalmers played for Glentoran in a home friendly match against Dukla Prague at the Oval, Belfast. Dukla were on a British and Irish tour – earning some hard currency during the "Cold War" era – during which they had already played Dunfermline Athletic and defeated Bohemians 5–0 in Dublin three days before the Belfast encounter. Transferred to the Northern Irish club for one day, Chalmers was one of four British players who guested for Glentoran in a match they lost 2–0. The others were Terry Neill and George Armstrong of Arsenal and Jimmy McIlroy of Stoke City. Chalmers lined up against eight players he would also face in the European Cup semi-final ties sixteen months later – Viktor, Dvorak,

Novak, Geleta, Strunc, Knebort, Masopust and Nedorost.

According to the Belfast Telegraph match report, a respectable crowd of 6000 turned out in "cold, far-from-pleasant weather" and watched. "With Glasgow Celtic centre-forward Stevie Chalmers in a similar determined mood (to Jimmy McIlroy), the 'stiffened' Glentoran attack gave the solid, well-drilled Dukla defence plenty of competition and the blank scoreline scarcely does them justice. Dukla, while never pulling out all the stops, impressed as a competent all-round team. Pin-point passing, with centre-forward Josef Masopust ... the perfect purveyor, was their most striking strength. Rarely was the ball used badly, there was no unnecessary running ... the Czechs' secret appears to be an unobtrusive effectiveness. One Oval old-timer put it beautifully: 'I couldn't spot a weak link'." It is worth noting that the bulk of the Glentoran team of that time achieved a drawn first-round European Cup tie with mighty Benfica nearly two years later in season 1967–68. The scores were 1–1 in Belfast and 0–0 in Lisbon, with Glentoran under the management of former Celtic player John Colrain, a player-coach who featured in both matches and scored Glentoran's goal from the penalty spot. As a result, Glentoran became the first British club to exit on the newly-introduced "away goals" rule.

SUMMARY OF GOALS AND APPEARANCES

Joined 6 December, 1966

NUMBER OF APPEARANCES (GOALS SCORED IN BRACKETS)

	L	LC	SC	EU	TOTAL
1966–67	21 (14)	–	5 + 1S (5)	3 (2)	29 + 1S (21)
1967–68	29 + 1S (21)	10 (4)	1	2	42 + 1S (25)
1968–69	29 + 2S (18)	8 (10)	7 (3)	5 + 1S (2)	49 + 3S (33)
1969–70	29 + 1S (16)	9 + 1S (5)	5 (1)	8 (2)	51 + 2S (24)
1970–71	25 + 1S (19)	3 + 3S (1)	7 + 1S (3)	5 (5)	40 + 5S (28)
1971–72	2 + 2S	1 + 1S (1)	–	1 + 1S (2)	4 + 4S (3)
	135 + 7S (88)	31 + 5S (21)	25 + 2S (12)	24 + 2S (13)	215 + 16S (134)

Abbreviations:

L = League; LC = League Cup; SC = Scottish Cup; EU = European competitions;
S = Appearances as a substitute.

Wallace also played in all three matches in the Inter-Continental Cup (World Club Championship) against Racing Club of Buenos Aires, Argentina, in October–November, 1967, but did not score).
He won the following major titles with Celtic:

    League Championship 1967–71 (inclusive)
    Scottish Cup 1967, 1969, 1971
    League Cup 1968, 1969
    European Cup 1967 (finalists 1970).

Pat Woods

Chapter 9

LIFE AFTER CELTIC

Leaving Celtic to join Crystal Palace came as a bigger surprise than leaving Hearts to join Celtic. In the previous month, September, I had played in both games in the first round of the European Cup against Denmark's B1903 Copenhagen and I felt I had thrown off a fairly slow start to the season and was playing quite well. There's no doubt that the first leg at Copenhagen had been a very poor performance by the team as a whole and a fair number of individuals. Even so, Lou Macari's goal in Copenhagen meant that if we could lift our game for the return leg at Parkhead two weeks later, we still had a better than reasonable chance of overcoming the deficit and going through to the next round. For the second leg, I was elevated from the substitutes' bench to start the game, played the full 90 minutes and my two goals helped us win 3–0 in front of 53,000 people at Parkhead and take the tie 4–2 on aggregate.

In the next round, we drew a relatively easy opponent in Sliema Wanderers, of Malta, with the first match to be played at Parkhead on Wednesday, 20 October. We travelled to the Seamill Hotel as usual on the Monday morning beforehand and relaxed during the afternoon.

Everything seemed normal as we enjoyed a quiet evening and went to bed around 10 o'clock. For the second time in my stays at Seamill, I was in a room in the annex, next door to the main building.

Around seven o'clock on Tuesday morning, there was a knock on our door and our trainer, Neil Mochan, came in. He didn't waste any time delivering his message: "Wispy, you have to shower and shave and dress with a collar and tie. You're going up to Parkhead with the Boss after breakfast." Immediately, I asked Neil what the problem was, fearing something had happened at home or to someone in my extended family. Neil said nothing was wrong and he thought it had something to do with Crystal Palace wanting to sign me and big "Yogi", John Hughes. Now I knew Yogi wasn't with the team at Seamill and began to think it was some sort of joke or "wind-up", so I laughingly told Neil to "get lost" and closed the door. He began knocking frantically on it and called out: "Wispy, I'm not kidding. You've got to hurry and have breakfast with the Boss in order to leave for Parkhead around 8.30am." Still confused, I didn't open the door again and Neil left. There were always "wind-ups" going on at Seamill.

Five minutes later, however, the phone rang. It was the Boss, who said: "Get yourself ready. Crystal Palace want to talk to you and the club would like you to talk to them." Without saying a word, I hung up, got ready and went down to breakfast to find the Boss already there. He signalled for me to sit at the table with him, Sean Fallon and Neil and, when I went over, he half-mumbled that we would be leaving in about 20 minutes. I sat down, had cup of coffee and a piece of toast but very little was said by anyone. By this time, other players were coming into breakfast. Several must have heard something was happening as they came up to me and said: "Where are you going?" All I could do was reply: "I don't know."

I felt empty. I had no idea what was going on and all sorts of things were racing through my mind. Why, for example, had the Boss not spoken to me about this beforehand? These things are not dealt with in the middle of the night; he must have known about it the day before. I thought to myself: Why had he not come to my room himself to say the club wanted me to talk to Crystal Palace? And why had he sent Neil Mochan to say it instead? I had long ago learned that at Celtic Park, the Boss was the man who made these sorts of decisions. It was all more than a little unsettling. Nevertheless, I tried to stay outwardly as calm as I could while I waited anxiously to see what would happen next.

About twenty minutes passed and then the Boss put his head round the dining room door and called over: "Are you right? Let's go". I joined him in his car just outside the hotel door and, with just him and me in the car, we set off for Parkhead. I'd made up my mind that I wasn't going to say anything or ask any questions until I knew more about what was happening. Then, about five minutes into the journey, he broke the silence. He said we would be going past Glasgow airport to pick up the chairman and manager of Crystal Palace, as they wanted to talk to me and "Yogi" about joining their club in the English First Division.

By this time, I was growing angry. Why was I being treated like this? I had never been in dispute with the club, I'd been a regular in the team and I could still get my fair share of goals. I didn't reply. He added: "Just talk to them and see what you think." Nothing else was said until we picked up the Palace people at the airport.

All the introductions were followed by a lot of small talk in the car as we travelled on to Parkhead. While the chit-chat was being exchanged, however, I was thinking to myself that no matter how little I knew about what was going on, my wife Olive knew absolutely nothing. So before we arrived at the ground, I decided to tell them I would like to call her before we went ahead with any talks. Bert Head, the Crystal Palace manager, said with obvious surprise: "Your wife doesn't know about what's going on?" I said to him: "I barely know myself. I only found out at seven this morning that something was happening!" After that, there was total silence.

When we reached Parkhead, it was Bert Head who asked me if I would like to telephone my wife, as the Boss had already disappeared into his office. I went into the main office and used the phone there to call Olive and explain as much as I knew. From the tone of her voice, I could tell she couldn't believe what was taking place. For my own part, too, I still couldn't get my head around it. At the end of the call, she simply said: "Well, just do what you think is best for the family." When I went into the boardroom, I'd already made up my mind that, if the offer was good, I would move on. And I'd reached that decision because I felt the way the day had gone – right from the very start – and how I'd been told of Crystal Palace's interest seemed to indicate I was no longer wanted at Parkhead.

Bert Head and Crystal Palace chairman AJ (Arthur) Wait were in the boardroom. When I sat down, Bert said: "Please, Willie, let me speak and go through everything we have to offer before you ask any questions." He spoke for about 10 minutes, covering wages, bonuses and all the extras I didn't have in my contract with Celtic, such as housing allowance, air travel and help with schools for the children. I accepted the terms and we shook hands on it. Bert then made a phone call to London and arranged for the club secretary to fly to Glasgow that afternoon to complete the contract.

As I came out of the boardroom, I met the Boss. "That didn't take long," he said. What did you do?" I told him I'd accepted their offer and, as soon as he heard that, he turned on his heels and took off. He did say something as he walked away but, to this day, I don't know what it was. But he didn't seem happy. Why? Beats me! I had travelled with Jock Stein from Seamill to Glasgow airport, where we had picked up the Crystal Palace representatives and – all the way – he had failed to say anything at all to me. It seemed pretty clear to me he had already decided I should move on! So, like all my moves before, I realised I should just get on with life and do my best at my new club.

After giving some thought to the totally unexpected events of that day, I remembered one particular conversation that had taken place between the Boss and myself only a few weeks before. Olive had attended one of Celtic's league matches and while she was waiting outside the main entrance at Parkhead to receive her ticket, Mr Stein approached her and asked her if everything was alright at home. Olive replied: "Yes. Why shouldn't it be? And why are you asking?" The Boss said: "Oh, no worries. It's OK. Just asking." He then turned around and walked through the front door back into Celtic Park. On the way home after the match, Olive brought up the subject with me and I told her I had no idea what he was talking about. After this, on the Monday morning at training, I went to the Boss's office. I found him alone and asked if I could have a few words with him. I brought up the fact that he had spoken to Olive and what he had asked her. His reply was: "Ah! Just rumours I heard." I then asked what the rumours were that he had heard. He said: "Oh, never mind." So I said to him: "I hear plenty of rumours about everyone at the ground –

A 17 year old Willie Wallace with Jim Storrie in 1957 playing for Kelvinside Thistle

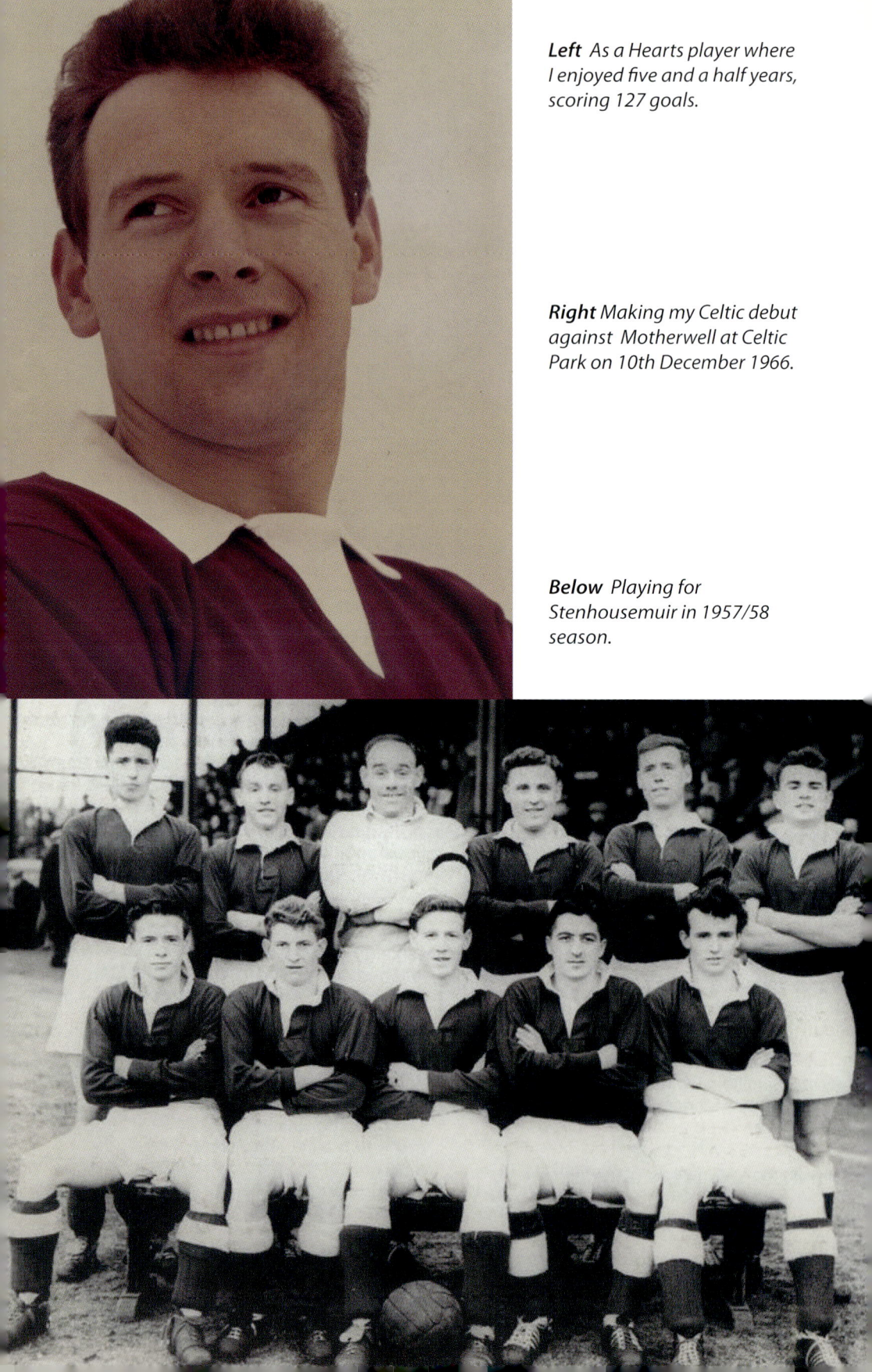

Left As a Hearts player where I enjoyed five and a half years, scoring 127 goals.

Right Making my Celtic debut against Motherwell at Celtic Park on 10th December 1966.

Below Playing for Stenhousemuir in 1957/58 season.

Above Right Jock Stein regarded Willie Wallace as a one man front line for Celtic

Below I loved every minute playing for Celtic.

Above THE BHOYS in a relaxed mood before kick off

Left Big Billy leading out a grand old team.

Below Yet another Celtic attack on the Milan goal.

Above *A goal must come and come it did !*

Below *Celtic pile on the pressure under a clear Lisbon sky.*

Above On the road to Lisbon - the Celtic programmes !

Right The best day of our lives !

Below Getting carried away by jubilant Celtic supporters.

Above We won the big cup and we brought it back !

Below All smiles with Tommy Gemmell.

Evening Citizen

IT'S PARADISE!

Exclusive

BILLY McNEILL

GREEN CITIZEN

Above The lorry drives around Paradise as we show off the European Cup !

Below Celebrations !

Top Left Not a bad collection of winners medals.

Top Right Jock Stein celebrating another Scottish Cup Final success at Hampden.

Left Tickets for the Lisbon final seemed to find their way into Celtic hands.

Below Walking out to pre-season Challenge match against Spurs at Hampden, August 1967.

Above *Celtic win BBC Sports Review team of the year for 1967....Celtic won everything in 1967.*

Below *Don't cry for me Argentina.*

Above Signing on for Crystal Palace with John Hughes

Above left After Celtic, as a Crystal Palace player.

Above Right Meeting the Big Yin- laughs with Billy Connolly in Australia.

Below The Lions Roar again !

Above Macaulay, Wallace
Wedding, 2nd April 1962
Left to Right
Mr Andrew Wallace,
Mrs Marion Macaulay, Willie,
Olive, Mrs Sarah Wallace,
Mr John Macaulay

Left Martin Hart and Olive's
Sister Hazel, Best Man and
Bridesmaid at Wallace/
Macaulay wedding

Above Willie, Madelyn, John Clark, Fiona Wallace and Olive

Left Madelyn and eldest grandaughter Brooke with Willie, Madelyn, Willie and Brooke

Below Todd, Lynn and Family Left to Right Lynn Wallace, Partner Todd Lewis holding TJ Lewis and Charlie Lewis in front

Left *Madelyn, Willie, Olive, TJ and Charlie at 50th Wedding Anniversary on 2nd April 2012.*

Below *With Olive at the 45th Anniversary celebrations in Brisbane- the Celtic support in Australia is truly amazing !*

including yourself – but I wouldn't go and ask your wife if everything was alright at home. I don't think it was the right thing for you to ask Olive without discussing it with me first." I turned to leave the room and, while I was walking out, I thought he looked mad enough to kill me! After this, there hadn't been a lot said between us, including on 19 October, 1971 – the day I left to join Crystal Palace.

John "Yogi" Hughes had also been transferred from Celtic to Crystal Palace on the same day. Together, we were invited to the Scottish League Cup final against Partick Thistle four days later, another match that Celtic were expected to win comfortably. Big "Yogi" and I had played for Crystal Palace in our 1–0 win against Coventry City on the Friday night and we travelled to Scotland by overnight train. On Saturday, we picked up our complimentary tickets at the front door at Hampden Park before taking our seats alongside the players who hadn't made it into the team. It was an awful afternoon. Celtic hit rock-bottom and went down 4–1 to a rampant Thistle side. I had been bitterly disappointed at leaving Celtic but as I looked at the devastation on the faces of my former team-mates after the match that afternoon, I wondered if my move south had come at just the right time in my career.

My stay at Palace was quite short but certainly sweet. I had always dreamed of playing against clubs like Manchester United, Liverpool, Everton, Arsenal, Tottenham etc and, in the twelve months I spent at Selhurst Park in London, I achieved my dream. It has always amazed me that I was transferred to Crystal Palace for £2000 more than my transfer fee from Hearts to Celtic. At the time John Hughes and I were sold to Palace, there was a journalists' strike so no other clubs knew we were available for transfer. I'm sure there would have been more clubs interested so the fee might have been even higher. It was a good bit of business by Bert Head and the deal must have suited the Celtic board and management. "Yogi" and I were far from "over the hill" and I firmly believe John would have gone on for a good few years more playing top-level football but he was very unlucky to receive a bad injury that finished his career. I went on to play successfully for another six-and-a-half years.

We were known as the "White Heather Club", as it was mostly Scots in the Crystal Palace team at the time. Along with "Yogi" and me, there was Jim Scott, John McCormick, Sam Goodwin, Gerry

Queen, Tony Taylor and others. Other quality players at Palace – not Scots – included Bobby Tambling, Bobby Kellard and goalkeeper John Jackson who, on his day, was one of the best goalkeepers I played with during my career. He was at least as good as any other in the English First Division at that time – and there were some extremely good goalkeepers in the early seventies.

Near the end of my first season at Palace, we played against Nottingham Forest, who sat in second-last place in the First Division table. For them, the match was crucial; they had to beat us to avoid relegation and stay up. The game was all the more interesting as big "TG", Tommy Gemmell, was by then playing for Forest. I remember Tom talking to me before the game and without for a moment suggesting any "funny business", I can recall him saying something like: "It's alright for you guys, you're safe now". We each wished the other all the best for the match and went into our respective dressing rooms. As things turned out, the game was pretty even with both sides having chances and then, in one of our attacks, Bobby Tambling beat his full-back, crossed a great ball and I met it perfectly with my head to give us a 1–0 lead. As much as they pushed forward later in the game, Forest couldn't score and my goal proved the winner. Forest were, therefore, relegated. I had mixed feelings about the result but when Tom and I had a chat over a beer after the game, he said it hadn't been this game that had relegated them but many others they hadn't won over the season – this had been just the final nail in their coffin. All the same, it wasn't exactly an enjoyable feeling to have been the one who had hammered it in!

I remember going in through the main foyer for the first and only game I played at Anfield, Liverpool. Standing there was their manager Bill Shankly, with a ball in his hands. As we walked past him, he said: "You Scottish boys are no' bad but you had better have a look at this ball now, for you'll no'' see much of it on the pitch!" He was right. We lost 4–1 – and I don't remember having even one shot at goal. But it was a great experience to play against Liverpool as they were a great side and "Shanks" a great man.

After completing my first season, I re-signed for two more. However, halfway through that second season, Bert Head was replaced as manager by Malcolm Allison. Just before Bert left, he told me that Dumbarton – then in the Scottish First Division – had made enquiries about me. Bert asked if I would be interested. After discussions with Olive, I agreed to travel to Glasgow for signing talks but there was a snag and I returned to London. Two weeks later, however, I did sign for Dumbarton and we moved back to Scotland. It proved a good move, as it wasn't too long before Palace were relegated.

The move back to Scotland made Olive happy. Not that she didn't like living in Brighton – where she had continued to play hockey with Brighton and Hove Ladies – but moving to Dumbarton meant we would be only half-an-hour away from my family at Kirkintilloch and Olive's family at Kilsyth. When we moved back to Scotland, we lived in the town of Dumbarton itself, the club providing a house while we looked around for one to buy. The house had been a church manse – the residence for the minister of the local parish – and built for the Church of Scotland in a deal with one of the local builders. As the church already had a manse, this one was spare. And it was only five minutes' drive from the club's ground, Boghead.

During my time there, Dumbarton had mixed fortunes against Celtic. I was full-time at Dumbarton and coached a group of young players who were able to train in the mornings. Occasionally, some of the senior players would also be able to train with us, depending on their shifts at work. In this group I had Ian Wallace, Tom and Colin McAdam, Murdo McLeod and Graeme Sinclair. All these boys went on to have great careers.

One of my first games against Celtic in Dumbarton colours was on 2 December, 1972. I managed to score but we lost the game 6–1 as Pat McLuskey chose that particular afternoon to score his only hat-trick for Celtic. On 30 March, 1974, Dumbarton played against Celtic at Parkhead. We played well in a 3–3 draw and it took a goal with just nine minutes to go from John "Dixie" Deans – who had been bought to replace me at Parkhead – to salvage a draw for Celtic. Young Tom McAdam, from my former coaching group at Dumbarton, also scored for Celtic that day and went on to have a distinguished career at Parkhead. I played my last game for Dumbarton against Celtic at Parkhead on 11 February, 1975, when the match again ended in a respectable draw, this time 2–2. Six or seven weeks later, I left for Australia to take up a two-year contract with APIA Leichhardt FC in Sydney. Two of the first-team players at Dumbarton, Roy McCormack and Kenny Jenkins, later came out to Australia to play along with me at APIA Leichhardt.

At Dumbarton, I got to know Dick, the groundsman, very well. Dick, it seemed, had been at Boghead for just about as long as the ground had existed. As it was built about 1872, that may be a slight exaggeration – but he had been around for a very long time! We became partners in playing the Pools every week, putting in a couple of quid each. I remember one particular Sunday morning when Dick phoned me up in what sounded like complete panic. We had seven score draws and were waiting for a late kick-off – Hartlepool v Somebody! Dick had already worked out he was going to buy the club, kick out all the "bums" (directors) upstairs and we were going to run the club our way. I could barely get him off the phone so I said I would be at the ground at 11am. When I turned up, I was expecting him to be running around sacking everyone but, mysteriously, he was nowhere to be found. I asked Bob, the physio, if he had seen him and he said: "Aye. He's in his wee room through the back". I opened the door slowly and there he was, head between his knees. Immediately, I asked: "How much did we win?" Slowly, he said: "Hartlepool was a hame win. Only one point, so we only get £1700 pounds". I replied: "That's no' bad" but, just as I uttered the consoling words, he jumped up and shouted: "But now we cannae get rid o' them upstairs!"

I remember attending a Dumbarton FC Christmas party at the local Dumbuck Hotel, a bow-tie event. TV star "Lonely" (actor Russell Hunter played "Lonely" in the series "Callan", starring Edward Woodward) was there and Olive and I were introduced to him in the reception area. Olive was wearing a beautiful, low-cut dress. He took my hand and said: "Nice to meet you, Willie" and then turned to Olive and said: "I like your simmet!". Those who know Scottish slang words know that "simmet" means a type of skimpy gents' vest. Olive definitely knew that and you should have seen her face!

During my first year at Dumbarton, I bought a piece of ground opposite my old house in the village of Condorrat and, over the next year, I built a new house. I was the contractor – or private builder – and I received tremendous help from some Celtic supporters who were also excellent tradesman. One particular gentleman was a close friend and famous pigeon-fancier from Croy, Jimmy Nash. His brother, Matt, did all my plumbing work and Jimmy's sons did all my brickwork. The electrician, Ian "Cowboy" Brown, from Kirkintilloch, was from another persuasion than Celtic but also did a great job. He had played a lot of junior football and I remember seeing him play for Rob Roy. By the way, the name "Cowboy" came not from him being a good shot with a six-gun but from the fact that his legs were a little bent. Ian was great to have around the place, always providing a joke or two and always saying he was a better player than me. I have the fondest memories of building that house – the "house that Celtic supporters built" – and will always appreciate the work done on it by all those who worked alongside me.

On 12 April, 1966, our first daughter, Lynn, had been born in Falkirk Royal Infirmary. As every parent knows, the birth of a first child is not only an extremely important event but brings a wonderful sense of excitement and awe. Mind you, there were some other captivating moments in the first 14 months of Lynn's life, such as her Dad joining Celtic, going on to win Scottish Cup, Scottish League and European Cup medals. It was an unbelievable period – and she slept through most of it!

Our second daughter, Fiona, was born in Falkirk Royal Infirmary on 9 July, 1970, and again the birth coincided with a memorable year of football. Celtic had won the First Division championship and League Cup and again reached the final of the European Cup. Blame it on a not very observant Dad but, until recently, I hadn't realised that both girls were born in the years Celtic were involved in European Cup finals.

CRYSTAL PALACE AND DUMBARTON: FACTS AND FIGURES

Crystal Palace: October 1971 – October 1972

WILLIE Wallace made his debut for Crystal Palace in an away League match against Coventry City at Highfield Road on 22 October, 1971, just three days after his transfer, along with John Hughes, from Celtic for a reputed combined fee of £50,000. The match was played experimentally on a Friday night, although the attendance was around 4000 below that of the start of the season.

Teams:

Coventry City: Glazier, Coop, Barry, Smith, Blockley, Parker, Young, Carr, Chilton, Mortimer, St John.

Crystal Palace: Jackson, Payne, Taylor, Blyth, McCormick, Pinkney, Tambling, Goodwin, Craven, Kellard, Hughes

(Wallace, sub).

Referee: D Nippard (Bournemouth).

Venue: Highfield Road, Coventry.

Attendance: 20,801.

The Daily Telegraph match report of 23 October described it as a match which "sadly lacked the finer skills." Tambling opened the scoring for Palace in the 7th minute with a hard, low, 25-yarder which was deflected past the unsighted Glazier by a defender. Coventry's equaliser – the match ended 1–1 – came from a St John strike from 10 yards after a Chilton shot "rebounded luckily off Young." The report in The Times noted that Wallace, who came on for Hughes in the 62nd or 70th minute (depending on which match report you accept), "scarcely had time to get the feel of things, but still almost scored with a header near the end."

SUMMARY OF GOALS AND APPEARANCES

Joined 19 October, 1971

NUMBER OF APPEARANCES (GOALS SCORED IN BRACKETS)

	L	LC	FAC	TOTAL
1971–72	27 + 2S (3)	–	2 (2)	29 + 2S (5)
1972–73	9 + 1S (1)	1	–	10 + 1S (1)
	36 + 3S (4)	1	2 (2)	39 + 3S (6)

Abbreviations: L = League; LC = League Cup; FAC = FA Cup; S = Appearances as a substitute

Dumbarton: October 1972 – March 1975

THE debut for Dumbarton came in their home League match against Dundee at Boghead on 14 October, 1972, just two days after Wallace's transfer from Crystal Palace for an estimated fee of £10,000. The home side opened the scoring in the 6th minute through the unmarked McAdam's header from a Wilson cross. Dundee equalised in the 46th through a Cushley own goal, the ball glancing into the net past Williams as Cushley rose with Duncan to meet a Houston free kick. Gordon Wallace put Dundee in front midway through the second half with a header from Houston's cross but McCormack equalised a few minutes later in controversial circumstances, with Dundee 'keeper Thomson Allan claiming the centre-forward had handled the ball before scoring. The match ended 2–2.

Teams:

Dumbarton: Williams, Menzies, Wilkinson, Jenkins, Cushley, Graham, Coleman, Wallace, McCormack, McAdam, Wilson.

Dundee: Allan, Wilson, Houston, Robinson, Stewart, Ford, I Scott, Duncan, Wallace, J Scott, Lambie.

Referee: EH Pringle (Edinburgh).

Venue: Boghead, Dumbarton.

Attendance: 5000.

The home fans appreciated the debutant, the Sunday Mail match report noting Dumbarton were "a side looking much improved with the inclusion of new signing Willie Wallace." The Sunday Post report said the newcomer "playing much deeper than in his Celtic days, brought composure and subtlety to the 'Sons' in midfield."

SUMMARY OF GOALS AND APPEARANCES

Joined 12 October, 1972

NUMBER OF APPEARANCES (GOALS SCORED IN BRACKETS)

	L	LC	SC	TOTAL
1972–73	24 + 2S (6)	–	3 (1)	27 + 2S (6)
1973–74	32 (3)	8 (1)	1	41 (4)
1974–75	26 (12)	6 (2)	3	35 (14)
	82 + 2S (21)	14 (3)	7 (1)	103 + 2s (25)

Abbreviations: L = League; LC = League Cup; SC = Scottish Cup,

S = Appearances as a substitute.

Pat Woods

Chapter 10

DOWN UNDER, DINGWALL AND DUNDEE: FROM PLAYER TO COACH

DOWN UNDER: APIA LEICHHARDT, 1975–76

Joining Apia Leichhardt in Sydney was a spur-of-the-moment decision taken during my second season at Dumbarton. By late 1974, with the Christmas and New Year season in full swing, the house at Condorrat I had started to build after returning to Scotland from London had been completed. I was coaching the club's full-time, first-team players one morning when three lads appeared at the ground, looking for a place to train. It turned out all three were first-team players from APIA Leichhardt FC, one being a local boy called John McGhee who had played for Dumbarton before going Down Under. I agreed they could train with us for the month or so they would be staying in Scotland.

It took only a few days of the boys training with us to see that their play was of a high standard and find out that APIA Leichhardt was one of the top clubs in Australia. Chilly as it was in Dumbarton, it was the height of summer in Sydney and, therefore, their closed season. John McGhee's parents lived in Dumbarton and invited Olive and myself to a Hogmanay (New Year's Eve) party. During the early part of the festivities, John asked me if I had ever thought of playing overseas. I told him about my time at Hearts – when I had thought of moving to Canada – and casually mentioned that if Dumbarton did not make it into the new Premier League, it was something I would consider. (Scottish football was restructured from two divisions into three, including creation of a new Premier Division, at the end of the 1974–75 season.) We had a great night at the party, went home and I didn't really give much more thought to my party discussion with John. Oh! By the way, just in case you're wondering about football players and parties, bad weather had meant our New Year's Day match was already cancelled!

At the next training session the Australian boys attended, John McGhee told me the APIA Leichhardt secretary/manager was on his way from Sydney to offer me a contract. The man in question was George Keith, who had been with Third Lanark before going on to play for APIA and Australia. I just had a little laugh, thinking John was winding me up but, sure enough, George arrived at Dumbarton two days later. Originally from the town of Clydebank, he was no stranger to the area. George travelled out to Condorrat with me and we had dinner, during which he explained what the club could offer me. This was the first time in all my moves that Olive was included in the talks. Mind you, at the back of my mind throughout our discussions was that this was not just a move "down the road" we were considering but a move "Down Under" – the other side of the world.

In the end, I agreed to all the terms he offered, with one provision: That I would wait to see whether Dumbarton would make it into the soon-to-be-created Premier Division. By late March, 1975, it was pretty clear they wouldn't so, around Easter, I travelled to Australia. By the end of the season, Dumbarton finished four places short of claiming a spot in the new 10-team top division.

I left London Heathrow airport on a Friday night and arrived at Sydney at 3.30pm on Sunday. I flew there with the Aussie airline Qantas, who flew Boeing 707s at that time, so we needed four stops – at Frankfurt (West Germany), Abu Dhabi (in the Persian Gulf), Bombay (India) and Perth (in Western Australia) – and then across Australia from Perth to Sydney's Kingsford Smith airport. All up, it took 36 hours and when I arrived I didn't know whether I was "Arthur or Martha" as I hadn't slept a wink in all that time. I was met at Sydney airport by the APIA team manager Harry Ambrose. We travelled by car across many suburbs of Sydney to the hotel where I was to stay until I could move into the flat the club had acquired for me. Harry would say: "Oh! This is where the Greeks live" or "this is where the Serbians live", then the Jews and then the Italians – on and on, just like we were visiting the United Nations. Finally, I asked him whether there were any Aussies living in Sydney. He laughed and said: "No, not many!"

We arrived at the Travelodge Motel in Ashfield, next door to the suburb of Leichhardt, where the APIA Club (the large social club associated with the football club) and football ground were located. The motel's manager was an Englishman, or "Pom", called Barry Roberts. Barry was a relief manager for Travelodge and had taken over just a few weeks before my arrival. He hailed from Bolton and was – and still is – a fervent Wanderers' supporter. He, like Harry Ambrose, was to become a very good friend. Harry told me that my new team was playing that day, kick-off time 3pm or just before I had landed. In keeping with the ethnic make-up of many of Sydney's suburbs and most of Australian football at that time, APIA Leichhardt was a club with very strong Italian connections and today's match had been against one of their main rivals, Pan-Hellenic, a club with strong Greek heritage. Harry knew I would be tired and had arranged for me to have dinner at the APIA Club that night, as the team always had dinner together after all their home matches. So I rested up for a couple of hours before setting off for dinner.

Despite APIA's "Italian connection", once more I had joined a club with a healthy quota of Scots. In goal was a chap called Dave McGuire, nicknamed "Spitfire" or the keeper "wi' nae hands". Dave was born in the city of Wollongong, south of Sydney in New South Wales, but his Mum and Dad both were Scots. The right-back was Bobby McGinn, who had played for Drumchapel Amateurs, and at left-back was Kenny Jenkins, who had been at Dumbarton. The right-half was the club captain and Australian national team captain Jimmy Rooney, who hailed from Dundee. Kenny Wilson was purchased one week before me from Carlisle United and he had also played for Dumbarton. There were two more Scots at the club, Brian Thom and Drew Dunlop, both formerly of Hearts. I felt as if I was back in Scotland when I sat down to dinner that first night – and the players were also in good spirits as they had beaten their "Greek" rivals 2–0.

My first game, a week later, was against a team called Western Suburbs, who were the closest club to our own ground. In Scotland, we would probably have referred to the game as a local derby. Not, however, in Australia, where our "derby" was based on ethnic rather than geographical rivalry. That was against the Greeks of Sydney Olympic FC, who were coached by Rale Rasic, a former Australian national coach who had guided the country to its first World Cup finals in Germany in 1974. The game against Western Suburbs was played on a cricket oval – yes, oval, with a hard wicket right in the middle of the field. The crowd was only a few thousand strong, although the venue was just up the road from our ground and the APIA Club. Apparently, our supporters wouldn't come to the Western Suburbs ground as they had to stand and were too far away from the action.

I felt terrible during that first match: Running through my mind all the time was "what am I doing here?" I thought: "There's no atmosphere and the football's scrappy because of the pitch." I don't remember much of the game but I do remember thinking that if someone had come up to me and said I could go home the next day, I would have been on that plane like a shot. And I was already missing my wife and two daughters. "Yes," I thought, "I've made my first mistake of my career." I had enjoyed playing for every one my previous clubs and here I was now, on the other side of the world and – there was no escaping the strength of my feelings – having major doubts.

The main problem at the beginning was that the coach of the club had been bypassed both with my signing and that of Kenny Wilson. The coach was a Scot, George Blues. I didn't know much about George before I joined APIA but he had been an APIA player himself before becoming the coach. I don't know what his relationship was with the football club's secretary/manager George Keith – the man from Third Lanark who had come to Dumbarton to sign me up – but it certainly couldn't have been very good. At training, Mr Blues did not say much or give me the impression he wanted me there. At first, I thought it was just me and things would improve as time went on. I was wrong; as time went on, things just got worse. We played our next game at home, where there were much better facilities than at the Western

Suburbs cricket ground the week before. I played up front again but didn't do so well. I think maybe the new environment and the jet lag were catching up with me; the body clock was upside-down, back to front and definitely needed rewinding!

We played our third game on a Sunday, away from home against a side called St George Budapest – of Hungarian origins – who, on the day, were to have a guest player, former England, Manchester City, Derby County and Bolton Wanderers' forward Francis "Frannie" Lee. As you might imagine, the match was a sell-out. With Frannie Lee's pedigree and Willie Wallace, ex-Celtic and European Cup-winner, due to appear, it made for great publicity in the newspapers on the Saturday morning and, fully an hour before kick-off, the ground was packed with 22,000 fans. But when the teams were announced, Frannie was not playing due to injury and Wallace and Wilson had been dropped to the bench! There was almost a riot and it was just as well there was a big police presence. The game began accompanied by constant "booing" and the punters wanted their money back. APIA lost 3–0, I didn't play and I didn't speak to anyone about the debacle.

At this time, my family were still back in Scotland and I was living in a hotel not far from the APIA Club and ground. Kenny Wilson was also living there, awaiting the arrival of his family. It was there that I woke up on the Monday morning after the St George Budapest match with a clear mind. I thought: Why would I have travelled 13,000 miles to sit on a bench? I could do that quite comfortably at home. So I phoned George Keith, who combined his role with the football club with also being part-time secretary at the APIA social club. His main office was at Auburn, a Sydney suburb one hour by train from our hotel, and Kenny and I agreed to travel to his office for discussions. I immediately told him I wanted a flight home by Wednesday. Then Kenny added that he did, too. Kenny's request took me by surprise, as we had barely spoken about our feelings. George was, of course, shocked and phoned the club president Jim Buyutti, organising a meeting between us at the Apia Club for five o'clock that afternoon.

When Kenny and I arrived at the club, we were taken into the boardroom to join George and Mr Buyutti. Coffee was served, everything was pleasant and friendly and I noticed as we sat down there was no coach present. I was first to speak, so I asked why George Blues wasn't there, as he was the guy who picked the team and should be given a chance to explain why he did what he did. I wanted to know why I was dropped and why he didn't speak to me before or after the game. I was answered very quickly by Mr Buyutti, who announced George was no longer the manager-coach of Apia Soccer Club, nor did he now hold any other position at the club. The president then told us the position of coach would be taken up by Phil Bottalico, a former coach at APIA Leichhardt and that he would like me to have some input into training and team selection. Not surprisingly, this threw me a little off-balance. Still, I asked if I could think about it overnight. Mr Buyutti agreed and said if I was still unhappy the next day, they would fly me home as soon as possible. I went back to the hotel with Kenny and we talked over a few things – mainly why we had been dropped, to which we still had no answers.

After giving a lot of consideration to everything I had thought about since the game and to what Jim Buyutti had said, I decided after all that I would stay for my two-year contract. But I didn't want to be involved in the management and coaching side at APIA; I just wanted to play. I also took into account that Sydney was a beautiful city and the APIA Leichhardt Football Club had certainly lived up to every part of their side of the deal so far. So, the next morning, I shook hands with the president and told him I would like to stay on as originally agreed, as a player. Over the next 18 months, my early doubts proved unfounded. We won the league in both seasons. At that time in Australia, they operated top-four play-offs at the end of each season to determine the champion team. We lost the "grand final" in the 1975 season but won it in 1976; we also won the Philips Cup in 1976. And I managed to score a few goals in both seasons but, as I had moved back into midfield, not as many as I might if I had still been playing as a striker.

After three weeks in Australia, I had already found a flat in a very nice suburb called Cammeray, situated on the north side of the city. I also had a job again – my first outside football since I was 18. I became a sales representative for a company called Westerveldt Sporting Wholesale, owned by a Dutchman called William "Bill" Westerveldt. He had been a professional footballer in Holland, New Zealand and Australia. Our main business was for Adidas (football) and Stellar International (tennis and squash) and my territory was the state of New South Wales. You can fit Britain into the state three times so –

not unreasonably, I think – I would only visit each area every six to eight weeks!

While on my travels, I would train with different sporting groups in the small towns I was visiting. It was usually with football clubs but, occasionally, might be rugby league teams or other codes. It didn't take me long to make many friends in the "bush", which also helped my sales figures as most of the sports store owners I dealt with either played or had played a sport themselves or were involved with local clubs. I would be back in Sydney by Friday, either driving or – depending how far out I was – I would leave my car in one of the towns and fly back to Sydney, returning to the country on the Monday morning to carry on my rounds. I really enjoyed the freedom, open spaces and big skies out in the country and, during a couple of school holidays, Olive and the girls made trips with me. In 1976, many country roads were made of dirt and some bush towns still had dirt roads and wooden sidewalks, even in their centres. I remember all four of us driving into the small town of Junee, population 4000, some 470km (290 miles) south-west of Sydney in the Riverina region of the state. It was just as I described – dirt street and raised wooden sidewalks. Olive thought we had driven on to the set of a cowboy movie and kept looking for John Wayne to ride down the street! It was certainly a long way from Kilsyth or Kirkintilloch.

Another trip I remember was with my boss, Bill Westerveldt. We had travelled to a small city called Tamworth, population 60,000, 420km (260 miles) north of Sydney in an area known as New England, for a three-day show on Adidas sportswear. We were staying in the Travelodge Motel and, after the first day's presentations, were relaxing after dinner when Bill suggested we visit the local club so he could play what we call the "fruit machines" and Aussies call "poker machines" or "pokies", for short. Bill had lost his right arm in a car accident – which ended his football-playing career – but he could still drive and generally do pretty much everything by himself. So we arrived at the club around 9pm, ordered a beer and had a look around. There was one guy playing a machine and the barman told us this poor chap had fed in around $400 and hadn't won a thing. After five minutes or so, he gave the machine a hard kick and cursed it for taking all his money. A minute or two later, Bill walked over to the same machine, put in a couple of dollars and won the $1000 jackpot.

The guy who had been playing the machine heard the bells ringing as the machine spilled out small mountains of coins, turned and saw Bill at the machine. In a loud voice, he said: "You one-armed bandits all f***ing stick together!" We all had a good laugh and Bill, always good-natured and generous, gave the guy a couple of hundred dollars of his money back. I had a lot of memorable trips in the Aussie bush with Bill Westerveldt.

My only sad memory was the death of the gentleman who was instrumental in my decision to come to Australia in the first place. As mentioned earlier, John McGhee had trained with Dumbarton during the Christmas-New Year period of 1974 and had asked me if I was interested in going to Australia. I had said "maybe" and things went on from there. Tragically, John was killed in a car accident in 1976. At first, it was thought he had minor injuries and he was kept in hospital overnight as a precaution. His spleen, though, had been ruptured and this had not been picked up by medical staff. During the night, his condition became much worse and the doctors were unable to save him. It was a very sad time for everyone at APIA Leichhardt, as John was one of the most likeable chaps you could ever hope to meet.

At the end of 1976 season, it was decided that, for the first time, there would be a new, national league in Australia. APIA, for political reasons, announced they would not apply for entry into the new league, so I decided I would return home. In the middle of making my arrangements to return, APIA told me they had received an offer for me from Hakoah, a club with Jewish origins which was later to become Eastern Suburbs and then the highly successful Sydney City. I discussed this with the president of APIA and reminded him of my original agreement with the club – that I had arrived on a free transfer and I would leave the same way. But he was adamant they would seek a fee as I was considered one of the best midfielders in Australia at that time and the board wanted money for me. I told him I would be going home and continued to make my arrangements.

The day before I was to leave, I received a phone telling me to go to the APIA Club and meet the president. He said the club would let me move if I wished and Hakoah representatives wanted to talk with me that afternoon. I explained to him that I was leaving for Scotland the next day and my personal belongings had already gone. His face broke into a smile and he said: "Let's have some lunch." So I had a very nice meal with him and left on the best of terms. I wasn't to know then that I would return three years later – as manager of the APIA national league side.

DINGWALL TO DUNDEE, 1977;
PLAYING DAYS END AND COACHING LIFE BEGINS

Arriving back in Scotland in January, 1977, I lived in Kilsyth with our relations the Harts, Hazel and Martin. Hazel is Olive's sister and Martin was my best friend and also best man at our wedding. Our girls joined their cousin, Lorraine Hart at Kilsyth Academy Primary school while I started looking for a job. After a week or two, I contacted Bertie Auld, then manager at Partick Thistle. Bertie asked what my fitness was like. I knew I had put on a bit of weight in Australia and had not trained or played for three months, so I started back the next day at Thistle's ground, Firhill. Within a short time, I started playing in a few reserve games and enjoyed them. Thistle were in the Premier League and at first I struggled with the pace of the games, which were played a little bit faster than in Australia. It was only a matter of a few weeks until Bertie let me know the Thistle board had, unsurprisingly, opted against signing me, having decided I was too old. Like it or not, I couldn't disagree with that as I was now 37. Apparently, Bertie was shrewd enough not to believe my repeated claims that I was only 26!

Ever helpful, however, Bertie suggested I should phone Morris Newton, chairman of Ross County in the Highland League, as they were looking for a manager, better still a player/manager. Morris was at this time in his thirties; I had known his father, Fred, from my days at Hearts and Celtic through a mutual friend Hugh Robertson, a businessman from Dingwall. I had first met Fred in Dingwall after playing for Hearts against Ross County in a pre-season match, in which I scored a hat-trick. Fred, a native of Blackburn, had been on the Ross County FC board and had started a bus company at Dingwall, which supplied transport to the Chevron oil company at Nigg Bay. Morris had become the owner of the bus company after Fred passed away.

I phoned Morris and got the job. My stay at Partick had been short but very sweet; it was great to be with "Ten-Thirty" again and, as usual, we had a few laughs along the way. The one I remember best was just after Bertie had sold Alan Hansen to Liverpool for £100,000 and, as a result, needed to find a centre-half. He had heard that Bolton Wanderers in England had a young central defender who was Scottish and homesick and might be available. Ian Greaves was manager at Bolton's Burnden Park at the time and Bertie had received a green light from his board to buy as long as the price was not over £8000. Bertie phoned Ian, asked about the player and how much he would cost. Ian said fifty-thousand wouldn't move him. Bertie replied: "Aye and I'm one o' them!"

As agreed, I travelled to the Highlands in March, 1977, to take over as Ross County player/manager. Due to the harsh winter weather, many games had previously been postponed and the club had eight matches to make up. I signed a two-year contract with County and made arrangements to buy a house in Maryburgh which belonged to the club and was being used by a player who was leaving at the end of the season. In the meantime, we lived at Fortrose, on the Black Isle, and the plan was to move into Maryburgh at the end of the season. Like a host of other plans I made in my life, it was destined never to come to fruition.

We had a hectic three months playing three games a week and managed to climb from third-last to third place in the league and played in one cup final and two semi-finals. The problem was part-time staff and injuries. One good result to come out of it was the emergence of Rab Geddes, an Inverness-born goalkeeper then 16 years of age who was to join Dundee FC just after I joined as first-team coach. Young Rab went on to have an extremely successful career in Scottish football. I enjoyed my three-month stay on the Black Isle and coaching Ross County. So many things happened during this time, I could write a book on this short period alone. I will always be grateful for the consideration given to me by Morris Newton and the board of Ross County FC in recognising that a move to Dundee FC to take the role of first-team coach was a great step up for me. They all agreed to release me from my contract and I moved to Dundee to join my old friend Tommy Gemmell, who was manager at Dundee, in July, 1977.

The move from Dingwall to Dundee's Dens Park marked the end of my playing career and the beginning of a new phase of my – and my family's – life. Again, it meant another upheaval for my wonderful, globe-trotting family, who always supported my every move at every stage. Little did they know that in another three years, we would be off once again to Australia to continue in football management – but that really is another story.

As I sit down and reflect on my career as a player over twenty years, I am amazed at what I achieved. As a young boy, I had just hoped I could do my best in any situation that presented itself. Everything that came in the years that followed just seemed to happen, as I had no great or guiding plan to follow. Of course, joining Celtic FC in 1966 will always be the best thing I ever did in football. Not only did we win the European Cup and also reach a second final, I was also part of a team that won every other honour available in Scottish football. I am, quite simply, proud to say I will always be a Celtic supporter and I am honoured to be part of Celtic Football Club's great and growing history.

Written by Willie Wallace

"I should point out to those who are too young to remember that this was in the days when the old façade of the ground still stared out at you when you walked up Kerrydale Street and the old building proclaimed that it was the home of Celtic Football & Athletic Club 1888. Further, the main- if not the only - car park was the one right in front of the ground that still stands there to this day. On European nights, the car park was choc-a-block with cars, and if getting into that car park was a slow laborious process then getting out of it after the game was sheer purgatory...an interminably long wait."

WILLIE WALLACE
A CELTIC LEGEND

BY BROGAN ROGAN TREVINO AND HOGAN

"So—with the game still on a knife-edge, but Celtic looking as if they were going to go through we left our seats and made our way out.

We had just gotten out of the stand and were stood opposite the main entrance when a huge roar went up accompanied by what sounded like a herd of elephant stamping their feet— clearly Celtic had scored and were now definitely through!!"

Chapter 1

WALLACE!

I remember quite clearly when my dad got a new car. It was a shiny new Vauxhall Victor and it had that new car smell and came with all sorts of gadgets that seemed very modern and exciting as a child—such as an electric aerial for the radio. The date was September 1971.

I specifically recall going with my father to collect it from the Vauxhall Show Rooms that were situated at New City Road near Dundasvale in Glasgow. It was my dad's second Vauxhall Victor in a row and so the sales manager knew him and I recall the chat surrounding the transaction was not limited to the business concerning, and the essential workings, of the new car.

There was considerable chat about...Celtic. That was on the Saturday...round about lunchtime.

The following Wednesday, Celtic were to play a midweek European game and it was a great thrill to be told that I would be going to the game with the old man.

It meant a drive across town in the new car—which was exciting in itself--- and it meant a trip to Celtic Park and a seat at or near the Directors Box...all on a school night too. This stuck in my head because my last visit to Paradise (again with my dad) had been a game against Clyde where Celtic had won by an amazing 9-1 and so a return to Celtic park was eagerly anticipated.

I had also been at Celtic Park for the last game of the Lisbon Lions when Ronnie Simpson had made a brief appearance before being replaced by Evan Williams, who was a distant relative—and again that would be against Clyde.

That just might have been my first time in the jungle—though it was to be by no means my last. If I remember correctly the South stand was under refurbishment and my father decided that we would go to the jungle and more or less stand where he used to stand when he was, if not a boy, then certainly a great deal younger.

However, on this midweek night I knew there would be no jungle. Instead there would be a seat in the stand close to the half way line with many faces that my dad knew sitting all around—including players, ex-players, players' wives and so on.

On this occasion the opponents weren't Clyde—This was a European Night and Celtic needed a win.

As the new car turned off London Road and into Kerrydale Street it paused as we reached the old school gates. Once there, the driver's window came down so that my dad could have a quick word with "The Jannie" from the school who would clearly not have recognised the car.

Once pleasantries had been exchanged, the Janitor guided my old man's new motor into the school, and helped my dad reverse it into position to be ready for leaving Parkhead when the final whistle blew.

This was an important part of proceedings because, as you shall see, we were not to leave right on the final whistle and my dad did not want to block anyone in and keep them waiting.

I should point out to those who are too young to remember that this was in the days when the old façade of the ground still stared out at you when you walked up Kerrydale Street and the old building proclaimed that it was the home of Celtic Football & Athletic Club 1888. Further, the main- if not the only - car park was the one right in front of the ground that still stands there to this day. On European nights, the car park was choc-a-block with cars, and if getting into that car park was a slow laborious process then getting out of it after the game was sheer purgatory...an interminably long wait.

Accordingly, the old fella had a long-standing arrangement with the school janitor that he would park in the school. This was an arrangement that had gone on for years.

Others would also park there—always the same faces—and always dealing with the janitor. Years later, I discovered that despite parking in that school almost constantly for a number of years, my dad didn't even know the janitors name! They just knew one another by sight and chatted to one another like long lost friends—without ever knowing each other's names!

Anyway, on the night in question, with the car parked, we walked up to the front of the stand. My dad would stand outside the ground and speak away to people he knew and eventually, after what seemed to me like an age, we went in to take our seats.

This was the second leg of a European tie and Celtic were trailing by two goals to one so the atmosphere was tense from the off.

The team had not played particularly well in the first leg, and although the mood of the crowd was optimistic as always, they were nervous.

That tension eased a little when Willie Wallace—who had been missing from the starting line up in the first leg although he would later come on as a substitute , scored in the first half to bring us back on level terms on aggregate—but we needed a winner. Not only that, the opposition were coming up the park every now and then, causing the Celtic defence problems and everyone knew that if they scored there would be a real problem. However, with the clock ticking down, Tommy Callaghan scored with a long header with about twelve minutes to go. The crowd went berserk and the singing started. Everyone was roaring the bhoys on.

The game was not over yet though, with the entire crowd realising that should the opposition score just a solitary goal then we would be heading for extra time - so the nerves and the tension remained.

Celtic were still leading by that solitary goal as we headed into the last ten minutes of the match. As the clock ticked on, my father announced that we were leaving early---- much to my dismay.

I can understand fully now why my dad wanted to leave early—and it was all because of that bloody car park!

For him, the trip to Celtic park was part passion and part business. A large part of his business at that time was flying Celtic fans to the away legs of any European tie and, as Celtic were regulars on the European stage at the time, business was good. There were a regular number of Celtic supporters who could be relied upon to go on each and every trip and who would follow the European adventures of Celtic no matter where they played.

However, these regular travellers included many who were businessmen and women of varying occupations. Many of these were publicans and others who would be leaving Celtic Park early on a week night to beat the traffic and to try and get out of that car park as quickly as possible. They wanted back to their pubs in time for closing at the end of the night. Others simply wanted away in order to beat the dreadful wait to get out of the car park.

My dad wanted to beat them out so that he could make a note of their shouts:

" Two for the next round Jimmy"

" Four of us for two nights Jimmy"

" There will be at least three of us Jimmy!"

And so on.

In this way he would know roughly how many aircraft to book and what size of plane would be needed—these were advance orders if you like and the people concerned did not need to know the dates of the game or the destination—they just followed Celtic in Europe wherever they went.

So—with the game still on a knife-edge, but Celtic looking as if they were going to go through we left our seats and made our way out.

We had just gotten out of the stand and were stood opposite the main entrance when a huge roar went up accompanied by what sounded like a herd of elephant stamping their feet—clearly Celtic had scored and were now definitely through!!

The crowd started to billow out in droves as people scurried for their cars in a mad rush.

I remember my dad shouting to one passer-by who was obviously in a hurry like everyone else:

"What happened?"

The man didn't even break his stride and carried on going but shouted a single word over his shoulder.

"WALLACE!"

No other words were needed.

Chapter 2

IN THE BEGINNING - THE ALL SEEING EYE

I am sure that many of you will be aware that there are occasions in life when something happens which just makes you smile involuntarily from ear to ear!

Well, when I was approached by the guys at CQN and asked to write something for this book, I couldn't see my smile but I could literally feel it—I could feel it all the way down to my ankles!

It is an honour and a privilege to be asked to contribute to this book on Willie Wallace. I say that partly for very personal reasons which I will reveal at the end of this piece, but also because the Wallace story is just one of those great stories— certainly a seldom told story— possibly an untold story in some respects...a wee gem that comes along only so often—perhaps just like Willie himself.

This is not just THE great untold Lisbon Lion story (although John Clark might have something to say about that), it is a story that every budding footballer should know, a story that every "unseeing" fan should read, and a story that many Celtic fans will be surprised at in many respects.

It is now almost 50 years since that day in Lisbon. 25th May 1967 ranks as arguably the greatest day in the history of Celtic football Club—sure everyone knows that...and the team that day trips off the tongue of supporters who were not even born at the time—with every player a hero.

Yet as Archie Macpherson hints in his wonderful contribution to this book, Willie Wallace is almost the forgotten player, the lost Lion, the one that we don't hear too much about and don't see in interviews too often. CQN Magazine, it should be recognised, did feature Willie on the cover of one of the early issues – so he is clearly a Celtic favourite over at CQN Towers.

Yes, he lives in Australia and has done so since the 1980's--- but that fact alone only partly explains why Willie has remained under the radar to a certain extent for all these years.

Willie Wallace was not the type of man or character to thrust himself into the limelight, bang his own drum, and seek publicity or self-aggrandisement. That is just not his style.

Yet even allowing for that, the Willie Wallace story has remained hidden yet obviously available for all to see, and it is a mystery to me why no sports journalist has sought to sit down and actively point out what is so glaringly obvious to anyone who cares to look.

Statistics never quite tell you the whole story, and I don't want to simply trot out a list of figures but in this instance the recorded statistics, once analysed, should really make the football fan sit up and take notice.

So much so—I am going to make the first of a number of bold statements:

Willie Wallace was Jock Stein's greatest EVER signing by a country mile—an absolute masterstroke and arguably ranks behind Henrik Larsson as perhaps the clubs greatest ever bargain!

Oh—and let me be quite clear about something, the last person you would ever hear make the claim that I have just made above would be ----well, Willie Wallace of course!

Again I refer to Archie's comments: While watching Willie play at Hearts, Archie saw a competent professional, a goal scorer, but as he openly admits he did not see a superstar or a player which stuck out in the crowd.

So what did Jock Stein see that Archie didn't? I think- and hope- I can provide an answer to that question, and in the course of the paragraphs below I will attempt to explain not only what I think Stein saw but also what he hoped to do with what he saw in the 26 year old Hearts striker.

Willie was a well-known figure in Scottish Football by the time Jock Stein came calling and it has often been reported that it was anticipated that Wallace would be moving to England or even to Rangers until something caught Stein's eye. Given that Willie had been at Hearts for 5 years and at Raith Rovers before that, surely Stein would have seen Willie at close quarters long before December 1966?

So what did Stein see that made him decide to bring Willie Wallace to Celtic Park?

Well, with the benefit of hindsight and a little bit of dogged research the answer becomes clear. Jock Stein saw a player who could have been nicknamed "The Bank" rather than Wispy, because right from his earliest steps of a long professional career, a manager, a team and a support could totally bank on Willie Wallace to do the business.

Further, "The business" concerned was not just the scoring of goals- though I will come to that later- it included the business of being a team player, following instruction to the letter, being a certain type of character, being a good trainer, and having a desire and a belief that would make you play with and against the big boys on the big stage.

Most importantly, Stein saw in Wallace someone who his already exciting forward line could play with—or perhaps I should say play even better with!

In short, Willie Wallace was the complete player. Not only could he win a game for you with his own individual contribution, but when added into the chemistry of the ingredients which were already available to Stein, and which would become available to Stein after Willie arrived at Celtic Park, he played a material part in making the Celtic team of the time an almost unstoppable forward moving force.

Someone who was around at the time and who can testify to the potency of the Celtic attack is Sir Alex Ferguson. Having played against this Celtic side many times, Ferguson would later talk about how the Lions squad had so many ways to hurt the opposition with skill and above all blistering pace. There were multiple goal threats from just about every outfield position but the forward line of the time was truly frightening—an absolute wealth of talent. This was a team that any defence in Europe was rightly afraid of—and with very good reason.

Consider this:

In Willie Wallace's time at Celtic Park he shared the forward line with the following players:

Bobby Lennox
Jimmy Johnstone
Stevie Chalmers
John Hughes
Harry Hood
Kenny Dalglish

If I add Willie and Bobby Murdoch to that list I will just have named 8 out of the 28 players who have scored over 100 goals for Celtic Football Club—more than 25% of the guys who over a 125-year history can claim such a feat.

Out of all of those named above, Willie played the fewest number of games for Celtic and had the most prolific strike rate. That alone is some claim and to achieve those statistics you had to be some player!

In fact Willie played fewer first team games than Frank McGarvey, Charlie Nicholas, and most of the other ton-up bhoys who wore the green and white shirt—and all at a time when Celtic were at their absolute zenith playing against the very, very best of opposition with the best defenders.

If I add some other names into the mix such as Joe McBride, Lou Macari, Bertie Auld, Charlie Gallagher, George Connelly, Jim Brogan, Vic Davidson, Tom Callaghan, David Hay and others who all played in the same team as Willie then you can see that the competition for places was fierce—really fierce.

So let me throw open a debate by way of stating a simple fact— an incontrovertible fact—a fact hidden in plain view just like Willie himself in many respects:

Between the date that he joined Celtic on 6th December 1966, and the day he left in October 1971, Celtic played 278 competitive matches. By my calculation, out of all those matches, Willie missed around twenty through injury, suspension or through not being eligible to play because of competition rules.

This then means that out of approximately 258 games when he was available, Jock Stein chose to play Willie Wallace in his side on 234 occasions, or to put it another way over 91% of the time--- and remember that in each of the seasons when Willie was at Celtic Park there would be occasions when Stein would play the kids – The Quality Street Gang--- to give them a taste and a feel for top flight football.

In short, from the moment Willie Wallace signed for Celtic, Jock Stein banked on him being in his forward line—he knew that Willie would do the job. He might not always perform in a spectacular way (though some of the goals were absolutely spectacular) but in an absolutely resolute, consistent, and professional way. You could take that to the Bank!

So pause, and go back to what Willie has told you in his own words:

There he was sitting on his own on that bench at Celtic Park waiting to see what the offer would be from Celtic only to be told by "Mr Stein" that these would be the terms and that he would get a six-month contract that would take him to the summer of 1967.

Of course initially Willie said no! He wanted to be played fair and square and as such thought the signing on fee was low.

I genuinely believe—for the reasons above and for those set out below- that Jock Stein was pulling a deliberate and planned fast one. He had no intention whatsoever of letting Willie go in six months as he had a prolonged plan for Wallace—that unfortunately would never come to full fruition. He only told Willie about the six months contract to ensure that his new striker really "did the business" in that period.

Further, between Stein and the representatives from Hearts it didn't take too long to sort out the signing on fee either!

I will come to what happened in that six months in a minute, but history now tells us that whatever Stein saw in Wallace the signing paid better dividends for Celtic football club than any bank.

"On 17th December 1966 Willie would score his first goal for Celtic when he headed in from close range after Joe McBride headed a Bertie Auld cross back across the six yard box. It had taken less than two games for the Big Man's vision to click! Interestingly the forward line that day included Lennox, Wallace, McBride, Chalmers and Auld.

On the day that Joe McBride broke his leg—Christmas Eve 1966--- Lennox, Wallace, McBride and Chalmers would all start, and on the same day Stein's dream team was wrecked when Joe McBride was badly injured."

Chapter 3

GOALSCORING AND MORE

Over a period of time, the myth has grown that Willie was signed to "replace" Joe McBride after Joe was injured on Christmas Eve, although, as we have seen, this is absolutely not true.

However, what is not widely appreciated is just what Stein originally wanted with Wallace. Stevie Chalmers would later openly admit that he was fearful of the Wallace signing and was afraid that he might lose his place in the team. Whilst that did not happen immediately, the injury to McBride certainly narrowed Stein's options when choosing just who to play upfront.

The big man's plans were however revealed to Club Captain Billy McNeill, and clearly it was a plan that Stein was very excited about.

Writing in his Autobiography, McNeill revealed that shortly after Wallace had put pen to paper, Stein came and talked to the team Captain about the new man in the squad. Willie was the last man into the Lions squad and clearly one of McNeill's team mates were going to have to make way for the new bhoy if he was going to play, and it appears the manager wanted to explain the position to his captain on the field.

In his book, McNeill goes on to say that Jock was very excited and explained that he believed that the combination of McBride and Wallace would be the most prolific and the greatest striking partnership in the history of the Scottish game--- and possibly even in Europe!

That was what the big man saw--- not just one player but two— where the combined talents of the two added up to far more than the totalling of their individual talents—this was to be a world class team within a world class team!

McBride and Wallace together were to be sensational!

On 17th December 1966 Willie would score his first goal for Celtic when he headed in from close range after Joe McBride headed a Bertie Auld cross back across the six yard box. It had taken less than two games for the Big Man's vision to click! Interestingly the forward line that day included Lennox, Wallace, McBride, Chalmers and Auld.

On the day that Joe McBride broke his leg—Christmas Eve 1966--- Lennox, Wallace, McBride and Chalmers would all start, and on the same day Stein's dream team was wrecked when Joe McBride was badly injured.

So let's stop there and examine another long held myth—or at least point something out that is not often talked about.
In season 1966/67 who was Celtic's top scorer?

Many will say Joe McBride but they will be wrong. Joe was certainly Celtic's most prolific scorer ending the season with 35 goals all scored before Christmas Eve. However, overall that season Stevie Chalmers scored 36 goals throughout the campaign—so he was the top scorer at Celtic park that season.
Remember that fact because I will come back to that later.
Ok—so who was Hearts top scorer?

Well—even though he left in December 1966, the answer is Willie Wallace—with 9 goals.

Between his arrival at Celtic Park on 6th December 1966 and 25th May 1967 Wallace would score another 21 goals in 30 appearances in domestic and European competition—making a total of 30 for the season.

Maybe that is what you do when you think that you might only be there for six months?

Although I think it will become clear that had Willie been given a four-year contract on day one the results and goals scored would have remained the same.

Throughout his period with Hearts Willie Wallace would be the Edinburgh side's top scorer every single year scoring as follows:

1961/62 12 goals
1962/63 25 goals
1963/64 28 goals
1964/65 25 goals
1965/66   9 goals

As you can clearly see, amongst the other things that Stein saw in Wallace at Tynecastle was a goal scorer and a prolific one at that.

Remember, that at this time Hearts were a good team and had been a club at the very top of Scottish football only a few years before. However they had passed their golden years by the early 60's.

This meant that they were not necessarily in the later stages of all competitions and they did not play in the later stages of European football every season, which in turn meant that they perhaps did not play as many games as say the resurgent Celtic under Stein—and for Willie Wallace every game presented a chance to score more goals.

Had Heart of Midlothian played more games in Europe or in the domestic cups during his spell there, then I have no doubt that Willie would have scored even more goals.

The following season at Celtic Park, Willie would score a further 25 goals, finding himself second in the scoring stakes to Bobby Lennox who hit the back of the net an amazing 38 times (more if you include The Glasgow Cup and friendlies) making him the third highest scorer in Europe for which he received the bronze boot.

In season 68/69, Willie Wallace would be Celtic's top scorer with 33 goals, and he would be top of the charts again the following season with 25 successful strikes.

However, that statistic of 25 goals in season 1969/70 hides the fact that Celtic were tearing teams asunder and scoring goals from all sorts of sources. Harry Hood had joined the club and was playing in a forward position. As a result he found the net 18 times that season, while John Hughes scored 14, Bobby Lennox 17 and a young man called Luigi Macari would enter the scene with an impressive 8 goals. In that same year, Kenny Dalglish would make his debut and virtually every other outfield player would weigh in with goals- Hay, Connelly, Gemmell, McNeill, Chalmers, Brogan, Johnstone, Callaghan, Auld, Davidson, Murdoch and Quinn would all get their names on the score sheet over the course of the season and very few of those scored a solitary goal.

In his last full season at Celtic Park (1970/71) Willie Wallace would miss 10 straight games between 19th August and 30th September. In between times The Celtic team on the field would score an amazing 34 goals including 2 from a young lad by the name of Paul Wilson, and Lou Macari netting an incredible 7 times!

Clearly, the young guys along with the impressive Harry Hood were setting a pace that would be hard to better.

Yet, by the end of the season Willie stormed back with 30 goals in 43 games to leave himself in second place in the scoring stakes behind Harry Hood with 33.

I will leave Willie's last season until later, but from the above it can be seen that Willie was an amazingly proficient goal scorer with both Hearts and with Celtic.

However, even those statistics do not tell the full story but for the moment lets return to most of the names given in the list of Celtic forwards Willie played with mentioned above.

If we look at goals scored in the top flight of the Scottish League throughout a football career you get the following:

Joe McBride	**221**
Stevie Chalmers	**173**
Bobby Lennox	**168**
Frank McGarvey	**127**
John Hughes	**116**
Charlie Nicholas	**115**
Kenny Dalglish	**112**
Harry Hood	**112**

Obviously Kenny Dalglish spent the majority of his football career in England and Charlie Nicholas went to Arsenal before heading back north to Aberdeen and eventually re-joining Celtic.

However, in considering Willie Wallace's stats you would not count his time with Stenhousemuir, Crystal Palace or Ross County—so where does he sit in this table?

Well it may be a surprise to some, but taking into account his time with Raith Rovers, Hearts, Celtic and Dumbarton—Willie tops this list with an incredible 223 league goals!

Separately, Wallace and McBride scored 444 league goals between them—yet together Stein thought that they would score even more!

Everywhere he went Willie Wallace scored goals.

"Further, don't be put off by the fact that Willie played in the Scottish league, as it can clearly be seen that Scottish Clubs were doing pretty well in Europe as demonstrated by the success enjoyed by Dundee in 1962/63 when they lost in the semi-final of the European Cup to AC Milan who in turn would defeat a great Benfica side in the final.

Equally, it should also be remembered that there is a very good argument to suggest that in season 1966/67 Scotland was the leading nation in terms of European Football!"

Chapter 4

BARGAIN

As Willie has said himself, he was keen to leave Heart of Midlothian and had been for well over a year. In that time, it is reported that clubs such as Sunderland and Stoke were interested in him and were prepared to pay around £80,000 for such a prolific goal scorer.

In 1968, Rangers would break the £100,000 transfer barrier in Scotland when they paid that sum to Hibernian for the free scoring Colin Stein.

This has to be measured against a couple of other transfers of around that time.

In 1960 Denis Law would join Manchester City for a transfer fee of £55,000, setting a new British record. Law spent one year there before Torino bought him for £110,000, setting a new record fee for a transfer between an English and an Italian club. Although he played well in Italy, Law found it difficult to settle there and signed for Manchester United in 1962, setting another British record transfer fee of £115,000.

He is best known for the eleven years that he spent at Old Trafford, where he scored 237 goals in 404 appearances for United over an

11-year period compared to Willie's 135 goals (for Celtic) in 235 appearances in just 5 years for Celtic.

In 1964–65, Law won the European Footballer of the Year award, and Manchester United won their first league title since Munich. Law's 28 league goals that season made him the First Division's top scorer. In the same year, Willie Wallace scored 25 goals for Hearts.

Another Scottish Player who was making his mark at the time was Alan Gilzean who would score more than 100 goals in the Scottish top flight as an important part of the successful Dens Park side, winning the Scottish league championship in 1961–62, reaching the semi-finals of the European Cup the following season and the final of the Scottish Cup in 1964, losing 3–1 to Rangers.

Gilzean then joined Tottenham Hotspur in December 1964 for a fee of £72,500 —although he was also wanted by Sunderland and Torino who were also interested in signing him. However, Gilzean was warned off playing in Italy by Denis Law after the difficulties Law had experienced playing there.

Gilzean enjoyed a glittering and long career as a Tottenham player, changing his style of play from a prolific striker to an intelligent and creative forward, forming a famed partnership alongside the legendary Jimmy Greaves. While Willie Wallace and Celtic were picking up the European Cup and every domestic trophy available in Scotland, Gilzean was a valued member of the 1967 FA Cup winning team, and he continued to be a regular first-team player despite the arrival of Martin Chivers in early 1968 from Southampton.

After strike-partner Greaves moved to West Ham United in March 1970, Gilzean and Chivers formed a new and equally successful partnership for Spurs.

In 1961, Joe Baker was transferred to Torino (yet again) for £75,000 from Hibernian. Baker was an English international and would go on to score over 100 league goals in both the English and Scottish Leagues.

On 7 February 1962, Baker was nearly killed in a car crash in Italy when he was driving his car with Denis Law in the passenger seat. Whilst Law was not badly injured, Baker's injuries were life threatening. When he recovered, he moved back to the UK by signing for Arsenal who paid a club record fee of £70,000 for him in July 1962.

In his time at Arsenal, Joe would score 100 goals in 156 games in all competitions, making him one of the club's most prolific goal scorers of all time. He would be top scorer for the club in seasons 62/63, 64/65 and 65/66.

At the start of season 66/67 Joe Baker was transferred to Nottingham Forrest for a fee of £65,000 - more than twice what Stein paid for Willie Wallace. Baker helped transform Forrest, so much so that in the same season that Celtic won everything, Forrest finished second only to Manchester United (complete with Law Charlton and Best etc) in the English League whilst a Spurs side lead by Greaves and Gilzean were one behind in third place.

Eventually, Joe Baker would return to Hibs and finish his career with Raith Rovers in 1974.

Compare all of these figures to what was happening at roughly the same time at Inter Milan where Helenio Herrera was building what became known as La Grande Inter—perhaps the most famous Inter Milan team of all time and one which was specifically put together to challenge the Di Stefano, Puskas, Gento lead Real Madrid and the Eusebio lead Benfica.

A large part of Herrera's plans focused on Louis Suarez who was a regular in a FC Barcelona team that also included Ladislao Kubala, Zoltán Czibor, Sándor Kocsis, Ramallets and Evaristo.

Suarez had won a La Liga and cup double in 1959, and a La Liga and Fairs Cup double in 1960. He was also in the Barcelona team that lost the 1961 European Cup Final to the all-conquering Benfica side managed by Bela Guttman who would go on to uncover the young Eusebio later that same season.

Suarez was also voted European Footballer of the Year in 1960 ahead of Ferenc Puskas, Uwe Seeler and Alfredo Di Stefano, and he would be runner up to Denis Law in 1964.

In 1961 Suárez became the world's most expensive footballer when Barcelona sold him to Inter for 250 million Italian lira, which equated to £142,000 at the time. This move saw Suárez become a regular in the Inter team that won three Serie A titles, two consecutive European Cups and two Intercontinental Cups—though he would miss the final in Lisbon through injury. Between 1961 and 1970 he made 328 appearances for Inter and scored 55 goals as a holding and creative midfielder.

It is against this background and these types of transfers that you have to measure the astuteness of Stein in securing the signature of Willie Wallace for a modest £30,000 in December 1966.

Long before that date, transfer values had risen in other places to around and above £100,000, and certainly by December 1966 the value of someone with Willie Wallace's already established record was way above what Stein paid.

Further, don't be put off by the fact that Willie played in the Scottish league, as it can clearly be seen that Scottish Clubs were doing pretty well in Europe as demonstrated by the success enjoyed by Dundee in 1962/63 when they lost in the semi-final of the European Cup to AC Milan who in turn would defeat a great Benfica side in the final.

Equally, it should also be remembered that there is a very good argument to suggest that in season 1966/67 Scotland was the leading nation in terms of European Football!

As we all know, Celtic won the European Cup and Scotland defeated the new World champions at Wembley with a team that included Willie Wallace. However, it should also be remembered that in that same year Rangers reached the final of the European Cup Winners Cup only losing in extra time to the Bayern Munich of Gerd Muller and Franz Beckenbaur, and Kilmarnock reached the semi-finals of the Fairs Cup losing out to Don Revie's Leeds United who in turn were defeated by Dinamo Zagreb in the final ------- and all this under the management of ex Celt Malky McDonald.

Accordingly in its time, Stein's purchase of Wallace—a proven goal scorer in a league which was producing good players that could attract interest in England and indeed Europe where higher transfer fees were paid - was a brilliant piece of business - so much so that years later many commentators would take the view that big Jock had actually stolen Willie Wallace from Hearts in a move that was akin to an act of theft!

Chapter 5

THE TEAM PLAYER

However, my argument that Willie Wallace was Jock Stein's greatest ever signing does not rely solely on his goal scoring record or the measly sum that Celtic paid to Hearts for such a prolific striker— the argument goes way beyond that.

Again, I stress what Archie McPherson says elsewhere in this book- namely that Willie is a quiet and modest man who is not one for the braggadocio when it comes to describing his own talents.

Football people are divided into two distinct groups—those who are playing and those who are watching. Of course there are times when those who play or have played must rank amongst those who will watch from the sidelines.

It has become far clearer to the spectator in recent years that those who play the game can sometimes see moves and patterns within a game that the ordinary spectator might miss for lack of being in a dressing room and having the benefit of a team talk given by the likes of a Stein, a Shankly, or a Busby or a Ferguson. Or,dare I say it,...... a Lennon.

With the advent of Sky Sports and seemingly endless football punditry, the average football fan is now far better informed about the tactics of the game and those small incidents that happen on the pitch which can have a huge influence on the game, but which many spectators may miss or fail to understand.

Needless to say one of the greatest watchers the game has ever seen was Jock Stein. I recall a comment made by Bobby Charlton who shared a TV studio with Stein when watching International football in later years. Charlton openly admitted that the experience left him in awe of Stein, not only because he was physically huge and dominant in any conversation, but also because, as far as Charlton was concerned, he saw things happening on the pitch either before anyone else noticed they were happening or he saw things that no one else noticed at all!

However, Stein was not alone in the watching stakes, and if you were good enough someone would notice.

This then brings me to an interview which Willie Wallace once gave on his career. In typically modest fashion, Willie advised that he never had any plan in his career. He never thought of himself as being any kind of superstar and he never planned the next step of his career or anticipated any transfer.

He simply played football.

When asked to describe or comment upon each stage and each step of that career, Willie said, "It just happened" and "There was no plan...it all just happened."

This is a statement that is both true and utterly misleading.

I have no doubt that Willie did not plan each and every step of his career, but at the same time I cannot accept the argument that it all "just happened" as that is just plain nonsense.

If you go back over Willie's own words you will see that even before he had reached the Junior Level of the game he was being asked by people to come and play for this team or that.

He had his choice of junior clubs whether that be Benburb, Kilsyth Rangers or whoever—and that is because there were those who watched the young Wallace and they liked what they saw.

By the way, as an aside, Willie has pointed out that he played for Benburb alongside Stevie Chalmers—well, within months of that occasion Benburb would also field a forward line which featured a young man called Joe McBride--- now there was a junior forward line to be reckoned with!

The point I am making here is that I think it was easy for those with knowledge who watched Willie from an early age to see that here was a player. A real player!

From the moment he became a professional footballer as a teenager, Wallace would force people to watch as he played and they could hardly fail to be impressed by the end product on show.

With Stenhousemuir he would play 50 games in his spell there— and in those 50 games he would score a creditable 23 goals...enough to force the watchers at Raith Rovers to have a look and make a move for him. The same thing would happen at Starks Park - Willie played, scored goals, got results for his club, and this time it was the Hearts watchers who looked on and decided to make a move for him.

Throughout his time at Stenhousemuir, Raith Rovers and Hearts, Willie Wallace had received and hoovered up a footballing education. He had played with experienced professionals who had been at the top of the game and had learned their trade--- and he learned from them. He had played in every forward roll and occupied every forward position under the eagle eye of men who were good coaches such as Jackie Stewart at Raith Rovers.

Stewart, would take Willie, Jim Baxter and others for extra training in the afternoons at Starks park—all with a view to making them better players with a better understanding of the game and how to play it.

Wallace had been a long term pupil of men who Jock Stein considered to be good coaches - and so when Stein came looking in December 1966 he saw far more than just a goal scorer. He saw a team player, a mature professional at 26, and someone who could influence his team with and without the ball.

In short, he saw someone who would make those around him play even better than they had been up until that point—especially Joe McBride.

However, it was not to be McBride who benefited first from the Wallace effect - It was his old team mate Stevie Chalmers who would revel in Willie Wallace's company on the field.

Take Big Jock's mention of Willie just after he had joined Celtic. Writing in the Celtic View a couple of weeks after his signing of Willie, Stein said the following:

"Willie Wallace has made a fine start with the club. Stevie Chalmers seems to have profited through his introduction, for Stevie has scored five goals in the two games in which Willie has taken part "

Notice the emphasis on the benefit to Chalmers as opposed to the highlighting of the fact that Willie himself had scored twice against Partick Thistle the previous week.

It is perhaps understandable at the time why some of the Celtic fans might have missed some of the essential elements of Willie Wallace's play and his value to the team.

After all the Celtic team of the time had some truly spectacular and memorable players.

There was the mercurial wizardry of Johnstone, who would draw the breath of spectators with his jinking runs, his bravery and his goals - he was the star attraction of the team. Yet, even with Jimmy, I can recall as a wee boy the crowd sometimes getting frustrated with him because he went to beat one man too many or because they took the view that he had held on to the ball for too long.

However, that would all change when the next time the wee man got the ball, he went by a defender or two, pulled a defence out of shape and then instead of hanging on to the ball as he did before he would slip a pass to a team mate who had loads of space because Jimmy had rent a defence asunder!

Whilst the moves before may not have come to anything, the opposition could never be sure of that and always had to worry about Jimmy getting past his man with the result that someone else would have to move out of position to go and "get him" - thus leaving another Celtic player in free space.

Then there was the equally mercurial Hughes! How often have I read that there were days when Yogi was simply unplayable? Those days when Big John suddenly took the notion that, yes, he could beat an entire team on his own with his size, strength and skill on the ball. He was a real impact player whose great days live long in the memory.

In addition there were Tommy Gemmell's galloping runs and thunderous shots from distance. This was a real flair full back who liked nothing more than rampaging forward and unleashing the most spectacular attempts on goal, which the crowd loved to see.

If that wasn't enough, there was the craft and guile of Murdoch and Auld. Bobby Murdoch has been described by Jack Charlton as the greatest passer of a football he has ever seen—better than Beckenbaur and better then Crerand both of whom rank among the very best. Helenio Herrera said of Bobby "when he plays - Celtic plays".

On the other hand Bertie Auld was all guile, cuteness, cleverness and cheek. Everything that Bertie did—from sitting on the ball, to sharp passes to striking goals or even to playing the role of the enforcer in the middle of the park - was exciting to see, watch and talk about.

And then there was Lennox - The Buzz Bomb - the fastest and greatest blind side runner the British game has ever seen. That blistering pace mixed with football ability would raise the roof of any stadium when the crowd saw Bobby take off.

Add to that Joe McBride's play and general ability, and Stevie Chalmers pace, never ending stamina and eye for goal, then what I have to say next will come as no surprise to many.

In preparing this piece I canvassed the views of some who had watched the Lisbon Lions team and asked about Willie Wallace in particular. Almost universally the same message was delivered—namely that Willie was a great player but he was overshadowed by the more spectacular players on the field of play, and away from the pitch this quiet unassuming man was overshadowed by the big personalities of say Auld, Gemmell and Johnstone.

Such comments were by no means a criticism, rather a confirmation that certain members of the squad immediately came to mind first in terms of the spectacular and perceived size of personality.

Yet, when you drill into the statistics—the goals measured against numbers of appearances and games played with different strike partners, and the performances of those strike partners with Willie playing just behind—a different picture emerges as the stats reveal a spectacular return for Celtic from one of the "quieter" men of the team.

As I said at the very start, you could take Willie Wallace to the bank even before he joined Celtic and certainly during his time there. He repeatedly scored goals and he constantly contributed to others scoring goals - end of story.

Stein clearly saw this efficiency and knew precisely what he was buying into when he got the chance to bring Willie Wallace to Celtic

Park. Further, Willie's attributes as a player were not missed by his team-mates either. The defence already knew all about Willie Wallace the goal scorer as he had no difficulty in hitting the back of the net against them in the past, and Bertie Auld said that Willie had proven to be a real pest when he had played against Celtic in previous years.

Billy McNeill would stress Willie's strengths in his autobiography, and would go on to point out that in his quiet way Willie was a bit of a hard man when it mattered and someone a defender could not take liberties with. McNeill mentioned that Willie would take care of himself and if someone chose to get a bit dirty with him, Willie would not complain - he would just bide his time and when the moment was right he would exact the appropriate retribution - in full!

Clearly, the Celtic captain and centre half thought Willie was a great centre forward!

However, the thoughts and reactions of his fellow forwards are even more noteworthy especially those who benefited the most from Willie's undoubted footballing brain in the forward half of the pitch.

Perhaps the thoughts expressed by Jock Stein in the Celtic View after Willie's second game with the club, mentioned above, are best reflected by Bobby Lennox or "Lemon" as Willie Wallace christened him after his name was misprinted in a newspaper!

Writing many years later the club's top goal scorer in Willie's first full season at Celtic Park had this to say of his newest team-mate of the time.

" Willie Wallace was another player who worked away quietly and instructively without an enormous fuss but he was hugely appreciated by his fellow players. He was a smashing all round player, a terrific goal scorer and talented enough to play in midfield if Bobby Murdoch or Bertie Auld were unavailable. He was also a lot of fun: great company off the park. "

When Harry Hood joined the side in 1969 he proved to be an inspired signing and contributed goals by the bundle and as I have mentioned above he would join that elite group who have scored more than 100 times for Celtic.

After joining the Celtic squad from Clyde, Harry would play up front with all the Celtic greats of the time as a partner - this list includes playing alongside Johnstone, Lennox, Chalmers, Deans, Dalglish and even Wilson at times but he is quite clear who his favourite strike partner was - Willie Wallace!

"I was lucky to play with a lot of great players in my time at Celtic - Kenny, Jimmy and Bobby, the list goes on - but my favourite team-mate was Willie Wallace. He was a great professional and when I was young and just in the team, he taught me a lot."

In Willie's last full season, Harry would be the club's top scorer with Willie just a few goals behind.

Interestingly that would be the only full season when Hood would play as the front striker. Like others he benefited from Willie playing just behind and as can be seen his goal tally soared.

When Willie left in October of the following season Harry was withdrawn from the front striker role and asked to play deeper leaving the front role to the newly signed Dixie Deans. I believe this to be significant as it is a role that Harry admitted that he did not enjoy as much as playing upfront, and eventually he would tend to drop back further into midfield especially after the full emergence of one Kenneth Matheson Dalglish.

As for John "Dixie" Deans - I will come to him later but it is interesting to note that in the past he has mentioned Willie Wallace as one of his football heroes!

Bertie Auld recognised Willie as a clever player and saw him as someone who was a real pain in the neck to play against having caused Celtic problems over the years. Like McNeill, he was also quite clear that despite his quiet manner, Wallace was no shrinking violet on the field, could not be intimidated and could finish a move in a flash!

However, for Stevie Chalmers, the arrival of Willie Wallace at Celtic Park meant one thing more than any other, space!

As mentioned above, Willie was undoubtedly a threat to Chalmers and the message from Stein to McNeill was that he particularly saw McBride and Wallace as a lethal combination. However, Stein also recognised right away that Chalmers had benefited immediately from Willie's team play, and after the dreadful injury to Joe McBride, Stevie and Willie would strike a regular partnership with Stevie ending top scorer in all competitions by the end of the season.

To an extent, the arrival of his old Rob Roy team-mate would herald what might be called an Indian Summer for Stevie Chalmers—and whatever the chemistry between them, both grabbed the chance to play effectively together with both hands.

In many ways it was an odd partnership. Neither was particularly tall or physically imposing for a striker. Both were quiet and modest personalities - if anything behind the scenes Stevie was quieter than Willie. Willie was known in private for being great company with a succession of jokes and wisecracks which revealed what team-mates would describe as a wicked sense of humour. However, neither carried the ego of the " star player" mentality that we often see in professionals today.

Both players had real pace and a good eye for goal given half a chance, and what Stevie Chalmers - and later others - benefited from was Willie's running off the ball and that ability to make space. Similarly, Willie Wallace revelled in the free running of Chalmers, Johnstone, Lennox and company.

When describing scoring the winning goal in Lisbon, many Celtic players will talk about how Jock Stein used to make his forwards practice turning shots and crosses into the net with the ball being swung in from both left and right. Practice - Practice - Practice! Whether the cross was high, low, floated or struck at pace, the forward line practiced the move in training - whip the ball into the box and the front guys had to convert (or should that be divert?) the ball into the goal.

In describing the Lisbon winner however, Stevie Chalmers starts with the fact that Stein asked his forwards - Wallace, Chalmers and Lennox - to endlessly run across and out of the penalty box to move the Italian's defence about and so make room for the midfield and fullbacks to come forward and pose a threat.

Stein knew Herrera's system and took the view that there was a system to beat it and that involved the forwards stretching and turning the very heart of the defence without the ball. As typical Italian man markers, where you went your marker went, and so, Stein theorised, in this way Celtic would make room for the midfielders to do the damage.

This system was followed to a tee. Chalmers at times would find himself dropping very deep to either get the ball or to pull his marker out of place in Lisbon but by the end of the game he describes his emotions and feelings by saying that he had had enough of that rigmarole and was now determined to get into the box.

The other Celtic players could see after the Gemmell goal that Inter were disorientated and were asking questions among themselves having been pulled hither and thither all around the pitch.

So, when it comes to describing the winning goal - which I am sure everyone can see in their minds eye, Stevie Chalmers points out something that may well have been missed by many.

As Tommy Gemmell shimmies and faints over on the left hand side before knocking the ball back to Bobby Murdoch for the cross come shot that would lead to Stevie's winning goal, Stevie points out that suddenly Willie Wallace makes a dash to the left running across the box towards Gemmell. The result is that the well trained Italian defenders instinctively go with him, one all the way and the other just a fraction as it appears that the threat may well come through Wallace.

Instead as we all know, Bobby Murdoch fires in a speedy ball and there in the area is the ever running Stevie Chalmers to do what had so often been done in training - divert or convert the ball into the net - and joy of joys for the front man, he discovered he had what was so rarely found by anyone against Herrera's Grande Inter ... a clear site of goal and space!

The European Cup winning goal was down to Stein's tactics, his vision of how to beat the Inter system, the endless practice of his players, their skill in converting a ball at pace, the ability to follow instructions for 90 minutes and more and to play unselfishly for the team using those tactics.

In this latter discipline, Willie Wallace excelled and various forwards at Celtic Park all saw it and benefited for it.

Ultimately, this would be a skill and a discipline that Jock Stein would miss dearly and there is a very good argument to say that Celtic Football Club would pay a heavy price for suddenly finding themselves without Willie Wallace.

"Whilst there is often talk about the quality Celtic had to face against Inter, the quality and the personnel of Dukla Prague are often forgotten in the Lisbon story. However in considering the true achievement of the Lions it is necessary to recognise just what a fine side they were. Further, in considering the importance of Willie Wallace in relation to the history of Celtic Football Club it has to be pointed out just how vital Willie was by now to Stein and his team especially in these two games."

Chapter 6

LISBON

To understand the road to Lisbon fully you have to go back three years to the European Cup Winners Cup of 1963.

This was a tournament which, although one rung below the European Cup where you would find Real Madrid, Inter Milan, Benfica and co, would feature great teams such as Barcelona, Hamburg, Manchester United, Tottenham Hotspur, Olympiacos, Olympic Lyonnais, Slovan Bratislava, Dinamo Zagreb, Sporting Club de Portugal, Fenerbahce and MTK Budapest.

Amidst all these great teams you also found Jimmy McGrory's Celtic featuring a line-up of familiar names - McNeill, Clark, Murdoch, Chalmers, Lennox, Johnstone, Hughes and Gemmell.

Celtic disposed of FC Basel in the first round by an incredible score of ten goals to one on aggregate with a Yogi Hughes hat trick away from home and goals from Divers, Murdoch, Johnstone and Lennox. Dinamo Zagreb fell next by four goals to two and again the scorers were from the familiar batch of players.

In the quarter Finals, Celtic beat Slovan Bratislava by a single goal both home and away with goals from Murdoch at home and Hughes away.

This then put the team in the semi-final against MTK Budapest, and after a 3-0 home win a European Final beckoned for McGrory and many of the team who would eventually take the field in Lisbon.

What happened next goes a long way to explain things that would take place in later years I believe.

Despite being the manager of Celtic, Jimmy McGrory did not pick the team nor did he spell out the team tactics in any given game. Instead he simply told the chosen team to "do your best" and so on.

Bob Kelly would make the decisions as to who would play and after beating Budapast at home he made the boastful statement " We've beaten them at home, now we will beat them away."

Alas, it was not to be, and unbelievably the young Celtic team would pay the price for being gung ho in Budapest and succumbed to a 4-0 defeat putting Budapest in the final instead of Celtic.

Had anyone with any sense at all been a student of tactics this would never have happened. You only had to look at the lessons from the previous round to see how dangerous European Football at this level could be. In the Quarter Finals, Manchester United had defeated Sporting 4-1 at Old Trafford only to get thumped 5-0 in Lisbon to find themselves dumped out of the competition having enjoyed a 3 goal lead after the first leg.

Sporting would go on to beat Budapest in the final but only after a replay as the teams drew 3-3 in the Heysel Stadium in Brussels and had to replay in Antwerp where the Portuguese won by a solitary goal.

In 1965/66 Celtic would lose out in another European Semi-final but this time under Stein. It was no consolation to lose to a very good Liverpool side managed by Bill Shankly, especially when Celtic had a perfectly good goal by Bobby Lennox written off—all because Lennox was too quick for the linesman's eye.

Being naïve in one semi-final and being robbed by a referee in another makes for scars that live long in the memory, and as they approached this semi-final of the 1966/67 European Cup the Celtic team and management wanted to make sure that they would not be thwarted for a third time - Dukla Prague or no Dukla Prague.

This was to be Willie Wallace's introduction to the European Cup. Earlier, Willie described his emotions as he watched his team-mates struggle to overcome Vojvodina Novi Sad in the quarter finals. Willie says he forgets who he was sitting beside but I can tell you that also sitting in the stand that night were Bertie Auld and Joe McBride and it is a racing cert that the three were seated together as they witnessed the nail-biting finish which ended happily thanks to Charlie Gallagher's magnificent left foot and Billy McNeill's equally magnificent head. The goal came with only two seconds to go!!

I have heard older Celtic fans say that they were never happier in their life than they were that night as they walked back along London Road. Even wedding days and births of children have been placed second to the feeling when the Serbian team succumbed to the old one two from Gallagher and McNeill. It was that night that made certain Celtic fans start to believe that Lisbon was on!

However, standing in the way was Dukla Prague and standing getting ready in the wings was Willie Wallace.

Willie has mentioned that he was desperate to play in the next round and in an earlier interview he said the following:

"I had been sitting beside the injured Joe McBride in the stand at Celtic Park to witness the astounding quarter final against Vojovodina and I thought "Wispy, this is the place for you". I wanted a slice of that. Believe me. I know all the lads would say the same thing, but the atmosphere generated by our support on those occasions was just breath-taking...quite staggering really".

As you are by now aware, the Saturday before the game at Celtic Park, Willie would find himself in the victorious Scotland team at Wembley along with fellow forward Bobby Lennox. Willie, himself, feels he played really well in that game, and it was a shot from Willie which was spilled by Gordon Banks, which lead to Denis Law tapping in.

However Lemon would be missing for the visit of Dukla. Instead Jock Stein brought in Willie and Bertie Auld from the stand, and chose Big Yogi in place of Lennox.

Whilst there is often talk about the quality Celtic had to face against Inter, the quality and the personnel of Dukla Prague are often forgotten in the Lisbon story. However in considering the true achievement of the Lions it is necessary to recognise just what a fine side they were. Further, in considering the importance of Willie Wallace in relation to the history of Celtic Football Club it has to be pointed out just how vital Willie was by now to Stein and his team especially in these two games.

Remember, Willie signed for Celtic on 6th December 1966 and the first leg against Dukla Prague would take place on Wednesday 12th April. It would be his 25th game for the club and his first in Europe.

It was by far the biggest game he had ever played in until that point.

Dukla Prague on the other hand were seasoned European campaigners having played regularly in the competition in the immediately preceding years where they were only bettered by such teams as Benfica, Real Madrid and Borussia Dortmund.

Further, they were regular champions of their country, frequent winners of their domestic cup competition, and they fielded a host of Internationals who were World Cup and European Nations veterans.

In addition, Czech football had to be admired throughout Europe. It was Czechoslovakia who had progressed to the World Cup finals in 1934 where they lost narrowly to hosts Italy and of course before and after the first world war one of the most influential people in Czech football was the long standing manager of Sparta Prague - who just also happened to have been the very first Celtic centre forward - Johnny Madden!

In 1962, the imperious Josef Masopust would lead a totally unfancied Czech side to the World Cup Finals again—this time losing to Brazil despite Masopust giving them a one nil lead early on in the game.

When Dukla came to Celtic Park on 12th April 1967 they had already disposed of Anderlecht including their talisman Paul van Himst, and Ajax who boasted the likes of Cruyff, Keizer, Nuninga and Swart. That was a Dutch side that had been sufficiently prolific to put 5 past Shankly's Liverpool who had beaten Celtic in Europe under controversial circumstances the year before.

Accordingly for the Czech's to dispose of Ajax they had to be a really good side.

In Goal for Dukla was Ivo Victor who would win 63 caps for Czechoslovakia and who the year before had played for his country against Brazil in the Maracana.

Victor would come 3rd in the 1976 European Footballer of the year Poll and was voted European Goalkeeper of the year in both 1969 and 1976. He was also voted in at number 24 in a poll of the all-time greatest goalkeepers of the 20th century.

At fullback was Miroslav Cmarada who would gain 6 international caps for his country and would join Dukla's hall of fame.

Next was Ladislav Novak. With 75 caps and captain for his country, Novak had appeared in the World Cup finals of 1954, 1958, & 1962— and had won 8 national league titles. Novak was a truly world class and very experienced defender. He would later go on to manage Dukla and the national team.

Vladimir Taborsky would end his career with 19 full caps between 1966 and 1972. He was only at Dukla for the two years of his military service and then went back to Sparta Prague - note that Dukla was the "Army team" and was actually pretty unpopular because they got all the best players when they did their compulsory national service.

Jan Zlocha was also on Military Service and played most of his football for Slovan Bratislava. This might explain why he gained only 4 caps, as Dukla players were favoured when the national team selections came around.

Jan Geleta was picked for Dukla Prague on 283 occasions and scored 27 goals. He was the Czech Footballer of the year in 1967 and so was right at the top of his form when he came to Celtic Park. He won 19 International caps.

Stanislav Strunc would score over 100 goals in 329 top flight matches - 65 of them for Dukla Prague. He was only at Dukla for the purposes of Military Service and played for the club between 1965 and 1972. He then spent most of his remaining career at his native provincial club - Plzen - where he is such a hero they named the stadium after him. He played for Czechoslovakia in the 1968 Olympics and won 3 full caps between 1966 and 1970.

Josef Nedorost twice won the league and twice won the cup with Dukla in Czechoslovakia but was a European specialist. His record in Europe is a goal every two games and he most famously once scored from 60 yards when playing against Valencia. Nederost was most influential in knocking Ajax out of the competition.

Josef Vasinovsky won 6 league titles and 4 domestic cups with Dukla and played in the 1960 Euro Championships for his country who came third in the competition. In all he would play in 32 European ties for Dukla and would score 5 goals.

Milan Dvorak could play all over the park and was deployed by Dukla in defence, midfield and attack. He made 261 appearances for the club and won 6 championships scoring 61 goals. He also played in the 1958 World Cup finals scoring twice. Overall he had 13 International Caps.

Finally there was the guy who has been described in other publications as true football royalty - Josef Masopust.

Masopust needs some explaining because this wasn't just a good player, or a great player - this was a great, great player and was of the utmost significance to Dukla Prague's success and in the thinking of Jock Stein.

Masopust won 63 caps and scored 10 international goals. He led Czechoslovakia to third in the 1960 European Championships and to the final of the 1962 World Cup. When others point out that he was the European Player of the Year—they do not adequately make the point as the phrase " European Footballer of the Year" just rolls off the tongue and disappears these days.

For a start he was the first ever player from the Eastern Bloc to win this award and was rarely seen by Western observers, as movement to and from Czechoslovakia was restricted. Accordingly he was only allowed to leave the country on official team business and as such, like all Eastern Bloc players, remained a bit of a mystery.

Further at the height of the Cold War some football chairman did not want their clubs even travelling to the Eastern Bloc. Bob Kelly, for one, would on at least one occasion kick up a fuss about Western clubs going to play Eastern bloc clubs.

To win the European Footballer of the year accolade, Masopust forced the great Eusebio into second place despite the Portuguese striker having a blistering season that year winning the European Cup against Real Madrid - at the end of the final no less than Ferenc Puskas handed Eusebio his shirt as if to pass on the baton of greatness. Such was the class of Eusebio. Yet he would be voted behind Masopust as the European player of the Year.

Third in the Footballer of the Year stakes was Karl Heinz Schnellinger the legendary German international. Gianni Rivera of AC Milan was 6th, Jimmy Greaves 7th, and Denis Law 11th.

The previous year, Masopust was voted joint tenth along with Bobby Charlton and Jose Santamaria of Real Madrid and in 1963 he would be rated 12th along with Paul van Himst and ahead of players like Cesare Maldini and Mario Coluna the captain of Benfica.

Pele named Masopust among the top 125 players ever to play the game and said of him "Masopust was one of the greatest players I ever saw, but it is not possible that he was born in Europe. With those explosive dribbles, he had to be Brazilian!"

Dukla Prague had played against FC Santos in 1959 in Mexico City in an invitational tournament, with Dukla winning 4-3 in a match that was described as "unforgettable". Masopust scored twice and was decorated as the best player of the game, giving a performance superior to the great Pelé.

In a poll to determine the greatest footballer to have worn the Czech international shirt, Masopust was voted the Golden player of the last 50 years and greatest Czech player of the 20th Century beating such contenders as Pavel Nedved, Antonin Panenka, Jan Koller, Karel Poborsky, and many others including Lubo Moravcik!

On 31st May 1962, Czechoslovakia would play Spain in the first group 3 match of the 1962 World Cup. By this time, Spain could boast the great Ferenc Puskas among their ranks along with Louis Suarez who was soon to go to Inter Milan as the most expensive player in the world, and the magnificent Gento and Santamaria of Real Madrid and many others.

However, against such stars it was Masopust who stole the show and it was his work that led to the solitary goal that gave the Czechs a surprise victory!

After the game, Ferenc Puskas was interviewed and asked for his views on the Masopust performance:

"I was surprised by how complete he was," Puskas admitted. "Luis [Del Sol] was one of the best midfielders there was at breaking up attacks, Suarez was a genius with his through-balls and Paco [Gento] was fantastic when running at fullbacks. But Masopust could do it all: win the ball, pass, and dribble and break into the box. He was an outstanding player."

Therefore when Stein's eleven took the field on 12th April 1967 they were to face a side who had players in their ranks who were as good as any in Europe and who posed a real obstacle to any idea of going to Lisbon for the final.

Both Archie McPherson and Willie have to an extent described what happened that night at Celtic Park in front of 75,000 spectators and so I won't go over old ground.

However, I would encourage every reader to view the You Tube footage of that game. It is black and white, a bit grainy, and it is 9 minutes and 34 seconds long. Here you will see just how good Celtic were that night and how good Willie Wallace was in particular!

As mentioned above, Willie was desperate to play in this game - absolutely desperate.

He is seen tackling, collecting the ball, laying it off, shooting, and running the channels - everything that has been described above.

As for the goals - he was involved in the winning of the ball for Jimmy Johnstone's goal and his first goal was a feat of sheer one touch predatory goal scoring as he placed the ball over the head of Victor to give Celtic the lead.

Willie's second goal came from a free kick about 25 yards out and was an absolute screamer.

Many will wonder why he was even in the vicinity to be involved in that free kick at all because what lives in the memory is that any free kick from that area and distance was the domain of Tommy Gemmell or maybe Bobby Murdoch.

However, just about three weeks before, on 25th March, Celtic travelled to Tynecastle to play Heart of Midlothian. This was the first time that Willie had been back to his old stomping ground since he moved to Celtic and of course the Jambo crowd soon let him know what they thought of his move to Glasgow!

Celtic would take the lead but then a free kick was awarded in a dangerous area offering a real opportunity for a second goal. In front of a baying crowd, Willie Wallace rocketed a shot through the wall and into the back of the net behind a helpless Jim Cruikshanks. 2-0 Celtic!

Now, at Celtic Park, with Masopust and the excellent Victor organising the defensive wall, Willie would strike again with devastating effect - and he was to have no idea just how much this goal would have a bearing on events to come.

As described by both Willie and Archie, Bertie Auld would place the ball while the wall lined up expecting a shot from behind Bertie. However, the grainy footage shows what a clever and well worked free kick this was. Just as Bertie fakes repositioning the ball, Stevie

Chalmers makes a run from right to left straight across the penalty box distracting the eyes of the defenders not in the wall and possibly Victor as well.

Note that running off the ball move, as it would come back again in future.

At precisely the same time, Auld slides the ball to his right suddenly and Willie lashes an unstoppable shot to the left of Victor who remains rooted to the spot!

This was an opportunist goal - something that was absolutely spur of the moment stuff from the ever-alert Bertie Auld and the accurate and opportunistic Willie Wallace!

Auld had said " Do you see the gap Willie?" slid the ball to Willie - and Willie saw the gap alright!

Bang! 3-1 Celtic.

Celtic had a two goal lead—and a vital lead it was too.

However, even with that lead Celtic continued to press with Willie Wallace playing out of his socks until the final minute.

Willie's performance that night was vital in getting Celtic to Lisbon - absolutely crucial and as I said at the very start was evidence, if evidence were needed by now, that in signing Willie, Stein was as good as going to the bank. He got an instant return on his money!

However that second goal - that one solitary strike - might just be the most important goal scored in the history of Celtic Football Club and it was a goal that would arguably change the game of football as it was perceived at that time for good.

First and foremost it gave Celtic a valuable two goal cushion and potentially altered the way that Jock Stein would set his side out in the second leg.

However, there were to be repercussions way beyond the reaction of the players on the field of play and the thoughts of the Celtic manager.

Let me explain:

My father had by this time started a travel agency and had flown some supporters to Nantes and Zurich in the previous rounds of the tournament. Flying into the Eastern Bloc for the second leg was not really an option, but Lisbon? Well that was a different matter!

He was of the opinion that if Celtic got to the European Cup final then the Celtic support would travel en masse to the final - if they could get there easily enough!

However that would take more than a little organising and could not wait until after the final whistle had blown at the end of the second leg in Prague on 25th April with the final exactly a month away.

Remember that at the time, mass air travel was in its infancy and the idea of a large travelling support journeying across Europe was completely unheard of.

When Real Madrid defeated Eintracht Frankfurt at Hampden a few years before the vast majority of the crowd were Scottish. Few if any Spaniards or Germans came to Glasgow. Subsequent European Cup finals had followed the same pattern with most spectators coming from the city or country that hosted the final.

However, my dad was of the view that Celtic fans would travel and so he decided that if Celtic were victorious in the first leg at home and had a good chance of progressing to the finals he would take a gamble and book planes to fly from Glasgow to Lisbon on and around the 25th of May. This would involve paying non-refundable deposits with the appropriate airlines - and obviously if Celtic fell in the second leg then the deposit money was lost!

Given the amount of money involved he was only going to risk the deposits--- If Celtic won at home by two clear goals, and it would be Willie Wallace who provided those goals on his European debut for the club.

Accordingly when the final whistle blew, there may have been celebration on the park and all around the terracing. However, when my old man, who was a lifetime long Celtic fan, came home from the game there would be a big intake of breath, a plane to London to book and a lot of organising to do.

For Jock Stein and his men though, they had one foot in the final and this time they were determined not to fail at the last hurdle!

Chapter 7

LIKE A LIMPET

I once read that Diego Maradona was in no doubt about the name of the toughest opponent he ever faced on a football field. Without any hesitation he would provide the same answer any time he was asked to name the guy who had given him the most trouble on the park—Lothar Herbert Matthaus.

On two occasions (1981 and 1986) Matthaus would be given the job of sticking to Maradona "like a limpet" with the view to preventing him dictating the game. On the first occasion the German performed such a task, he was no more than 20 years old and received rave reviews for doing such a great job. A great defensive job, despite being an attacking and creative midfielder who would score his fair share of goals.

Almost 15 years earlier, Jock Stein would turn to another attacker and creator and ask him to do a similar "limpet" job on Josef Masopust in the second leg of a European Cup Semi-final.

Masopust was, as we have heard, nearing the end of his days in top class football, and at the end of season 68/69 he would be allowed to leave his beloved Dukla and play out the last two seasons of his career in Belgium with a degree of success.

However, in April 1967 he was still the central cog in the Dukla Prague wheel and from his position in midfield it was he who made the side tick - and Jock Stein wanted to make sure that he did not tick effectively against Celtic.

Masopust was known for breaking runs forward - described in the press reports of the time as the Masopust slalom - and for his crisp intelligent passing of the ball. It had been one of his runs up the park in the first leg that eventually led to confusion in the Celtic defence allowing Strunc to score in the 44th minute.

Accordingly, Stein decided he had to be man marked and more or less sat on for 90 minutes! Stop Masopust and in many ways you stop Dukla!

In choosing who he wanted to perform this task he opted for Willie Wallace - withdrawing him somewhat from the forward line and putting him in midfield instead to joust with Masopust.

As everyone now knows, the second leg in Prague would not be a footballing spectacle, and at times it would best be described as a gritty, backs to the wall, performance by Celtic whereby they got the job done with none of their, by now, customary flair.

Stein and Celtic also had to keep an eye on the referee Mr Gottfried Dienst from Switzerland. While he was considered to be the best referee in the World at the time, this was the same official who had taken charge of the 1966 World Cup Final at Wembley and had awarded a goal to Geoff Hurst which many thought was not a goal at all.

Dienst had been the man in the middle for the 1961 final that saw Benfica defeat Barcelona to become champions and the 1965 final that saw Inter lift the big cup at the San Siro when they defeated the almost ever present Portuguese. Very few referees have ever taken the final twice - in fact Dienst was one of only 4 officials ever to do this.

He was also only one of two referees who would officiate for both the World Cup final and the European Championship final, and it was those European Championships that would lead to his greatest controversy.

His officiating in the 1968 European Championship final was marred by real controversy. In that game, a 1–1 draw between Italy and Yugoslavia which was played in Rome, Dienst came to be accused of favouring the home team. The final was replayed later (the Italians winning 2–0) in a game refereed by the Spaniard José Maria Ortiz de Mendibil.

By 1967 Dienst already had a reputation of being a "home" referee.

In deciding to deploy Wallace on Masopust Big Jock will have gone through the options.

Bertie Auld would be an obvious choice to do a job on the Czech midfielder, but if Bertie was over keen or his fiery temper got the better of him, the official might find an excuse to take Celtic down to ten men, which would undoubtedly spell disaster.

Bertie's partner in the middle, Bobby Murdoch, was most effective playing deeper, and Stein would not want him trailing all over the park after the tricky Masopust and so leave his Celtic team out of shape.

Bobby Lennox and Jimmy Johnstone were extra cover on the wings. If they could get forward - great - but they also had a defensive job to do in front of Jim Craig and Tommy Gemmell.

Accordingly Stein opted for the man who he had described as the equivalent of a whole forward line when he signed him. Remember Bobby Lennox saying that Willie was good enough to drop into midfield and do a top class job, and both McNeill and Auld pointing out that Wallace could take care of himself physically and was no soft touch?

Well these qualities plus Willie's pace, stamina and ability to follow instruction convinced Stein to play Wallace on the Czech playmaker.

Willie has said that Stein told him to let Masopust know he was there early - to give him a wee dunt to let him know that Willie was there and would be there throughout the game.

There was no way in the world that Josef Masopust had not received such treatment before and in his own book Bertie Auld would stress that his Celtic team-mate played Masopust fairly all day whilst effectively negating his influence on the game.

Accordingly this second performance of Willie's was just as valuable in getting Celtic to the final as his two goals in the first leg.

If ever Jock Stein was to get a great return for his money, then he got it out of Willie Wallace in the two semi-finals with Dukla. It is at least arguable that cometh the hour cometh the man and that Celtic would never have been in Lisbon if it were not for Willie Wallace!

The man himself will, in all likelihood, not thank me for saying that, and will highlight the fact that it was the whole team that took them to Lisbon rather than one performance. Equally, without Gallagher's corner and McNeill's header in the previous round, Willie may not have even got the chance to play in the European Cup of 1967!

However, there is no doubt that the semi-finals of the European Cup belonged to Willie Wallace and no Celtic fan should ever forget that because without him Lisbon was by no means certain.

The entire tie, home and away, could be summed up by simply saying Willie Wallace 2—Josef Masopust Nil!

Before leaving the story of this tie there are two things I have to highlight.

I have never read any account of the second leg in Prague by any of the Lions without them mentioning the disappointment shown by Josef Masopust in not progressing to the final. Everyone to a man has commented on his refusal to shake hands at the final whistle and his attitude towards Willie in particular.

Equally, everyone again acknowledges that this great player put that disappointment behind him very quickly and made a point of going out of his way to apologise for his surliness and then going on to congratulate Celtic wishing them all the best for the final.

This story has been repeated so regularly by the members of the Celtic team that it is quite clear the incident and the player made a lasting impression on them. It is to the credit of the Celtic team that no one has ever even thought of criticising Masopust for apparent churlishness. On the contrary, the Celtic players who have written and talked about the incident have said that they would not have blamed Masopust for his behaviour and would have thought no less of him had he not taken the decision to apologise very quickly, shake Willie's hand, and wish them all the best for the final.

However, I have to end this section with a Masopust story, which may explain his actions at full time, and which more likely, explains his complete volte face and the decision to apologise immediately and wish his conquerors well.

As we have seen, Josef Masopust was the European Footballer of the year in 1962.

Masopust was the star man of an unfancied Czech team captained by fellow Dukla Player Novak, and his skill was instrumental in dragging his team all the way to the final against Brazil. However progress to that stage was thought most unlikely especially as the Czechs were drawn in the same group as the holders at the start of the tournament along with Spain and Mexico.

Having won their opening match, Czechoslovakia would play the holders Brazil in the knowledge that another surprising victory would put them in a great position to progress from a very difficult group.

It is in this game, that the man from the Eastern Bloc with all the skill would do something that made both footballers on the park and the footballing public in general stare in astonishment.

Before half time, Pele would be badly injured leaving him virtually hobbling on the sidelines as a spectator and of no use to his team at all - he would take no further part in the competition at the final whistle.

However, from time to time the ball would be played out to him out of sheer instinct and he was virtually unable to control the ball and play it back to a team-mate.

In the middle of the Park, Brazil fielded the magnificent Didi and it was Masopust's job to go head to head with him.

The Czech player kept the irresistible Didi quiet as Czechoslovakia held Brazil to a shock 0-0 draw, however it was a match in which his class showed both professionally and personally.

This was the pre substitution era and with Pele severely injured and forced to hobble helplessly around the field there were numerous chances for Josef Masopust to win the ball without fear of challenge. However, when the ball went towards the Brazil No10 the elegant Czech No.6 refused to challenge his opponent at any time despite the importance of the game and the opportunity for a fantastic result.

In a show of true sporting integrity Masopust simply allowed another Brazil player to collect the ball from Pele rather than make a challenge.

"It was a gesture I will never forget," said Pele afterwards.

Pele's team mate, the legendary Djalma Santos who would play in four World Cup finals remarked at the time: "It was moving to see the respect with which Masopust treated the situation. It was not just respect for Pele but for the entire Brazil team and the tournament. He was a great player and, moreover, a gentleman."

Whilst I appreciate that this is a book about Willie Wallace it has to be said that at times sport throws up a true great and Josef Masopust was truly great in every single way. Although second to Willie Wallace when it mattered most to Celtic. So that is one of the two things I have to highlight.

The second is that this game was played in the afternoon of 25th April 1967 and there was no television coverage, and so back home everyone was tuned into the radio commentary provided by a certain Archie McPherson.

When the final whistle went and Archie proclaimed, " That's it! They've done it. Celtic are in the final of the European Cup!"--- Well with my old man in London potentially chasing planes for the final, my Mammy just burst into tears!

Chapter 8

WIN FOR THE SAKE OF FOOTBALL

Bryon Butler the former Daily Telegraph football correspondent and BBC Radio Commentator described the European Cup Final of 1967. I can't find the exact quote but he said something along the lines of: " This was good and against evil. Dark against Light. Night against Day. Hope against Despair. Stein's Celtic came as if from nowhere - and they had to win - for the sake of football!"

The Victory in Lisbon meant many different things to many different people.

For many of the Celtic support, both those who were there and those who were back home wherever home may be, the victory meant the culmination of a long journey for the football club that was started as an idea at a meeting in St Mary's Hall on 6th November 1887. It was almost beyond the belief of many that the club were now Kings of Europe, yet prior to the final you would be hard pressed to find any Celtic fan that was not confident of victory against Inter Milan.

For Willie Wallace, it was the culmination of a different type of journey. The boy, who had started playing football at school in

Kirkintilloch, had journeyed through school team football, to a boy's brigade team, to junior football with Kilsyth Rangers, then through part time Stenhousemuir, to Raith Rovers, Heart of Midlothian and now with Celtic.

In the preceding few weeks Willie had played for Scotland when beating the World Champions at Wembley, won the Scottish League, made his debut in the European Cup scoring two goals, and had been the Celtic hero in the Scottish Cup final at Hampden scoring goals number 18 and 19 in the course of just 26 games for Celtic.

To cap it all, he would end the 12th European Cup final a winner and leave the field of play, mobbed by fans having been held aloft by the Celtic faithful, and wearing nothing but a jock strap!

...And all of this happened on a 6 month temporary contract! It is a story that is scarcely believable.

Many years later, when celebrating the anniversary of that day in Lisbon, Willie and his team mates would celebrate together in memory of that famous win and more than once he would repeat something time and again with obvious pride and total conviction.

"As a team, we didn't fear anyone - we believed that on our day we could beat any team we played".

I say again, Willie Wallace is no braggadocio, no big headed boaster or blow hard, and so when he says that he and his colleagues could have beaten anyone in their heyday then this is no idle boast or words of wishful fantasy.

Further, there are very few in the world of football—whether they are from Scotland, England, Ireland or anywhere else in Europe or beyond--- who would disagree with him.

Football is a team game and at any given time and in any particular era there will be a number of very good if not great teams - and not all of them can be proclaimed champions of Europe. Yet the bhoys from Scotland were crowned kings of Europe and shortly after Willie Wallace left Celtic Park as a player four and a half years later, the club would be in yet another semi-final attempting to reach their third final in five years.

Accordingly, May 25th 1967 could certainly be said to be the date when the world came to realise that Jock Stein, his team and Celtic Football Club were indeed a match for anyone else on the planet and would be for a number of years to come.

For a footballer who has trained, worked, played, trained and worked to achieve something in football - and who has been lucky enough to earn a living from playing football - realising that you are part of the best team in Europe must be a brilliant feeling and a very satisfying achievement.

I have no idea how that would feel of course but what I can describe is the pride I feel in that achievement as a Celtic supporter.

I can honestly admit that whilst Willie and Co were playing their socks of in the Estadio Nacional, I was back home in Glasgow watching the telly and from the 8th minute on I was hiding behind the couch!

I was far from certain that my heroes would win especially after going a goal down so early in the game. At the time, this fear was just the fear of a child who did not want his team to lose.

When you consider and analyse the facts surrounding Inter Milan at the time there were good grounds for being afraid—unless of course you were actually in Lisbon where, I am told, as the game unfolded, everyone just knew that Celtic would prevail.

Inter Milan had been the European Cup Winners twice in the previous three years in season 63/64 and 64/65.

This was the era of La Grande Inter and to this day it is regarded as the period when the club was at its height and at its most successful.

Their manager, Helenio Herrera, was regarded as the best manager in Europe and had been brought to Milan with the specific intention of building a team that would challenge the then dominant Real Madrid for the European title. As such, Herrera was given access to hitherto undreamt of funds to establish a world-class team and he did this with great success.

However such success was achieved at a cost and it was true open entertaining football that paid the cost as Herrera's incredibly skilful team would at times abandon all flair and panache in favour of adopting the dreadful Catenaccio system of stealing a goal and killing the game.

Yet Herrera was not the inventor of the dreaded Catenaccio, merely its most successful exponent. The system had been invented by an Austrian coach named Karl Rappan and his original system was implemented using 4 fixed defenders, playing a strict man-to-man marking system, plus a playmaker in the middle of the field who played the ball together with two midfield wings.

However, Herrera would modify this system to make it even more defensive and stultifying - especially after his team had taken a lead - and so forcing opponents to chase the game whilst facing what seemed like a wall of defenders.

To make it ever more difficult to score against this Inter side, Herrera added a fifth defender, the sweeper or libero, behind the two centre backs. This sweeper or libero acted as the free man and he would deal with any attackers who managed to find a way through the two centre backs or who managed to get away from them or their full backs.

Accordingly, as soon as Inter scored, any opposing team found themselves facing a full back five with at least a deep lying midfield three in front of them and as often as not that defensive midfield three would easily become a four or a five who would look to counter attack on the break - if they needed to!

It took Herrera fully three years to perfect his team formation and his playing staff, and in successive years Inter would finish the league in 3rd, then 2nd and finally in 1st place taking them into the treasured European Cup which they then won in successive years displacing the great sides of Madrid and Benfica.

As a result, Herrera - who would be the only man ever to manage Barcelona three times - and in three different decades - would be given the title " Il Mago" - The Magician!

However, the magician's tricks would bring a success that would mean absolutely stultifying the abundance of natural talent he had at his disposal---------- and what talent that was.

As previously mentioned, when Herrera arrived at Inter from Barcelona he quickly brought with him the European Footballer of the year Louis Suarez who was the most expensive footballer in the history of the game at the time.

At the Camp Nou, Suarez had become a hero at inside right and was lauded for his creativity, his attacking flair and goals. He made 122 appearances for the Catalans and provided a return of precisely one goal in every two games scoring 61 times.

Yet on arrival at Inter, Herrera immediately took steps to convert him into a deep lying midfielder, and while his performances were absolutely excellent, in his 256 league appearances over the next 9 years, he would find the net only 42 times - reducing his scoring rate to less than one in every six games. However such was Suarez prowess and skill he would be voted as runner up in the European Footballer of the year poll on two further occasions and would feature almost constantly in the top ten or twenty players over several years.

Suarez would miss the game in Lisbon, though Herrera refused to confirm whether he was playing or not in his team sheet, with the result that Stein told the officials that unless he received confirmation of the Inter line up, his team would not be leaving the dressing room!

In addition to Suarez being absent, Herrera would also be without the Brazilian Jair de Costa who had starred in previous tournaments and who had been an Inter stalwart. Jair had left the club for the moment, although he would return in later years and even face Celtic in a future semi-final. Eventually he would move on and make his way back to Brazil where he played alongside Pele for FC Santos. To replace Jair, Herrera would rely on Domenghini who had cost a mere £116,000 from Atalanta the previous year!

However, when the Italians did take to the field, they provided the following formidable line up.

Giuliano Sarti would play 357 Serie A Games winning 3 championships, 1 Coppa Italia, 2 European Cups, 1 European Cup Winners Cup and 2 Intercontinental Cups. Sarti had already collected a championship and a Cup Winners Cup medal with Fiorentina before he joined Inter and he would play beneath the sticks for Italy on 8 occasions. In Lisbon, he would be Inter's man of the match. On leaving Inter he would have a short spell at Juventus.

Tarcisio Burgnich would make 467 appearances for Inter over 12 years and would be one of the rocks of their defence. With 66 caps for Italy, Burgnich was reckoned to be among the best defenders in the world. He would help Italy to the 1968 European Championships and would be in the World Cup squads of 1966, 1970 and 1974. Despite his 5 Scudetti, two European Cup Winners medals and all those caps, he would be reduced to chasing Jimmy Johnstone's shadow in the heat of Lisbon.

Giacinto Facchetti - an Inter legend with more international caps than virtually the whole Celtic team with 94 International appearances in which he wore the captain's armband no less than 70 times. Facchetti had started his career as a centre forward and was viewed as the greatest attacking fullback in the world when given the chance.

At 6'3" tall he was a commanding figure in any team. Facchetti won four Scudetti in 1963, 1965, 1966 and 1971; one Italian Cup in 1978; two European Cups in 1964 and 1965; and two Intercontinental Cups in 1964 and 1965. He was always there or there abouts when it came to votes for European Footballer of the Year and he would rank as runner up behind Eusebio in 1965. Facchetti would go on to be an Inter executive and employee for many years until his death at the age of sixty six.

In Lisbon, he would have to cope with the movement and pace of Bobby Lennox.

Armando Picchi was the Inter Milan Captain. Previously a full back, Herrera converted Picchi into the sweeper or Libero. He would play behind the traditional back four and sweep up anything that got past them. Picchi would only gain 12 International caps because his libero roll did not suit the Italian National team's style and so he was not even included in the 1966 World Cup squad. However at club level, he would win the Italian title 3 times, The European Cup twice and the Intercontinental Cup twice. He would take the field for Inter 257 times over a seven year period. Unfortunately in 1968, Picchi would fracture his pelvis in an international match against Bulgaria and this hastened his retirement and his move into management.

Gianfranco Bedin would play 211 Serie A games for Inter over a ten year period whilst playing at the very peak of European Club Football making 310 appearances in total with 23 goals from defensive midfield or defence. He would then go on to make 112 appearances with Sampdoria scoring 6 times.

Aristide Guarneri would be picked at the centre of the Italian International defence on 21 occasions. For Inter Milan he would man the defence on 333 occasions and formed a formidable partnership with Picchi. He won 3 league titles, Two European Cups and two Intercontinental cups with La Grande Inter.

Angelo Domenghini performed in 164 games for Inter Milan and scored 54 goals. He also had spells at Cagliari, Roma and Atalanta and made 398 appearances in top flight Italian football all told. He was a significant member of the Italian squads at the 1968 European Championships and the 1970 World Cup. He had previously won The European Cup, two league titles and two Intercontinental cups with Inter and had won the Coppa D'Italia with Atalanta scoring a hatrick in the final.

Sandro Mazzola scored twice to beat Real Madrid in the 1964 European Cup Final and was in the side that won the big cup again the following year against Benfica. He would play for Inter throughout his entire football career as an attacking (when allowed!) inside right. Ultimately his career lasted some 17 years during which he made 417 league appearances and scored 116 goals. By the end of his career, Mazzola had won four Serie A titles (1963, 1965, 1966 and 1971), two European Cups (1964 and 1965), two Intercontinental Cups (1964 and 1965), one European Championship (1968) and was top-scorer in Serie A in season 1964-65. His total of 70 international caps may well have been more were it not for his great Milanese rival Gianni Rivera as at one time the resident Italian manager decided that he could not play Mazzola and Rivera in the same team. Accordingly for a period, Mazzola would play in the first half and Rivera the second. Throughout his career, Mazzola would regularly be nominated for the title of European Footballer of the year and often finished in the top 20 players. His highest ranking was 2nd. Rivera on the other hand won it!

This game may well have held a very special resonance for Mazzola. His father had been a top class footballer and his last ever match had been in the Estadio Nacional. Tragically, after that game, Mazzola Senior had been killed in an air crash.

In 1966/67 Renato Cappellini was the Italian under 23 player of the year. He had not made many appearances in previous seasons and in all he would only make 50 league appearances for the Milan club scoring a more than respectable 18 goals for a side that was deemed to be ultra-defensive.

Cappellini had won the Scudetto the year before, and would move to A.S. Roma in 1969 with whom he would win the Anglo Italian Cup in 1972. Twice his country capped him. At that time Italy had a preponderance of strikers such as Luigi Riva and Pierino Pratti, but in the European Cup of 1967, Cappellini had developed a habit of finding the net.

Mauro Bicicli was called in for the injured Suarez in the final of European Cup. Bicicli was nicknamed the Bicycle because of his speed and his name. He had three different spells with Inter and was brought back by Herrera specifically for the 1966/67 season. Overall he scored some 19 goals for Inter in 159 starts and was already the holder of a league winner's medal when he took the field against Celtic. In 10 starts in the European Cup he had scored 3 goals.

Mario Corso was nicknamed "God's left Foot". Corso was another player who regularly featured as a nominee for European Footballer of the year. He played as a midfielder, won 4 league titles, two European Cups and two Intercontinental Cups .He played a total of 502 games, scoring 94 times. His speciality was his striking of the ball with that famous left foot at free kicks.

Corso, despite clearly being one of the best players in Europe, would never play in The World Cup Finals being overlooked repeatedly when it came to that tournament. However, he has a remarkable record with Inter Milan—he worked for the club in one capacity or another for 53 years!

This was the team that Celtic would face and defy to win the European Cup.

Willie Wallace had faced Inter Milan before. In November 1961, during Herrera's first season at the club, Hearts had drawn Inter in the second round of the Fairs Cup. The Italians had won 5-0 on aggregate recording a win by a solitary goal at Tynecastle and then scoring 4 in Milan.

The goals for Inter across the tie came mainly from English Centre Forward Gerry Hitchins who would be the club's top scorer that season, but some of the squad that had played for Inter at the start of the decade were now experienced European Champions. Mazzola, Facchetti, Picchi, Guarneri, Corso and Bicicli had all been in the squad at the time.

However Inter now faced a different Willie Wallace. He had scored in Europe for Hearts prior to his move to Celtic Park, but now he was a Celtic player and was in a rich vein of form in front of the net. It was his goals that had seen off Dukla and in between the two semi-finals it was Willie's goals that would see Celtic lift the Scottish Cup.

In 1961, Gerry Hitchins had scored 19 goals in the season. In 1967, Willie Wallace had scored 21 in six months! Clearly when considering his tactics, Helenio Herrera would have to consider the threat posed by Wallace and his fellow strikers - Chalmers and Lennox.

To get to the final, Inter had scraped by Torpedo Moscow in the first round by way of a Voronin own goal. Having progressed by four goals to one in the second round against Vasas of Hungary, Inter now faced the might of Real Madrid in the quarter final. In Milan, Inter won by a solitary goal from Cappellini, before producing the result of the round by winning 2-0 at the Bernabeu with another Cappellini strike and an own goal from Zoco. Against CSKA Sofia, Facchetti gave Inter a lead both home and away before the Bulgarians equalised and once again it was the on form Cappellini who scored the goal in the play-off that took Inter to Lisbon.

In all Inter had scored 11 goals to get to the final while Celtic had scored 16 while playing one game less.

Another contrast between the two sides was the fact that until the week before the Lisbon tie, both clubs had had the chance of a clean sweep of every competition they entered in that particular season. However, by the time the teams took to the field in Portugal, Celtic had swept the board in Scotland while Inter had lost in the Semi Final of the Coppa D'Italia and had been beaten to the league. Accordingly the European Cup was their only chance of gaining silverware that season - something that was surely an incentive if incentive be needed.

What was perhaps an added incentive for the Celtic players was the support.

As I have mentioned before, it was not the norm for a club to take a big travelling support to a European Cup final but no one knew better than Inter Milan how much of a difference a home support could make. The 1965 final between Inter and Benfica had been the subject of some speculation with the suggestion being that the Milanese had succeeded in negotiating that the final take place in their home ground.

This was something that had irked many in Portugal and so it was to be anticipated that many of the local Portuguese fans would be none too sympathetic towards Inter - and the Benfica fans in particular may well have been more than happy to support anyone against Inter.

However, Lisbon was to be the first time that any European city would play host to a mass travelling support for a major club final, and it was the first city to witness the effect and attitude of the massed Celtic support abroad.

Subsequent press reports would say that Celtic had taken anything between 7,000 and 15,000 fans. Of these two figures, the latter is certainly closest but in truth there were likely to be far more than 15,000.

For my father's part, he had been in London when the final whistle went in Prague and at the appropriate time he had called back to Glasgow from a phone box in the Tottenham Court Road.

Back in his office, on Glasgow's Dumbarton Road, my mother and all the rest of the staff listened to Archie McPherson's voice describe the tense game against Dukla over the radio - complete with crackles and all.

By the time my dad called in my mother could barely speak and all he heard was her sobbing at the end of the phone-line. Not unnaturally he concluded that Celtic had lost by two clear goals so he tried to sooth her feelings by saying that she was not to worry - they had lost some money but it was not the end of the world.

He was in mid-flow when my mum managed to blurt out " We Won! Celtic are through to the final" – they had done it!

Those words would be the starting pistol to send him off on another round of meetings where he tried to persuade companies with aeroplanes worth millions of pounds to lease them to an unknown man from Glasgow for a couple of days for the purposes of flying people to a football match in Lisbon!

When he went into the offices of a certain Freddie Laker and made this request, the receptionist told him to take a seat and promptly advised Mr Laker that there was a madman in reception who wanted to hire every plane the company had around 25th May in order that he could fly football fans from Glasgow to Lisbon. The receptionist advised Mr Laker to stay in his office while the gentleman was removed by way of an Ambulance!

Fortunately, Freddie was no dummy and with a quick phone call to the Daily Express he discovered that Glasgow Celtic were indeed in the European Cup Final and would play either CSKA Sofia or Inter Milan who would play the following night!

On that news my dad was ushered in to the office to see Freddie Laker who told him that at certain times in the past Laker too had been viewed as a madman!

The net result of all of this work is that my Father's company would fly 17 plane loads of fans to Lisbon. Other companies would fly as well and fans would go by scheduled service, by boat, by car, by train and by any other means possible!

The need to fill those planes would need a publicity push and so fervour was whipped up in Glasgow and Scotland generally about the number of fans going to Lisbon. In turn, this persuaded more and more fans to explore the possibility of getting to the final. There were reports in the paper that some people had sold their house to pay for the fare - others had been paid out by an insurance company after making a claim. Others had won the pools!

Some of the stories were true - some were carefully constructed plants with an element of truth - but all served the purpose of creating "Lisbon fever".

John Quinn of the Glasgow Evening Times would persuade the paper to allow him to commission a green and white Hillman Imp to lead a cavalcade of cars from Glasgow to Lisbon.

The result was that thousands and thousands of Celtic fans were in Lisbon with their banter, huge smiles, plenty of drink and a total and utter belief in their team.

My dad's customers were met at the airport by a fleet of green and white buses all of which had a large sign sending greetings from Glasgow Celtic Football Club to the people and the city of Lisbon.

Accordingly if the Inter Milan team were somewhat amazed by the site of the Celtic Players singing for it's a Grand Old Team to Play for in the tunnel - they were in for a surprise when they came on to the field of play as it seemed that to a man the whole stadium was supporting the men in the green and white hoops!

"Not for the first time Willie Wallace would play a role that was all about "team" rather than personal glorification. Bertie Auld would describe the running of the front three as totally and completely selfless! Billy McNeill would echo those sentiments and as mentioned before Bobby Lennox would highlight the fact that Willie always did what he was asked without question and in a quiet but effective way – constantly - and that this was something that was wholly appreciated by his team mates."

Chapter 9

PREPARATION AND TACTICS

Prior to the game, Jock Stein had taken the Celtic team to Seamill and amongst other things the team watched video footage of the Real Madrid v Eintracht Frankfurt from Hampden. Stein wanted the whole team to see the quality of the football and the style of what had been considered as the world's greatest football match.

In the sun in Lisbon, Celtic would play in a style and in a fashion that would make the football world sit up and take notice of the class of the Glasgow club. At the same time the performance would sound the death knell for the Catenaccio.

Stein's tactics that afternoon are of great interest in that he wanted to constantly turn the Inter defence.

After Inter had taken the lead with the penalty by Mazzola, Billy McNeil, John Clark and Ronnie Simpson would be virtual spectators.

However further up the park there was constant green and white motion.

One paper would describe Tommy Gemmell constantly coming forward down the left as being like a big blonde Celtic tom cat scattering Inter defenders like Italian pigeons!

Similarly, Jim Craig would come down the right and forage forward regularly - in spite of certain instructions from Stein!

In the middle is where the game would be won, and so Bertie Auld, Bobby Murdoch and particularly Jimmy Johnstone would see plenty of the ball. Johnstone, in particular, would weave, twist, turn and jink all over the park taking the ever present Burgnich with him.

The Italian international shadowed wee Jimmy everywhere so much so that he turned back in on himself so often that he must have met himself coming back the way and always asking "Where did the wee guy go?"

However, what concerns us here is the running of the front three - Chalmers Lennox and Wallace.

Jock Stein relied on the excellence of the Italian defence and the Catenaccio system in planning its downfall.

Stein was aware that these guys were amongst the greatest man markers in the world and their defensive system was such that it demanded that the defenders follow the opposing strikers everywhere. In particular, these same defenders would be instructed to concentrate on Celtic's main scoring threats - Chalmers and Wallace - who would be expected to hover in and around the penalty area.

Guarneri and Bedin would look after the central two, and Picchi would play his Libero roll thus snuffing out the perceived threat.

Except Stein planned differently. The Instructions to Wallace, Chalmers and Lennox were to constantly move OUT of the penalty area taking three defenders with them whenever they could thus leaving gaps in the defensive wall. With Lennox and the advancing Gemmell causing Facchetti problems down the left, with Johnstone pulling Burgnich all over the field from the right, and Wallace and Chalmers constantly running and dragging Guarneri Bedin and Picchi around - the midfield would find holes to exploit if they by-passed Mazzola, Domenghini and the Bicycle.

In essence, Stein used the Catenaccio mentality to show anyone and everyone how to dispose of that system forever.

Not for the first time Willie Wallace would play a role that was all about "team" rather than personal glorification. Bertie Auld would describe the running of the front three as totally and completely selfless! Billy McNeill would echo those sentiments and as mentioned before Bobby Lennox would highlight the fact that Willie always did what he was asked without question and in a quiet but effective way – constantly - and that this was something that was wholly appreciated by his team mates.

Despite being one goal down the Celtic team could see the effect of the game on the Italian champions. Celtic were by far the dominant team both in terms of territory and possession, but of greater importance they were the dominant team in terms of tactics. It was Celtic who were dictating the tempo and shape of the game and dragging the Inter players out of shape and around the pitch despite Inter Milan's lead and their resorting to the defensive Catenaccio.

As we all know the goals came from Tommy Gemmell in the 63rd minute and Stevie Chalmers in the 84th minute and Celtic would be European Champions with each of the Scottish heroes taking home a coveted winners medal.

No report from that match, no review or commentary would ever say that Celtic were not wholly entitled to their victory, which in one European review was described simply as "breathless!"
It was the perfect end to the perfect season.

In the season that Willie Wallace joined Celtic they won every single event they entered - even Quizball on the BBC - and they would end up as the BBC Sports Team of the Year which was presented at the annual Sports Review of the Year programme by Sir Matt Busby.

They would end the season having played a total of 64 games (including two friendlies against Manchester United and Real Madrid) winning 53 times, drawing 8 and losing just 3---- twice to Dundee United! In all they scored an amazing 200 goals.

This was the form of champions. European Champions! For Willie Wallace though the Celtic journey was only just beginning.

However for Inter Milan the game would effectively spell the end of La Grande Inter and the Catenaccio system. They ended the season trophy-less and when the following season did not go to plan, Helenio Herrera was sacked—strangely he was replaced by Herberto Herrera who had been the coach of Juventus from 1964 to 1969 winning the championship for Juve in 66/67.

Before leaving Lisbon it is worth considering something further concerning Inter Milan.

The quote from Jock Stein about playing attacking football in such a way that made the neutral want to support Celtic is well known.

However he also criticised Herrera's brand of football as a waste of the supreme talents of the players he had at his disposal.

Yet Herrera was a pioneer at the time. He was the first high profile coach who made a big impact on a team with his methods. For example while people would talk about Di Stefano's Real Madrid at the same time they would talk about Herrera's Grand Inter.

Herrera would break new ground with his training methods, his dietary practices for each player and his motivational talks and messages. However, his legacy would not be without considerable controversy, which may or may not have affected the 1967 European Cup final in one way or another.

The referee for the Lisbon game was Mr Kurt Tschenscher from Germany and he was viewed as one of Europe's top officials. He had previously refereed a European Cup Winners Cup final and in the later stages of the European Championships, and one of the semi-finals in the same competition the previous year. He would later go on to be the man in the middle during the group stages of both the 1970 and 1974 World Cups. In 1971, Tschenscher officiated at Pelé's final professional match, at the end of which he received the final jersey worn by the Brazilian.

It did not matter, but in this match the German made some odd decisions. Specifically he gave Celtic two indirect free kicks inside the penalty box - something that I have never heard of happening in a match since - and more importantly he denied Celtic a penalty after the most blatant foul I have ever seen by a goalkeeper, when Sarti clearly grabbed Willie Wallace's leg about two yards from goal. Not only should it have been a penalty but Inter's star man should have gone for the early bath!

Now I raise the performance of the man in black because in the intervening years it has been repeatedly suggested that Inter had a long standing practice of getting far too close to referees with gifts and what some saw as bribes.

The Italian football association would mount various investigations into a number of teams including Inter Milan and in later years there would be literally hundreds of taped telephone conversations, which would implicate the great Facchetti (by then a senior inter official) in having regular contact with referees in a manner, which might be classed as unethical.

Bill Shankly's Liverpool would complain about very strange decisions when playing against Inter - decisions that were in the eyes of Shankly truly inexplicable - so much so that there was open speculation about the referees being bribed.

Now these allegations have never been proven although the Italian Football Association did later make a comment that Facchetti had been guilty of rule breaches. However none of this was ever alleged against Herrera.

However, Ferrucio Mazzola brother of Sandro has made very substantial allegations.

Ferruccio was a fringe player at Inter during the Herrera years and he has claimed in a book that not only did La Grande Inter seek to influence the decisions of referees by way of bribes, but that Herrera was also drugging his team with amphetamines and wee white pills!

Sandro Mazzola, Mariolino Corso, Luis Suarez, Tarcisio Burgnich, Gianfranco Bedin, Angelo Domenghini, Aristide Guarneri as well as Ferruccio Mazzola eventually testified with regard to these allegations before an investigative Tribunal in Rome where evidence was provided.

The majority of the Inter players would deny or at least dismiss as insignificant what Ferruccio had to say, yet he persisted in his allegations when matters came to court.

Ferruccio would go on to say:

"I was part of that Inter too. I've seen with my eyes how players were treated. I saw Helenio Herrera providing pills that were to be placed under our tongues. He used to experiment on us bench players only to later give them to the first team players. Some of us would eventually spit them out. It was my brother Sandro that suggested to me that if I had no intention of taking them, to just run to the toilette and spit them out. Eventually Herrera found out and decided to dilute them in coffee. From that day on "Il Caffè Herrera" became a habit at Inter.

He went on: " I believe (the pills) are amphetamines. Once, after a Caffè Herrera, it was prior to a Como vs Inter (1967), I suffered 3 days and nights in a state of complete hallucinations, just like an epileptic. Nowadays, everybody denies this, even Sandro...

Since I have decided to speak out, (Sandro) and I simply don't talk to each other. He says that dirty laundry should be washed at home;

on the contrary, I believe that it's right to speak out, above all for a number of my former team-mates, a number of which are either very sick or dead.

The first (to die) was Armando Picchi, captain of the team. He died aged 36 due to a cancer. Then came Marcello Giusti, a reserve player, who died of a brain cancer during the 90's. Carlo Tagnin, a great player that would never refuse a pill, since he wanted to further his career as long as possible, he died in year 2000.

Mauro Bicicli and Ferdinando Miniussi have left us respectively in 2001 and 2002. Enea Masiero, with Inter from 1955 to 1964, is undertaking chemotherapy, whilst Pino Longoni is in a wheel chair."

Mazzola would then go on to make other allegations and when it came to Giacinto Facchetti he said:

"I was sued by Inter President Mr Facchetti. All the players of that team, I mean all the players that are still alive, have a choice to testify. I just want to see if they won't have the courage to say the truth under oath.

I was once very friendly with Facchetti but let's just leave him out of this, because I'd have to mention heavy stuff. If I wanted to cause real damage to Inter, within the book, I could have added a number of other episodes. I could have added details about fixed matches and bribed referees, especially in Cup ties........."

There would indeed be a great scandal about Inter in 2006 but it did not touch on the Grande Inter period nor the European Cup Final of 1967. However Inter and Giacinto Facchetti were severely damaged by the allegations.

Regrettably, the former 6'3" attacking fullback would die at the age of 66 in September 2006 and was President of Inter Milan until the day he died having previously been technical director, board member, worldwide ambassador and vice president. He had fought a long battle with pancreatic cancer.

Facchetti did indeed sue Ferruccio Mazzola for defamation in relation to his allegations...and lost!

Chapter 10

LIFE AFTER LISBON - CELTIC AND THE WALLACE YEARS

On 2 September 1967, a few months after the Lisbon triumph, a bus full of Celtic supporters left from "The George Bar" in Bridgeton Main Street heading for Aberdeen where Celtic were due to play in a league cup tie.

The Bus, with a full complement aboard, left at 7.00 a.m and the enterprising patrons had taken out the whole back seat which was converted into "The Bar" for the journey. Around Cumbernauld, one elderly man who had consumed a few was already showing signs of over-indulgence and by Stirling he pointed out the window and asked "What's that, son?"

"That", came the reply "Is Wallace's Monument".

He was pleasantly surprised with this reply and said "Christ! They wurny long in getting' that up"!

Whilst the Wallace monument was not erected to celebrate the feats of a footballer, from season 67/68 onwards the feats of Willie Wallace in a green and white shirt would warrant a monument of sizeable proportions in football terms.

For the next 3 years or so, the Celtic forward line would effectively be spearheaded by Willie Wallace plus one other - and the one other could be any one of Lennox, Chalmers, Macari, Hood, Hughes, Johnstone or the returning McBride.

However, Jock Stein was to add a further name to the list of potential partners for Willie by signing the mysterious Pat McMahon immediately upon his return from Lisbon.

The McMahon story reads like a piece of Boys-Own fiction and ends as mysteriously as the George Connelly story.

McMahon began his football career just like Willie at local Scottish team Kilsyth Rangers. While with Kilsyth Rangers, he wrote to Celtic off his own bat asking that the senior club take him for trials.

When he received no encouragement, he packed his bags and moved to London where he worked for the GPO. In April 1967, Kilsyth Rangers reached the Scottish Junior Cup finals but found that they were short of players so they sent McMahon a telegram asking him to play for them in the cup final as a last minute replacement for an injured player. The young fella answered the call, travelled back to Glasgow and performed splendidly, helping Kilsyth win the cup. Celtic, now European Champions, responded promptly to this performance and signed him immediately—just two days after the final in Lisbon.

In other words, Willie Wallace - the man supposedly signed on a temporary short term contract - would appear just about constantly in a Celtic shirt and was regarded as an automatic pick for the club whilst starring alongside all of the above players at any given time - including the recently signed young man who had once played for his old junior team Kilsyth Rangers!

Such was Willie's regularity in the team at this time that the actor, author, and Celtic fan John Cairney described Wallace during this period as a "Stein favourite" and so it would be fair to say that at this point Celtic's strike force was Wallace plus one of the above.

In season 67/68 Willie would weigh in with 27 goals including three hat- tricks and in a game against Kilmarnock he would score 4 of Celtics 6 goals. Between February 14th and March 30th 1969 Celtic would play 9 games and in the course of those games Willie Wallace would score an amazing 14 goals. Yet he would not end the season as top scorer. That honour went to his pal Bobby Lennox who scored 23 goals in the last twelve games of the season taking his tally for the whole campaign to an astonishing 44 if you include Glasgow cup games.

Willie's goals would include one which helped Celtic knock Rangers out of the League cup in a 3-1 victory, and he would have no difficulty scoring against his former clubs—especially Raith Rovers who must have been sick of the sight of him as he found their net 4 times.

Interestingly one of those hat-tricks would come on the day that Pat McMahon would make his debut as an inside forward for the club. The game was against Partick Thistle in the Glasgow Cup and Celtic would win 5-0 with Willie getting his hat-trick and the unknown debutant scoring the other two!

A fortnight later, Celtic travelled to Pittodrie in the league cup and promptly despatched Aberdeen by 5-1 with young McMahon scoring again. One week later, Celtic defeated Clyde in the league at Celtic park and McMahon unbelievably scored again - the first of Celtic's three goals that day!

Next up was a 6-2 defeat of Ayr United - and yes you have guessed it - McMahon was yet again amongst the goal scorers! The Celtic fans thought that this was another stroke of Stein genius and that this young man was going to go on to be a real superstar.

In the next two games he did not score and was then dropped never to play another single first team fixture all season!

In fact he would start only one more senior game for Celtic - in the following season's League Cup Quarter Finals against Hamilton Accies - where yet again he promptly scored in a 4-1 victory. That was on September 25th. He was not heard of again until he made a substitutes appearance on 18th January the following year when he came on against Dundee United in a league match - and scored!!

Thereafter he would never play for Celtic again—and within a short time was on his way to Aston Villa with Tommy Docherty on a free transfer! Apparently he took the huff at being dropped and was shown the door by Mr Stein!

The opening game of season 68/69 would find Celtic face Rangers in the League Cup at Ibrox on 10th August. Rangers went down to a 2-0 defeat with Willie bagging both goals. The two sides would meet again at Celtic Park later in the month for the second encounter in a group stage which saw the sides play home and away. Celtic and Willie Wallace warmed up for the second encounter with Rangers by taking on Partick Thistle on 17th August at Paradise, where Willie would run amok with all four Celtic goals. The following week, in front of 75,000 fans Wallace would again put Rangers to the sword with the only goal of the game.

He had essentially started season 68/69 where he had left off the previous season - he just could not stop scoring - especially in big games such as those against Rangers. In all Willie would score 31 goals including the odd penalty when Tommy Gemmell was not available for duty - something that should be borne in mind for future reference.

In the European Cup, Celtic would come from behind having lost 2-0 in St Etienne to win 4-0 at Celtic Park and so progress to the next round against Red Star Belgrade.

The game at Celtic Park on 13th November would see Celtic at their very best with Willie amongst the scorers in the 5-1 victory which saw Jimmy Johnstone give a dazzling display in return for supposedly avoiding the flight to Belgrade.

The return match was on 27th November and although Red Star pulled a goal back, Willie Wallace was on hand to score an important away goal just to ensure that everyone knew which club was to progress.

The European adventure that year would end at the quarter final stage when Celtic were undone by the eventual winners AC Milan losing out to a solitary goal from the forever dreaded Pratti, however they completed a domestic treble with Willie among the scorers in the Scottish Cup semi-final against Morton and in the league cup final against Hibs.

The 1969/70 season would see the names of Harry Hood and Luigi Macari make regular appearances on the Celtic team sheet - giving the fans a new song to sing with the help of a tune from George Harrison.

Hood in particular would be prolific in the early part of the season and clearly enjoyed the role of playing as the main striker just in front of Wallace - as we have seen before he would later say that he loved playing alongside Willie and that he learned most from working alongside the very experienced Wallace.

However, Celtic were changing in personnel. Joe McBride had moved on and Steve Chalmers was to suffer an injury and not unsurprisingly was to feature less in the starting 11.

As well as Hood and Macari there were other new faces making appearances in the forward line such as Tommy Callaghan and on occasion a young Kenny Dalglish and Vic Davidson.

This then left Willie Wallace as the "senior" striker in the team and again he would be an almost ever present. He would grab important European goals against Benfica and Fiorentina and throughout the league campaign was on target regularly, ending the season as Celtic's top scorer.

However, it should be noted that this Celtic team saw goals from nearly every forward position in abundance with Hood, Lennox, Macari and a rejuvenated John Hughes all scoring freely.

However, the season would end with huge disappointment when Celtic could not overcome Feyenoord in the European Cup Final in Milan and lost to Aberdeen in the Scottish Cup Final.

By this time, the Celtic fans had had a few years to get used to the idea of European travel in support of their team - and Europe had had a few years to get used to the fact that where you got Celtic you also got their huge support.

For the 1970 final, my father's company were to fly 31 separate flights to Milan all full of Celtic fans anticipating a repeat of Lisbon. Other companies also had flights from Glasgow and yet more fans would make their way to the game by car, train and every other means—the turn out of the Celtic faithful was huge - yet again.

Many fans this time went to the host city for a night or two and were staying in the Milan Hilton and other top class hotels going all the way up to Stressa on Lake Maggiore from where a fleet of buses would take them into the city centre and the San Siro for the game.

Celtic did not play well on the night and were undone. Most of the players and the fans believe that the team would have beaten the Dutch side in a replay or on another occasion. For me, however, two things strike me looking back at that game.

The first was the odd decision of Jock Stein not to play Harry Hood in the final - instead relegating him to the substitute's bench. Hood and Wallace had formed a formidable partnership - remember Jock's comment to Billy McNeill when Willie signed for Celtic? Saying he thought that a Wallace/McBride partnership would be potentially the greatest in Europe?

Given that Harry and Willie playing together had been Celtic's most potent goal threat all season I have no idea why Stein chose to change the set up. As we shall see, the pair combined even more lethally the following season!

Anyway, it was not to be and we are left looking back on Milan as what might have been - maybe should have been!

However, that trip to Milan was to leave me with one of my most abiding memories of a football occasion and which went a long way to formulating my view of the Celtic support in the eyes of others.

The day after the game I distinctly remember a whole host of Celtic fans sitting in cafes along one side of a square somewhere in the Milan city centre.

Suddenly you could hear the bellowing sound of numerous Feyenoord fans and their deafening claxon horns that were ringing out proclaiming their victory the night before. Hundreds of Dutch fans billowed into this square and sat more or less opposite where the Celtic fans were sitting and for a short period the atmosphere was somewhat tense as the Dutch were absolutely intent on celebrating whilst the Celtic fans were deep in disappointment.

However, the most amazing thing then happened.

A group of Dutch supporters appeared with trays full of beer and as the remaining Feyenoord fans struck up in unison these Dutch guys walked clean across the square and started handing out beers to the seated – and by this time astonished—Celtic supporters. " CEL----TIC" " CEL—TIC" " CEL—TIC" came the cry from the Dutch on the other side of the square while the impromptu waiters handed out the beer to the seated Celtic fans.

That one incident has stuck in my mind ever since and remains to this day one of THE reasons why I love European football and the camaraderie and joy that it brings. Further, it emphasised for me that being a Celtic fan was to be something special in Europe. We don't care if we win lose or draw - and neither do most Europeans - if you are a Celtic fan then you will be lauded, applauded and appreciated in Europe - for me that was the lesson of Milan 1970.

In his last full season with Celtic Willie Wallace would score 30 goals despite missing more games than in any of the previous seasons with the club. He and Harry Hood were on Fire with the former Clyde man ending the season as the clubs top scorer with 32 goals. Further goals were coming from all the usual suspects - Lennox, Johnstone, Macari,

Hughes and contributions from Callaghan, Davidson, Connelly, Davie Hay and even Paul Wilson who had started to make his way into the team.

However at certain stages in the season the score sheet simply read Hood-Wallace-Wallace-Hood as Celtic marched towards the title again.

The European adventure would once again end at the hands of the Dutch. Although this time it would be Johan Cruyff's Ajax who would see off Celtic by 3-0 in Amsterdam although Celtic would win 1-0 at Celtic Park in the return with a Jimmy Johnstone goal. To be fair, Celtic were only one behind for the majority of the game in Amsterdam, and two late goals made the result a far better result for the Dutch.

Before that, Willie Wallace had added more European Goals against Kokkola and Waterford continuing his record of scoring in Europe in the course of every season with the club. Once again Willie was happy to take a penalty if he was on the field of play and Tommy Gemmell wasn't although Harry Hood was also adept when it came to spot kicks as he would take three during the season to Willie's solo score against Dunfermline.

Celtic lost the league Cup Final to Rangers by a single goal but would win the Scottish Cup yet again when they defeated the League Cup Winners in a replay with goals from Macari and Hood with his third penalty conversion of the season.

In the last 11 games of the season Willie Wallace and Harry Hood would each find the net 7 times and Bobby Lennox would score 5 times as the Celtic domestic juggernaut rolled relentlessly onwards.

" Eventually White's relationship with Stein would deteriorate to such an extent that he would completely fall out with Jock Stein altogether. Towards the end of Stein's time at Celtic Park, White would be remembered for the awkward looking photograph where he is shown shaking hands with the incoming Billy McNeill, with Stein standing helplessly looking on between McNeill and White. The photograph is made all the more awkward looking as White shakes hands with his left hand—his right arm having been badly damaged when he accidentally walked into a spinning aircraft propeller blade years before."

Chapter 11

AND IN THE END - A MYSTERY

When the man raced by my dad and I on that September night in 1971 and shouted simply "Wallace!" none of us—not even Willie—could know that he had just scored his 134th and last goal for Celtic.

By the start of season 1971/72 Willie Wallace was 31 years of age and the previous season he had scored 30 goals for the club including goals in Europe - as usual.

As mentioned above, in the last dozen or so games of the previous campaign, Willie and Harry Hood had scored 14 times between them and were clearly the top two scorers at the club.

However, by the start of the next campaign Stein faced a problem - in fact several problems - some of which were good, and some of which were not so good.

The good problems came in the form of his playing staff. The score-sheet at the start of 71/72 would demonstrate the nature of one of the problems because it read as follows for the first few games:

Johnstone, Dalglish (Pen)
Lennox
Hughes, Hay, Dalglish

Dalglish, Callaghan, Lennox
Dalglish, Lennox, Hay, Macari
Lennox, Macari, McNeill, Callaghan, Murdoch, Dalglish
Macari, Hood, Callaghan, Wallace

Clearly, Celtic had uncovered a new young talent in Kenneth Mathieson Dalglish and this was the season he was to make his mark.

However, it should be noted that all of the above score sheets came in the league cup where sometimes it was considered that the competition was not as tough as in the league and Scottish Cups— and certainly nowhere near as tough as in Europe.

Noticeably Willie's goal was to come in the league cup quarter final and it was to be his last domestic goal in a Celtic shirt. It was the only match that he had so far started during the season and he would not start another match of any kind for 4 weeks afterwards.

Essentially he had lost his place and was relegated to the subs bench from which he made three appearances.

One of those appearances was in Celtic's first European Tie of the season, which was played away in the city of Copenhagen against the Danish Champions BK 1903 Copenhagen.

Fielding a "younger" less experienced Celtic side than in previous years, the Celtic performance that night has been described as lacklustre and lacking spark, with Celtic going down by two goals to one against a team that everyone had expected them to beat.

Willie would make an appearance at half time in that game, when Jock Stein chose to take off Jimmy Johnstone who had somewhat annoyed his manager. As a result, Jimmy was unceremoniously given the hook, and on came Willie!

Now stop and consider this. With the exception of the defeat to Dynamo Kiev in the season 1967/68, Celtic had progressed to the later stages of the European Cup and had always only been beaten by a team that had either won the competition outright or had been defeated finalists. AC Milan, Ajax, Feyenoord------ and the expectation was that the Glasgow side would be there or there abouts again.

Accordingly, despite the away goal from Lou Macari, the defeat to Copenhagen and the quality of performance was seen as a disappointment.

Perhaps it was for that reason Jock Stein decided that Willie Wallace should start in the home tie at Celtic Park? Maybe he saw that when it came to Europe, he needed the senior striker with all his craft and guile on the park against the champions of other countries—for this was most definitely not the league cup!

As you know, just as he had done several years before on his Celtic European debut against Dukla Prague, Willie Wallace- the man who had been out of the team for a month - stepped up to the plate with two goals and Celtic were through!

That result would see them go on to play Sliema Wanderers of Malta, Ujpest Doza of Hungary and finally old foes Inter Milan in the semi-final.

It is in no way a criticism when I point out that Kenny Dalglish did not score a single goal in Europe that season whereas goals did come from Hood, Lennox, Macari and even Jim Brogan - as well as the ones from Willie and Tommy Callaghan.

Equally, Celtic's top scorer for the season would be Dixie Deans with an astonishing tally of 27 goals in a few short months - but none of them would come in Europe. Further, where Harry Hood had weighed in with 32 the previous season, he would contribute just over half of that number in the season that Willie Wallace left the club.

However, if the arrival of the prodigious Dalglish posed a good problem for Stein, I believe that in the background he faced a problem of an entirely different nature - and this time it was not a good sort of problem at all.

Before the home match with Copenhagen at Celtic Park, the old ground would resound to the sound of silence for a period of one minute so that the club could pay its respects to Sir Robert Kelly who had died after a long fight with cancer. The man who had appointed Stein, and who had virtually ruled the club for 3 decades, had died.

In the past, Kelly had played a major part in picking the team before Stein had arrived, and even during the Stein years he would on occasion come into the dressing room to address the players before a game - though Stein would then tell his players to " forget all that" and provide his own team talk.

However, Kelly had been an interferer and perhaps there were other "interferers" on the Celtic board who were now prepared to flex their muscles at least a little.

I fully admit that what I am about to say is part speculation on my part but at the same time I am convinced that there is some substance to the following theory.

The circumstances of his transfer out of Celtic Park as narrated by Willie Wallace are very strange - and when taken together with other facts that are now well known - they may be viewed as even stranger still.

There is no doubt that by September/October 1971 Jock Stein was quite happy to part company with John Hughes and to let him leave Celtic Park. Stein made it clear to Hughes that his time had come and when Crystal Palace agreed to sign Hughes, then as far as Stein was concerned Big Yogi was a gonner! Except for one problem—Hughes did not want to leave!

By his own account, John Hughes put it to Stein that he wanted to stay and fight for his place only to be told by the Celtic manager that there was no question of that and that if he did not agree to go to Crystal Palace then he would never play for Celtic again as Stein would simply not pick him—ever!

Jock was already in the throes of breaking up the Lions squad by this time. Ronnie Simpson had retired, Bertie Auld had gone to Hibs and Stevie Chalmers and John Clark had been allowed to head down to the tail o' the bank with Greenock Morton. Now Yogi was to get on his way.

The long serving Hughes, who had been at the club since the late 1950's, had always been a favourite of the board and in the past Stein had been asked just why Yogi was not playing on any given day.

However, that was from Sir Robert Kelly who had recently died—now the control of what was the Celtic Football Club board passed to Desmond White who had up until then been the club secretary.

White was an accountant by profession but he had other business interests including a substantial business that involved the renting out of slot machines to public houses. His family had a long tradition of being involved in the affairs of Celtic Football Club and now Desmond was to take over Bob Kelly's mantle as the principal director although he would perhaps not be as visible as his predecessor in the public eye or in the football corridors of power.

Eventually White's relationship with Stein would deteriorate to such an extent that he would completely fall out with Jock Stein altogether. Towards the end of Stein's time at Celtic Park, White would be remembered for the awkward looking photograph where he is shown shaking hands with the incoming Billy McNeill, with Stein standing helplessly looking on between McNeill and White. The photograph is made all the more awkward looking as White shakes hands with his left hand—his right arm having been badly damaged when he accidentally walked into a spinning aircraft propeller blade years before.

Further, It would be White who would be responsible for the complete PR disaster when the board offered Stein a menial and insulting job with Celtic Pools once they had decided to replace him with McNeill as manager.

Desmond White was very much a throwback to times past. So what had White to do with the departure of Willie Wallace from Celtic?

Well I openly admit to some speculation here and all and anyone is free to disagree with my conclusions.

First of all, with no disrespect to Desmond White, he held a business and monetary view that immediate cash was king. It had long been alleged that Desmond would determine the declared size of the crowd at Celtic Park on a match day by simply taking a look and estimating the crowd size rather than by relying on any scientific means or logical calculation.

His offices at No 28 Bath Street sat above the Blue Lagoon fish and chip shop at the corner of West Nile Street and Bath Street and it was from here that he would oversee all business dealings including those of Celtic Football Club.

Entrance to the office was by way of a flight of stairs on Bath Street. They were gloomy stairs leading to an even gloomier office, which, once through the door, were lit with a solitary unshaded light bulb. White himself sat in a rear office that was lit with a slightly more powerful light bulb, but the entire impression given in these premises was one of austerity and impoverishment - these were not offices which were kitted out with a view to suggesting a surplus of funds - or ambition in the corporate world. They were functional at best, and just plain dingy if you are being honest.

Next it should be noticed that both Willie and big John would be out of the Parkhead door almost immediately after the death of Robert Kelly. Yet there is clearly a difference between the two transfers albeit the players went to the same club.

It is clear that Jock Stein wanted to transfer John Hughes. He had clearly told him that he was leaving and where he was going to, leaving Hughes little option to say anything about the matter at all. Clearly there had been discussions between the two clubs about Hughes prior to Stein speaking to Hughes himself and there had been ongoing discussions in the background that would then allow Stein to break the news to Hughes that a deal had been done. Those discussions did not take place out of the blue or happen all of a sudden although they did take place without Hughes' knowledge.

I don't believe that the financial discussions would have been between Stein and his counterpart at Crystal Palace - they would have been between Chairman and Chairman, and with Robert Kelly being terminally ill for some time that meant that the discussions would have been between the Chairman at Crystal Palace and Desmond White. It would have been White who discussed and agreed the figures and indeed the players to be transferred.

In considering that very issue - the players to be transferred - remember that the season before Willie Wallace had been prolific in forming a striking partnership with Harry Hood scoring 30 goals. Whilst he was now 31 he was still at the peak of his powers and more importantly he had bags of experience unlike the other players who were vying for a start in the forward area.

In terms of seniority or length of service or experience the nearest rival would be Bobby Lennox who was much more a wide left player utilising his speed and blindside running which had always been a great weapon for Celtic and a real problem for opposing fullbacks. Willie and Bobby were not the same type of player at all and offered the manager different options altogether.

Willie played either at the front of the line or just behind the main striker and this meant that the men who would be in direct opposition for a place would be the younger Hood, who could be played further back in the midfield, the younger and smaller Macari or the even younger and emerging Dalglish. At this stage in the career of all of these players, none offered the experience that Willie Wallace offered and none had Willie's goal scoring record going back over a number of years.

Yet there is evidence that even with all of these options Stein knew that he needed more cover for the striking role—whether that be on the domestic field or in Europe.

Given the fact that Stein wanted to offload Hughes, had released both McBride and Chalmers, and had lost another source of regular goals in Auld, The Big Man had already started to make moves in the transfer market.

It should be remembered that Willie Wallace had wanted to leave Hearts for some time before he joined Celtic and that he had even made noises to the Edinburgh club about emigrating to make a new life for his family in Canada.

Now, another player in Scottish Football found themselves in a similar position.

John "Dixie" Deans had been at Motherwell for a period of over 5 years—indeed he had been sent off when playing for the steelmen on the day that Willie made his Celtic debut.

Now, by his own account, Dixie was contacted by a journalist come well known fixer and friend of Stein's with a message. He was to tell Motherwell he wanted to emigrate...to Canada.... And this would facilitate a move to Celtic Park!

Deans was a totally different type of player and personality to Willie Wallace. Dixie was a front line striker. He was not as mobile around the pitch, nor as versatile in terms of being able to play in all the forward positions and was far bigger and chunkier in his physique. Further he was mercurial in temperament and had a poor disciplinary record having been sent off for the early bath on many occasions - very often for what he said to the man in black as opposed to his robust play. He was also not the greatest trainer (by his own admission)- and with no disrespect to him at all - he was not the hard working model professional that Willie Wallace was. Dixie was a completely different character in the dressing room when compared to Willie and that should be remembered especially when that dressing room was full of young and impressionable footballers who were setting out on their careers.

However Stein thought he could play and that he would get the best out of him, and in truth Dixie would later accept that the stern Stein regime was just what he needed.

Stein was set to lose a big physical specimen in Hughes and I believe he was set to replace him in the squad by the not quite as big, but physical and chunky Deans - I don't believe that Willie Wallace even figured in Stein's eyes in this "in and out" equation.

Further, Jock Stein also knew that Deans would cost less than £20,000, and figured that he was going to get more than that for Hughes - and so such a deal would balance the books at worst or show a profit.

All of that is so far and so good, however I now return to Willie's account of how he came to know about any interest from Crystal Palace.

You will recall that the entire squad - with the exception of John Hughes - was at the usual training camp at Seamill in Ayrshire when Willie Wallace was suddenly told at six am to accompany Stein back to Glasgow at very short notice and with no explanation being given for the trip.

Further, the information imparted by Stein to Willie in the car journey was quite specific - representatives from Crystal Palace were on their way and THE CLUB would like you to talk to them. Stein didn't say "it might be worthwhile your talking to them" or "I want you to talk to them" or anything like that. He said "The Club" wanted Willie to talk to Palace - and with Robert Kelly now dead "The Club" at this stage and in this sense at least meant Desmond White!

Was this White flexing his muscles as the new chairman and letting Stein know that he would have a say in matters? Remember that there was every good reason to accept John Cairney's opinion that Wallace was a Stein favourite as up until the end of the previous season Willie was virtually ever present and with good reason as the goals per game tally easily demonstrated.

Remember too that when Willie met with the Palace representatives at Celtic Park, Stein left them in private for a brief period. However, the discussion and meeting was very short and by the time Stein returned to the boardroom Wallace was already out of the room and when asked by Stein what had happened, he informed his manager that he agreed to sign for Palace, sparking surprise in Stein who turned on his heel and ran back down the corridor to who knows where.

Are those the actions of a man who is happy or content with what he has just heard? Or are they reactions of someone who suddenly needs to speak to someone because he has just been told of a situation that represents an unexpected problem that needs sorting?

Whatever the explanation for Stein's behaviour something was up and he was clearly not acting in a calm manner that would suggest that he was in control of proceedings.

At no time in Willie Wallace's account does he say that he received any encouragement at all from Stein to agree to terms with Palace - Stein simply said the club wanted him to just speak to Palace. Contrast that attitude with the experience of Hughes who was quite clearly told by Stein that he was leaving and that his time was up in no uncertain terms.

Does anyone really believe that Jock Stein was in any way reticent about selling a player or moving any of the Lions on? No Chance. He would have been as brutal and blunt and frank as he had always been. If it was your time to go then he would have told you – plain and simple!

However, would Stein be as brutal and blunt to a new chairman—especially someone with whom he did not enjoy the greatest of relationships? After all that chairman was technically his boss! If White had told Stein that he wanted Willie Wallace to speak to Crystal Palace could Jock Stein have refused any such request?

Further, if this was White's first sojourn into any type of transfer discussions--- how would he react to a suggestion by another chairman that he would be interested in signing one of Celtic's players? Would he consult Stein before giving an answer or would he call the shots and make up his own mind about who could speak to whom?

Coming so soon after the death of Robert Kelly, I think Stein was simply outmanoeuvred by White. Even though £50,000 was a ridiculously low price for Wallace and Hughes, the fact that Stein could get a replacement striker for £17,500 would leave White with what he would see as a tidy £30,000 plus in the coffers - and that is something that would appeal to White big style whether Stein liked the position or not!

I think there is further evidence for suggesting that Stein did not want to sell Wallace at the time and it comes partly from results and selections, and partly from something that Stein said himself when he signed Deans.

First of all, it is all very well to highlight the blistering start to season 71/72 by a young Kenny Dalglish, but of course Stein had seen such a phenomena before. You will recall the Boys Own story of Pat McMahon who had all the talent and appearance of being a

Celtic great in the making. However, McMahon, who had made as spectacular a start as one could, eventually disappeared without trace first to Aston Villa and then on to the soccer fields in the USA where he apparently still lives.

Further, while Macari and Dalglish performed admirably on the domestic front they were untried in Europe—and when they did play, in the away leg to Copenhagen, The Celtic team did not fire as of old—in fact they struggled. Macari would go on to play well in Europe that season scoring vital goals against Ujpest Dozsa of Hungary in particular, but he was still relatively untried at European level.

Make no mistake, the performance in Copenhagen was not just down to Lou Macari and/or Kenny Dalglish. The fact is that the makeup of the Celtic side was shifting and it was shifting too fast with too many changes and not enough experience.

Accordingly, when Copenhagen came to Celtic Park, Willie Wallace was reinstated up front from the start and was described in the press as leading the line splendidly. However, that did not cover up the fact that Celtic still struggled that night and it was not until Tommy Callaghan scored with a header from virtually the edge of the penalty box 11 minutes from time that Celtic and the crowd could relax - at least a little. Until then, had Copenhagen scored - as they threatened to do - Celtic were in danger of losing out to the away goal and going out of Europe.

Willie Wallace's first goal that night was described as "opportunistic" in the press and would have reminded his manager and the board of Directors that guile and experience do make a difference in football. The second was described as having been scored "by the clever Wallace"- was there ever a time when Willie Wallace was not a "clever" player?

After Copenhagen, there was no way of knowing who Celtic would draw in the European Cup and it was eminently possible that they would draw even stiffer opposition than the Danes. Accordingly, with a European campaign to fight, would this be the time when Stein would want to off load your "clever" and "opportunistic" striker with experience in the European forum?
I don't think so!

There is no doubt that Jock Stein could have handled the Wallace situation better—and even less doubt that he had his time again he would have handled it very differently. Asking his wife if everything was alright at home was an outrageous act and was rightly challenged by Willie at the first opportunity. It was sheer impertinence and indeed stupidity on the part of the Celtic manager. Yet I wonder if the question was well intentioned?

Was Stein merely confirming what he already knew - namely that Willie was a happily married family man with small children who was happy to see out his time in the locality and in the community he had always known?

Did Stein think that Willie was the kind of guy who could be tempted by the bright lights of London?

I wonder if Jock Stein believed that when Willie Wallace sat down with the men from Crystal Palace, he would listen to what they had to say - no matter what they had to say - and then politely say "Thanks, but no thanks" which would then strengthen Stein's hand with his new chairman?

As a football man, did Stein believe that Willie would willingly swap the Celtic set up of the time—complete with European Football, titles, cups and medals, for a struggling and unfashionable Crystal Palace?

No, I think there is evidence that Stein believed that Willie would say no and that he could then go back to Mr White and say there was no deal to be done thus getting Jock Stein out of a jam with the new Celtic chairman.

That is what I believe was meant to happen.

Whatsmore, Willie Wallace has confirmed that he had not wanted to leave. Willie would in fact have been happy at Hearts had they given him a little more money. He was not the kind of player who was for ever on the lookout for a move and at Celtic he was perfectly happy.

He only agreed to the move to Palace because he felt that the unexpected journey from Seamill to Glasgow was a sign that he was no longer wanted at Celtic Park!

But he was wanted--- he was wanted by Jock Stein in particular!

Dixie Deans was never a replacement for Willie Wallace - he was an altogether different type of player. More over the role Stein perceived for Deans would be revealed shortly after Dixie signed for the club.

Stein said of his knew striker " Dixie can do a job in the Joe McBride style and that's all I am looking for".

Do you remember Stein's words to Billy McNeill - " I see the combination of Wallace and McBride as possibly the greatest partnership Scotland has seen - maybe in Europe".

Was Dixie originally targeted with a view to being brought in to play with Willie at least some of the time, in the Joe McBride style? Were Macari and Dalglish meant to learn how to play the second strikers role from the "clever" Wallace? Both would go on to fulfil precisely that role with huge distinction in later years - but were they really ready to play that position at the highest level in early 1971?

The effect of Willie's departure could perhaps be seen in the League Cup Final of 1971 when Celtic were unexpectedly drubbed 4-1 by Partick Thistle. Willie and John Hughes had just left the club and clearly there would have been a sense of absence in the dressing room.

It is widely accepted that Celtic just did not turn up that day, with Harry Hood in particular being described as abysmal in comparison to past form. However, that explanation does not take into account another factor, which is that Dave McParland, the crafty Thistle manager, could see a set of tactics, which would ruffle the former European Champions.

Remember that the Hampden stage was new to the Thistle players who had nothing to lose as they were clear underdogs. The Celtic team on the other hand included young players too but as Celtic players they had everything to lose.

McParland's first tactic was to make sure that Jimmy Johnstone was made ineffective and this was achieved when future Celtic player Ronnie Glavin gave wee Jimmy such a dunt that he had to leave the field of play after only twenty minutes.

Celtic were now without the wizardry of Johnstone and another of their experienced players. Jimmy was still one of their most potent weapons and after he left the pitch, Celtic were a shadow of the great team of Europe, with the result that Partick Thistle's youth and gung ho attitude saw then rip Celtic apart in terms of goals while Celtic just did not have the guile afield to get them back into the game!

Oh for a clever and opportunistic Willie Wallace!

However, perhaps the greatest loss to Celtic as a result of Willie's departure was yet to come.

Sliema Wanderers of Malta proved easy opposition in the European

Cup and Celtic would not face a real test until they met Ujpest Dozsa who were only narrowly despatched with goals from Macari.

Next up however were up with their old foes - Inter Milan at the business end of the tournament - the Semi-Finals.

The Inter team of 1971/72 contained some familiar names:

Facchetti; Burgnich; Jair, Bedin, and, Mazzola were all still there— Jair having returned to the club now had the chance to face the team he had missed playing against in 1967.

Celtic also had players who had performed in Lisbon, yet the team had a very different feel to it from the Lisbon Lions team:

Williams; Craig, and McCluskey; Murdoch, McNeill and Connelly, Johnstone, Dalglish (Deans 61 mins), Macari, Callaghan and Lennox.

Having secured a no scoring draw in Milan, Celtic would bludgeon Inter Milan for the full 90 minutes and all of extra time at Celtic Park but they could not get the breakthrough. Oriali would shadow Johnstone everywhere (presumably Burgnich did not fancy a repeat of 1967) and this time the Inter defenders were able to shut the wee man out of the game most of the time.

While Celtic pressed and pressed they could not find the room in the penalty box to make the breakthrough and with half an hour to go Stein withdrew Dalglish and replaced him with Dixie Deans. Facchetti had out-muscled Bobby Lennox all night and Dalglish and Macari just could not find a way through, though clearly Inter were on the back foot with Evan Williams a virtual spectator.

So—I pose the question: What would Jock Stein have given that night for a Willie Wallace with his craft, cleverness, and opportunistic instinct? Where in that line up of Celtic players do you see the experience in scoring in Europe -even Harry Hood is missing?

Perhaps this is even more cruelly highlighted when it came to the new method of deciding such games - the penalty shoot-out!

When Dixie Deans strode forward to take Celtic's first penalty it should be noted that in practice matches in training, Deans had taken literally hundreds of penalties and had never missed once!

However, this was not a practice match and as journalist Raymond Jacobs would write this was "an awe¬some responsibility for a player without any previous experience of the tensions at this level of the game, let alone a sudden-death situation."

What would have been the line-up had Willie Wallace still been at

Celtic Park that night? Would he have started? Would he have been on the bench and if so, would he have made an appearance as a substitute rather than Dixie?

The answer is undoubtedly yes he would - for his craft, his guile and his cleverness and movement off the ball.

It would have been Willie's 8th or 9th game against an Italian defence at the top level and he had already scored 13 European goals for Celtic.

Crucially however, you will recall that Willie had always taken penalties in the absence of Tommy Gemmell.

Of course we have no way of knowing if Celtic would have beaten Inter Milan to reach their third European Final in 5 years if Willie Wallace had played, nor do we know if Celtic would have defeated Ajax in the final in Rotterdam - especially as the superb Ajax side had defeated Celtic 3-0 the year before, although the score line flattered the Dutch somewhat, and a final over one leg is a very different proposition to a two match tie.

What is certain, as Jock Stein would later admit, was that the decision to sell Willie Wallace - whoever made it - had been a mistake and potentially cost Celtic very dearly indeed. It robbed Stein of a prolific and experienced striker at a time when such a player was crucial to the advancement of the team -especially in the later stages of Europe.

For the record, Inter would lose 2-0 to Ajax in Rotterdam and Dixie Deans would go on to score over 100 goals for Celtic in less than 200 games showing a terrific ability in front of goal in the Joe McBride mould. However he would not score as many goals as Willie Wallace nor have quite the same effect in Europe.

Had Deans and Wallace formed a pair even for a year or two? Then who knows?

A Postscript to this tale of Inter Milan comes by way of a personal story:

Following the game at Celtic Park there was a meeting of officials and representatives of the two clubs at the Central Hotel in Glasgow - also represented were representatives for Ajax and the other defeated semi-finalists - Benfica.

The topic of conversation was the unavailability of hotel rooms in and around Rotterdam on the date of the final, with the Inter representatives in particular concerned that there seemed to be no possibility of any sizeable Italian support being able to find a bed for the night in Holland. Perhaps there was a suspicion that the Dutch were engineering a situation whereby Ajax would play in front of a partisan "home" crowd.

However, eventually it became clear what in fact had happened. In anticipation of Celtic reaching the final my father had reserved every possible hotel room in Rotterdam! Had Celtic defeated Inter then the largest Celtic invasion of Europe to date was planned—certain that in the home of old foes Feyenoord—the travelling Celtic support would have been welcomed and encouraged against Feyenoord's great rivals Ajax.

All of the hotel reservations were handed over to those representing Inter as it would be their fans that would be going to Holland.

Dixie's penalty going over the bar came at a cost of around £30,000 and more in lost revenue as a result!

My dad, let alone Jock Stein rued the day when Celtic would part company with Willie Wallace!

" Willie talks of the sheer bundle of fun that was Jimmy Johnstone at his best:

" Hey Willie do you see the blonde in the stand?"

Willie looks from the pitch and can only see a sea of faces

"Willie! Look at the blonde in the stand!"

Willie continues to stare like a twit.

"Willie, do you not see the blonde in the stand?"
And of course Willie couldn't—because wee Jimmy had never seen any blonde in the first place!"

Chapter 12

LIFE GOES ON

Willie Wallace left Celtic and carried on with his career at Crystal Palace, Dumbarton, Partick Thistle and Ross County before deciding that the long term future for him and his family would be to emigrate - not to Canada - but to Australia where he had played for a couple of years towards the very end of his playing career.

Down under, Willie coached, opened a sports shop, played golf and generally set about living the life that he made for himself having been a professional footballer in the 50's, the 60's and the 70's.

I think there is something very romantic in the notion of the wee boy who was born in Kirkie after the war years and who loved playing football so much that he went on to be a professional player which in turn led him to a land down under in search of the better tomorrow for his wife and family.

It is a career that is devoid of the stunning riches that today's footballers enjoy, and it is a career that speaks of steady progression through ever better teams until it hits its peak with Celtic and the European Cup Final.

In the course of that career, Willie graced the same football pitch as some of the greatest names to play the game—Charlton, Eusebio, Coluna, Best, Law, Di Stefano, Gento, Masopust, Mazzola, Rivera, Bremner, Giles, Baxter, Moore, Macari, Dalglish not to mention Simpson, Craig and Gemmell, Murdoch, McNeill and Clark, Johnstone, McBride, Hughes, Connelly, Hay, Auld, Lennox ,Hood and more.

He was the scorer of a spectacular number of goals and the Celtic View and other publications of the time would show photographs of Willie unleashing a powerful shot with the caption "A Wallace Special" as his powerful shooting with either foot became a trademark. Willie would tell you that one of his favourite goals came against Kilmarnock at Rugby Park in a game where Celtic were absolutely dominant. It was Celtic's third or fourth goal and a Wallace rocket ended a move which had started back at the 18 yard line and involved fantastic build up play before Willie issued the Coup de Grace in front of goal.
I have seen old footage of that goal on VHS video and it is something to behold.

However, what comes across from Willie's own words most is that Willie clearly enjoyed his time in football. As you can see from his stories he enjoyed the camaraderie of the dressing room and the fun that comes with sharing a close friendship with team-mates and fellow players. Throughout his career Willie enjoyed a laugh, whether that be at Stenhousemuir, Raith Rovers, Hearts, Celtic or beyond. Clearly that camaraderie is something that is important in creating a happy and successful team and perhaps more importantly it is something that is necessary in life generally.

Willie talks of the sheer bundle of fun that was Jimmy Johnstone at his best:
" Hey Willie do you see the blonde in the stand?"
Willie looks from the pitch and can only see a sea of faces
"Willie! Look at the blonde in the stand!"
Willie continues to stare like a twit.
"Willie, do you not see the blonde in the stand?"
And of course Willie couldn't—because wee Jimmy had never seen any blonde in the first place!

In my opinion Willie's story is a great story as it shows how one man made it to the very top in football by regular steady progression as opposed to the many stories of someone suddenly being catapulted to the top as an overnight sensation with all the mad trappings of fame and wealth that we often see today.

Instead Willie Wallace's story is the story of a true footballer who worked hard at his game, gave all for his club on every occasion, reaped tremendous success but always with a sense of who he really was and with his feet on the ground.

Can you imagine any top class footballers today that would keep a car for such a long time that it notched up over 200,000 miles on the clock? Not a chance!

There is also no doubt in my mind that throughout his career, Willie always played for team Wallace - namely wife Olive and their two daughters. They are just as strong a team today with Olive playing a huge part in getting this book published. Yes he was a footballer, but he was simply working away to provide a decent standard of living for his family, and at the end of the day the footballing journey would lead the Wallace family to Australia--- something that could not be imagined in Willie's school playground in Kirkintilloch or in Olive's case Kilsyth.

Willie Wallace was a player- a great player - a team player. Someone that you would be proud to have in your team for his abilities on the park and his demeanour off the park. According to his team mates he was great company, always funny and up for a laugh - and in life a laugh is important.

Willie won both winners and losers medals in the European Cup Finals. He won international caps - although why he did not win more is an absolute mystery, and he won Scottish League, Scottish Cup, Scottish League Cup and Glasgow Cup medals. He played in Edinburgh Derbies, Glasgow Derbies, Internationals, Top Flight European games and many great stadiums—although he will confess to disliking if not actually hating Broomfield the former home of Airdrieonians. It was just not the same as Wembley or Hampden or the San Siro - too right it wasn't! Willie should have tried the spectators "facilities" - luxury it was not!

More importantly Willie Wallace won the admiration and affection of his fellow team mates and those who were lucky enough to see him play wherever he went in his career - from the oldest to the youngest - and sometimes it is what a star footballer does off the field that leaves a lasting impression and maybe makes a future fan.

I have always loved football, and watching football, especially the idea of European Football. I grew up with Celtic in Europe at the very highest level. Given my own personal background I came to love the feeling of excitement you get when at an airport or boarding a plane to go and watch football in an exciting foreign city, where you could walk about before a game and take in the vibe of just being a Celtic fan. There is a thrill at every football match, home or away, but the whole experience of following Celtic across Europe has always been extremely special for me and it is something that lives with me to this day.

Willie Wallace and his team-mates undoubtedly played an unwitting part in how I now come to view football in the European forum and the feeling of excitement that has lingered with me now for decades.

However, to close there is one final pertinent and personal story to tell which explains why I had an involuntary and automatic smile on my face when I was asked to contribute to this book and all I would say is that recounting it here is my way of saying thank you to someone after a period of around 45 years or so.

A small boy stands in a crowded airport with his mother - he is six years old and is more than a little bit whiney. He has recently received a Polio vaccination to which he has had a bad reaction and as a result he has not been particularly well.

The Illness would pass, but for the moment he is clearly under the weather - and a child under the weather can be challenging in a public place - especially a foreign one.

The airport is full and it is hot, sticky and uncomfortable - making the small boy all the more irritable and demanding.

Suddenly, the doors open and the Celtic team arrive, filing into the airport in two's and three's, all with bags and hold-alls waiting to check in for their flight. They are perhaps not in the best of moods— Argentina has not been a good experience for anyone connected with Celtic.

The small boy wants to see, but he is too small to see through or over the crowd.

"Lift me up mum, lift me up!" he demands.

His mother dutifully obliges and lifts him in her arms so that he can see the footballers who are only a matter of feet away across the crowded airport.

He is still clearly out of sorts - wriggling and squirming in his mother's arms.

Without warning, one of the players makes his way over to the woman and the little boy and exchanges a few words;

"Hello son- how are you doing?"

"He is not very well" replies his mother

The footballer makes a bit of a fuss of the wee boy who is shy and curls into his mother's arms - he is too shy to speak but recognises that this man has come to speak to him and is being kind. The player and his mother exchange a few words and pleasantries, before the player goes away again saying "Cheerio Son".

As he leaves, the boy's mother says, " Do you know who that was?"

I still hear a six year old's voice say;

" YES—THAT WAS WALLACE!"

Buenos Aries Airport- November- 1967.

Willie Wallace--- The heart of a Lisbon Lion.

Jim McGinley, April 2013

"He had more than paid his way to Lisbon and was now part of that proud line of players on the 25th of May 1967 walking into the Estadio Nacional, burnished both by the sun and the optimistic hordes in green and white. The game, the skills employed, the superiority of Celtic, the fight-back, the running qualities of everybody involved and the tumult of victory at the end have been well-documented both by me and many others. But a strange legacy developed for Willie Wallace personally. Somehow or other he did not seem to flourish in the limelight. He was a modest man, whose nickname Wispy not only described his soft-spoken manner but also was a reflection of his quiet personality. Others became spokesmen for the team and seemed naturals for the job, in particular the captain Billy McNeill and the irrepressible Bertie Auld. Willie was not cut out for such a role."

A TRIBUTE
by Archie Macpherson

Willie Wallace won his first senior medal on the very day I started my broadcasting career. It was the 27th October 1962. While I was embroiled in trying to make sense of a lower division game at Douglas Park Hamilton, on that pleasant afternoon he was treading the light fantastic at Hampden Park, in an excellent Hearts side, to lead them to their fourth Scottish League Cup trophy. To this day I still wonder if he experienced some of the tension I felt, which had nothing to do with our totally different challenges that football represented for us that day, but which stemmed from what was happening in the rest of the world. How could anybody, including a fit athlete and prolific goal-scorer like Willie, not be affected, even heading for a cup-final, by the headlines in newspapers which declared that a nuclear war could be imminent as American warships were heading to intercept Russian merchant ships on the high-seas, carrying missiles? Such a challenge would amount to an act of aggression, the Russian leader Khrushchev had stated. That Saturday represented the scary nadir of the Cuban missile crisis.

Willie, me and the rest of the world, did survive though and one of the joys of that survival was to be in Lisbon five years later to watch him trot out in green and white as a fully-fledged member of that troupe of skilled performers, now colloquially known as the Lisbon Lions. His progress from success at Hearts to the ultimate platform of European football, combines elements of fairy-story, brilliant effort and even a healthy dose of serendipity. Before that fateful Saturday in 1962 I had seen him play in the occasional league game for Hearts and was struck by his pace and that clean finishing style which at times made the difficult seem ridiculously simple and accounted for him being Hearts top scorer in the first four seasons after his signing from Raith Rovers in 1961. But having said that, he did not immediately leave an impression on the mind then of somebody who would fit regularly into the finest club team we have ever seen in Scotland. He seemed to me at that time a highly professional club player who lent the distinct impression he was enjoying his football and could be around Tynecastle for years, even though rumours abounded that Rangers were interested in him.

But at that time when Rangers were in ascendency in Scotland almost any player was linked with them. So I did not give it much of a passing thought although some in the media continued to conjecture about Rangers. So when an announcement came from Celtic Park in 1966 that Jock Stein had scooped the striker up and carried him off ,like young Lochinvar did his betrothed, we were set back on our heels.   Why Wallace? What did Stein have in mind? That was the refrain amongst my colleagues, some of whom obviously had been disappointed that he had not eventually ended up at Ibrox.   Now through the succeeding years a rightful perception grew that Jock Stein would frequently upstage Rangers, and ultimately embarrass them by either nipping in first to sign a player which everyone had suggested was Ibrox bound, or so panic them that they would go out and be forced to buy a player after hearing of the so-called Stein interest. And of course as one of the most cunning of managers of all time, he did play that political game .

But this Wallace signing was in the earliest stages of the Stein era , long before the political adroitness of the big man reached full flow. Despite, in retrospect, many thinking this was simply a snatch from Ibrox, it was just the purchase of an asset which Stein guessed would pay dividends. It is said he remarked to a friend on the day the transfer was completed that he had signed a whole forward line. That was certainly true, because the image I have of the pre-Celtic days at Tynecastle, was not of somebody stuck through the middle but of a fluency and speed that saw him roam right across the Hearts forward line. And let us recall that the manager who took him to Tynecastle, the famous Tommy Walker, might have looked and sounded like a merchant-banker from Charlotte Square but obviously saw in Wallace the need for flexibility in a modern approach, and that the Hearts manager was of the same mind-set as Stein about the value of such a versatile player.

However, there is one game which comes distinctly to mind, where I witnessed him displaying abject misery on the field along with the others in maroon. It was on the afternoon of 24th April 1965. It was the day Jock Stein was to win his first managerial trophy for Celtic in their 3-2 victory over Dunfermline at Hampden in the Scottish Cup Final. On the other side of the country in Edinburgh the league championship was at stake. All Hearts required to do that day was draw with Kilmarnock and the title would be theirs for the third time since the end of the war. They were hot favourites to do so, which is why Tynecastle was filled to capacity. As a fledgling broadcaster I was very fortunate to end up with this title decider, for the senior commentator at the time George Davidson was covering the Scottish Cup Final at Hampden. What I did not realise was that in the old shed at Tynecastle they had pillars which obstructed the views of both cameramen and commentator which made my task even harder than I had envisaged.

But it did not blot out entirely the reason why Hearts failed. They froze. And they were playing against a side which was well organised in defence and led on the field by a great defender in Frank Beattie, and from the sidelines by Willie Waddell who framed his philosophy on solid defending and robust play. So Willie Wallace was like the rest of his colleagues that day. They all looked like they were chasing shadows as I recollect , as they went down 2-0. The problem for him on that afternoon, was that he was a marked man and simply could not get the right service. That free-running which I had seen previously never really surfaced. So in terms of public focus, both he and Hearts seemed to disappear off the scene after that day and in fact the club were never to win the league again.

What might have eluded the attention of the press in the West of Scotland, obsessed as they truly are with selling the Old Firm to their public, was that Willie had seen service in European football as Hearts had played in both the European and Fairs Cups. He had even played against Inter-Milan managed by a new lad called Helenio Herrera. All that would have been noted by Jock Stein when he came to prepare for the future after that Scottish Cup victory in 1965. Of course he would have had to hand the bare statistics which reflected the potential he was taking on. Wallace before he left Tynecastle had scored an incredible 91 goals. But there were others around who were potential goalscorers as well as Willie. In other words the new man at Celtic Park could have gone in many directions for recruitment. It is here that serendipity conceivably played a significant part.

Something occurred on a foreign field which led to circumstances that by accident turned out to have a pleasant outcome for Willie Wallace and perhaps an even significant one for Jock Stein. It was when Jim Craig was sent off in Celtic's game against Dinamo Kiev on the 26th of January in the European Cup Winner's second-leg tie. Craig was kicked by his opponent and retaliated by giving the Dinamo player a mouthful. To his astonishment he was sent off . Jock Stein asked him to apologise to the chairman Bob Kelly who demanded the highest standards of his players and regarded a sending-off , particularly in Europe, as a stain on the club's record. As Craig felt he had done no wrong he refused to apologise. Three days later after a horrendous and delayed journey back to Glasgow and incredibly a training session at Celtic Park at eleven o'clock on the Friday night they travelled to Tynecastle the following day to take on Hearts. To his astonishment Craig was dropped, on the instructions of Bob Kelly, Billy McNeill was shunted to right-back with the late John Cushley moving into his position at centre-half.

And for a head-start Hearts lost George Miller who was stretched off after only five minutes. Celtic were therefore playing against ten men for the rest of the game. But Hearts real asset was up front. For Willie Wallace tore the tired, re-arranged Celtic defence apart even though in the early stages of the game one of Scotland's famous football journalists, Rex Kingsley wrote, 'It looked as if Hearts could only get into an attacking picture by bribery.' Willie changed all of that. Cushley was no match for the whippet-like speed and swivelling abilities of the Hearts striker. Rex described Willie's first goal in terms which remind you of the later rubric Braveheart ,when he wrote of his strike in the 36th minute, ' William Wallace lifted up his sword.' What in fact he had done was bring down a high cross from right-winger Johnny Hamilton, outwit Cushley, cut in between Billy McNeill and John Clark before slamming the ball behind Ronnie Simpson. After John Hughes had equalised Willie again eluded Cushley to score a second and just before the end with the score standing at 3-2 in Hearts favour Willie hit an upright with a shot which denied him a hat-trick. It was a virtuoso performance.   In fact it was one of his finest at Tynecastle and could hardly be ignored. This was more than looking at the statistics of the player, which was easy enough for anyone to do, this was the real thing, the action of a man who had given an unwitting audition to the eager eyes of a certain manager.

Now think of the sequence of events. Had Jim Craig not sworn at an opponent on a foreign field, had the chairman not taken umbrage at the sending off, had he not been dropped as a result, had Billy McNeill not been moved to a position he did not relish, had the players not had a cruel energy-sapping nightmarish journey back from the Ukraine and been on their knees, that game might have worked out differently and Willie might not have been so prominent. But that afternoon resolved any doubts in Stein's mind about the player and, incidentally, led to an internal change at Celtic Park which with the backing of Desmond White gave Stein complete control of team matters without any interference in the future from the chairman, as in the Craig issue.

I have to say I cannot recall the first game Willie played in a Celtic jersey after that. But I do remember well the first season there for him and the complete confidence he had in slotting in with mates who eagerly combined with him, as if they had known each other from the school-playground upwards. So now we were quickly realising just how perceptive Stein had been in acquiring him. I observed the goals accruing which are too numerous to identify. But mention Dukla Prague to me and I think of Willie Wallace for two entirely different reasons. It was his first European game for Celtic. And he played his part, both as a scorer and as a team player.

When I went to Celtic Park for the first-leg of that European Cup semi-final on 12th April 1967, it was for a radio commentary, with

George Davidson, my colleague on the television platform. I felt that I had experienced one of the finest finishes ever seen at Celtic Park in the tie before when I did the television commentary and tried to lift my voice above the clamour in the old Jungle as Billy McNeill scored the winning goal in the last seconds of the game against Vojvodina. Could this one against Dukla be any more dramatic than that? Willie Wallace helped provide the answer.

His two goals in the second half are as indelibly fixed in the mind as that Vojvodina winner. Dukla were strong and organised but twice caught out by Willie's alertness. The first one came at 1-1 in the 59th minute. I can still see Tommy Gemmell trying to emulate American football's Hail Mary pass by a long, speculative punt, high into the dark skies, and it falling just beside one of the Dukla defenders, just inside the box, who was utterly surprised by Willie's one touch goal, the ball slipping off the side of his foot passed a stunned goalkeeper. He was even more stunned 6 minutes later and had to stand rooted to the spot after Bertie Auld cutely sent a quick, short square-pass from a free-kick to Willie just outside the box and again with one touch he swept it past the surprised and unmoving keeper into the net. That did it, 3-1.

But his contribution in the second-leg had an unusual aspect. A myth developed after this match played two weeks later. It was based on the fact that Jock Stein allowed a theory to be developed amongst the press that he had ordered his team to defend. That simply was not the case. As Bobby Lennox reported accurately to me, as well as others, but put succinctly by him, ' If big Jock asked us to defend then I must have missed the team talk.'

What in fact had happened was that Dukla, a very fine side, had played well and the Celtic defending was outstanding, with Billy McNeill playing probably his finest match. Celtic had been forced on to the back-foot and in that respect football instinct took over and it was every man to the pumps, including Willie, who proved in that match what a team player he was. For here was an attacker, if ever there was one, deciding to shadow one of Europe's finest midfield players Masopust, the Dukla captain and effectively negating his famous forward thrusts. He was everywhere with him, as I recollect and Celtic were now on the cusp of a famous achievement on the back of the 0-0 draw.

He had more than paid his way to Lisbon and was now part of that proud line of players on the 25th of May 1967 walking into the Estadio Nacional, burnished both by the sun and the optimistic hordes in green and white. The game, the skills employed, the superiority of Celtic, the fight-back, the running qualities of everybody involved and the tumult of victory at the end have been well-documented both by me and many others. But a strange legacy developed for Willie Wallace personally. Somehow or other he did not seem to flourish in the limelight. He was a modest man, whose nickname Wispy not only described his soft-spoken manner but also was a reflection of his quiet personality. Others became spokesmen for the team and seemed naturals for the job, in particular the captain Billy McNeill and the irrepressible Bertie Auld. Willie was not cut out for such a role.

It was only natural that he lapped up the adulation like the others, but seemed, all the time to me, to be quite content to let the others sum up the emotions of that fateful day. As a result of that feeling of staying in the background and of course ultimately going off to Australia to live a major part of his life he is not identified with the Lisbon triumph as readily as some of the others, perhaps also because he made a late entry into the European campaign. But that is only to the general public. To the avid lovers of Celtic he is as treasured and revered as any of the others. Nobody deserved that special place in the sun any more than Willie Wallace.

Archie Macpherson, May 2013

25 MAY, 1967: THE BIRTH OF THE LISBON LIONS

CELTIC 2–1 INTERNAZIONALE,
Estadio Nacional, Lisbon, 25 May 1967.
Scorers: Mazzola 7 pen, Gemmell 63, Chalmers 84.
Referee: Kurt Tschenscher (West Germany).

CELTIC: Ronnie Simpson, Jim Craig, Tommy Gemmell,
Bobby Murdoch, Billy McNeill (c), John Clark, Jimmy Johnstone,
Willie Wallace, Steve Chalmers, Bertie Auld, Bobbie Lennox.
Squad also included: Jim Brogan, John Fallon, Charlie Gallacher,
John Hughes, Joe McBride, Willie O'Neill.
Manager: Jock Stein; Assistant Manager: Sean Fallon;
Trainer: Neil Mochan.

INTERNAZIONALE: Giuliano Sarti, Armando Picchi (c),
Tarcisio Burgnich, Aristide Guarneri, Giacinto Facchetti,
Gianfranco Bedin, Mauro Bicicli, Mario Corso,
Angelo Domenghini, Alessandro Mazzola, Renato Cappellini.
Manager: Helenio Herrera.